Imprints on Native Lands

Imprints on Native Lands

The Miskito-Moravian Settlement Landscape in Honduras

Benjamin F. Tillman

The University of Arizona Press Tucson

The University of Arizona Press

www.uapress.arizona.edu

Library of Congress Cataloging-in-Publication Data

Tillman, Benjamin F. (Benjamin Farr), 1969–
Imprints on native lands : the Miskito-Moravian settlement landscape in Honduras / Benjamin F. Tillman.
p. cm. — (First peoples : new directions in indigenous studies)
Includes bibliographical references and index.
ISBN 978-0-8165-2454-9 (cloth : alk. paper)
1. Miskito Indians—Missions. 2. Miskito Indians—Land tenure.
3. Miskito Indians—Agriculture. 4. Moravians—Missions—Honduras—History.
I. Title.
F1529.M9T55 2011
972.85004′97882—dc22

2011005497

Publication of this book was made possible, in part, with a grant from the Andrew W. Mellon Foundation and by funding from the AddRan College of Liberal Arts at Texas Christian University.

Manufactured in the United States of America on acid-free, archival-quality paper containing a minimum of 30% post-consumer waste and processed chlorine free.

16 15 14 13 12 11 6 5 4 3 2 1

For Rosa Maria Tillman

Contents

List of Illustrations ix

Acknowledgments xi

1. Introduction 1
2. The Setting: Mosquito Coast Geography and the Moravian Missionary Impetus 10
3. Miskito Settlements: Change and Continuity 36
4. The Overt Moravian Landscape: Churches and Compounds 65
5. From Top to Bottom: Moravian Modification of Miskito Housing 86
6. Missionaries for Christ, or Early Prophets of Sustainability? Moravian Influence on Miskito Agriculture 104
7. Uncommon Ground: The Material Culture of Miskito Cemeteries 117

Conclusion 145

Appendix A: 2001 Census Population of Selected Settlements in the Department of Gracias a Dios, Honduras 151

Appendix B: Scientific Names of Selected Vegetation 153

Appendix C: Settlements with Catholic, Baptist, and Church of God Congregations 155

Appendix D: Settlement Names 159

Appendix E: Names of Selected Miskito House Parts and Construction Materials 165

Notes 167

References 169

Index 183

Illustrations

Figures

1.1 The Mosquito Coast of Central America 2
1.2 Miskito settlements studied in the Department of Gracias a Dios, Honduras, 1998 5
2.1 Diffusion of the Moravian Church on the Mosquito Coast, 1849–1970 28
2.2 Moravian membership growth in Honduras, 1930–1995 33
3.1 Raised footpath and stilt dwellings in Kruta, 1998 39
3.2 Sticks protecting newly planted fruit trees in Walpata, 1998 45
3.3 Sketch of Cocobila, 1998 49
3.4 Cocobila, 1996 49
3.5 Sketch of Belén, 1998 50
3.6 Sketch of Krata, 1998 51
3.7 Houses on beach ridges, and elongated ponds, 1998 52
3.8 Sketch of Kaurkira's center, 1998 53
3.9 Sketch of Raya, 1998 54
3.10 Sketch of Tikiuraya, 1998 55
3.11 Sketch of Laka Tabila, 1998 56
3.12 Sketch of Lisangnipura, 1998 57
3.13 Sketch of Mocorón, 1998 58
3.14 Sketch of Puerto Lempira, 1998 61
3.15 Sketch of Ahuas, 1998 62
3.16 Sketch of Brus Lagoon, 1998 63
4.1 A stage-one church in Katski Almuk, 1998 70
4.2 A stage-two church in Twitanta, 1996 71
4.3 A stage-three church in Ahuas, 1998 72
4.4 Hierarchy of Moravian centers, 1998 76
4.5 Sketch of the Kaurkira Moravian compound, 1998 78
4.6 Sketch of the Cocobila Moravian Compound, 1998 79

4.7 Sketch of the Brus Lagoon Moravian Compound, 1998 81
4.8 A portion of Brus Lagoon's compound, 1998 82
4.9 A Moravian seal on the Puerto Lempira church door, 1998 84
4.10 A map, a Moravian seal, and decorations inside the Tasbapauni church, 1996 85
5.1 A split-bamboo-walled home in Piñales, 1996 90
5.2 A Cocobila home with a suita thatched roof, 1998 90
5.3 Sketch of a typical dwelling frame 94
5.4 Sketch of a typical floor plan for a house and external kitchen 95
5.5 A yagua-and-zinc home with external board-and-bamboo kitchen, 1998 96
5.6 A board-and-zinc home with full-length gallery, 1998 97
5.7 Distribution of roofing materials, 1998 98
5.8 A Miskito woman assembling suita thatch, 1998 99
5.9 A large modern home in Cocobila, 1998 102
7.1 Selected cross styles in Honduran Miskito cemeteries, 1998 126
7.2 Cross orientation in Miskito cemeteries, 1998 127
7.3 A child's grave in the Palkaka cemetery, 1998 130
7.4 Canoe burials in Sirsirtara, 1998 137
7.5 Grave sheds sheltering cement tombs in the Brus Lagoon cemetery, 1996 138
7.6 A grave house in Palkaka, 1998 139
7.7 "Less traditional" and "more traditional" cemeteries, 1998 141

Tables

1.1 Settlement name and number, as shown on fig. 1.2 6
2.1 Moravian Church expansion in the Honduran Mosquitia, 1930–1999 31
4.1 Moravian churches in Mosquitia: Orientation and construction materials 67
4.2 Hierarchy of Moravian centers 75
7.1 Cemeteries with open views 124
7.2 Selected material culture traits in Miskito cemeteries 134

Acknowledgments

I express my gratitude to all those who, in one way or another, aided in the publication of this book. I am especially indebted to the many Miskito who welcomed me into their homes, provided food and shelter, guided me on trips to their villages, and patiently answered my many questions. To them I say *tengki pali*. I also express appreciation to the Puerto Lempira staff of MOPAWI and CODEFOR, for their assistance with lodging and transportation. Without their help I would not have been able to visit several remote Miskito villages. Elmor Wood, Natán Pravia, Atto Wood, Carla Boscath, and Tom Keough provided translation from Miskito to Spanish, for which I am grateful. I thank the Instituto Geográfico Nacional of Honduras for sponsoring my research, and Noé Pineda, Mario Argueta, Fernando Cruz, and Osvaldo Munguia, who provided assistance in various ways during my stay in Honduras.

I also thank Vernon Nelson, archivist of the Moravian Church Archives in Bethlehem, Pennsylvania, and his staff, and Julie Bartholomew, who graciously provided accommodations for my family during our stay in Bethlehem. A Fulbright dissertation grant and a Robert C. West award from Louisiana State University provided research funding, for which I am grateful. Dr. Bill Davidson offered guidance on my dissertation, for which much of this research was originally conducted.

I am indebted to Loren Baxter for producing the maps and figures on computer, to Steve Sherwood for reading an earlier draft, and to Daniel Williams, who retyped tables and read previous drafts. I thank Dr. Allyson Carter at the University of Arizona Press for her patient support, and the Press's anonymous reviewers, who made valuable recommendations. I also thank the University of Arizona Press staff and Lisa Williams, who copyedited the manuscript.

Finally, I express appreciation to my family, including my parents for their encouragement, and most importantly to my wife, Rosa Tillman, who typed the initial draft, for her patience and encouragement. Photographs and translations are the author's unless otherwise noted.

Imprints on Native Lands

CHAPTER 1

Introduction

ON MARCH 14, 1849, a German couple sailed into the lagoon of Bluefields, Nicaragua. Unlike other Europeans of that era, they did not come to the Caribbean coast of Central America in search of riches. They were Moravian missionaries, the first in Central America, and their purpose was to "spread the word." The Moravian missionary effort among the Miskito began at the invitation and encouragement of German political leaders who attempted to establish a colony on the Mosquito Coast. Although the colonization scheme never materialized, the missionaries thrived, employing a three-pronged approach consisting of proselytizing, medical treatment, and education to convert the majority of the Miskito population. As a result of Moravian missionary efforts, the Mosquito Coast of eastern Honduras and Nicaragua is one of the largest regions in Latin America where Protestants make up the bulk of the population (fig. 1.1).

Latin America has been a Catholic stronghold for centuries. In recent decades, however, Protestantism has experienced rapid membership growth, particularly in Brazil, Chile, and Guatemala. While scholars including Clawson (1984, 1989), Annis (1987), Martin (1990), Stoll (1990), Stoll and Garrard-Burnett (1993), and Garrard-Burnett (1998, 2000) studied this religious change from economic, historical, political, and sociological perspectives, no study focused on subsequent changes in the settlement landscape because of Protestant missionary efforts. The Moravian Church of the Mosquito Coast of Central America represents an early Protestant missionary effort to successfully gain adherents and eventually create its own distinctive landscape.

This book shows how Moravian missionaries modified the Miskito settlement landscape in eastern Honduras—particularly village form, housing, agriculture, and cemeteries. The Miskito-Moravian settlement

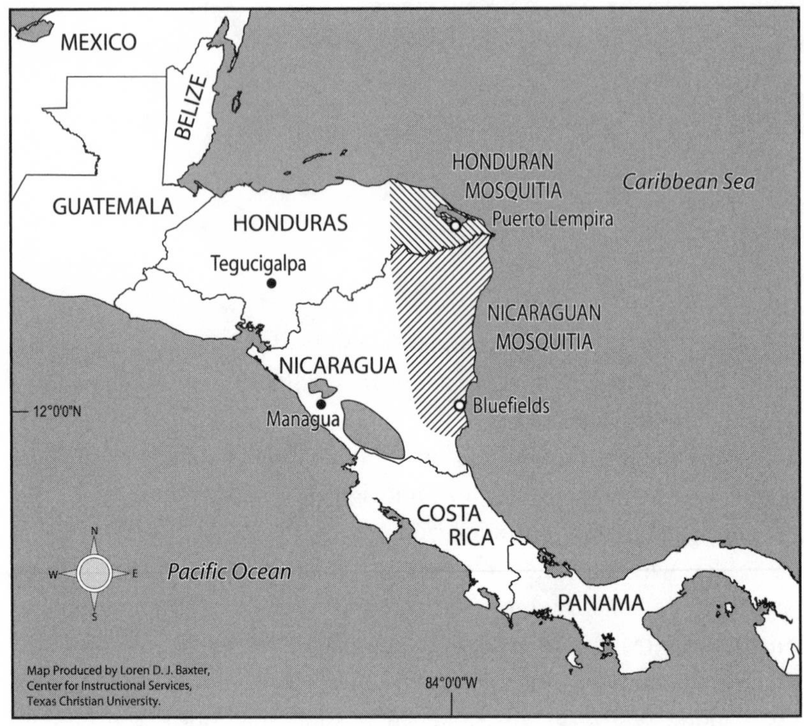

1.1 The Mosquito Coast of Central America (adapted from Tillman 2005).

landscape of the Mosquito Coast now stands in stark contrast to Catholic landscapes found elsewhere in Central America. This study illustrates how colonial practices, such as the use of missionaries as an arm of colonization, affected the region even though the desired colonization never occurred. This book also advances our understanding of the role of religion in creating ethnic landscapes, and of the historical and cultural processes involved in the development of a Protestant cultural region within otherwise predominantly Catholic Central America.

Anthropologists, historians, and cultural ecologists produced earlier scholarly books on the Mosquito Coast and emphasized the Nicaraguan portion of it (Floyd 1967; Helms 1971; Nietschmann 1973; Dozier 1985; Naylor 1989; von Oertzen, Rossbach, and Wunderich 1990; Hale 1994; Gordon 1998; Dennis 2004; Pineda 2006). However, while all writers acknowledge Moravian missionaries were a major cultural force in the region, no research, until now, documented the geographic spread of the Moravian Church or detailed its influence on Miskito settlements. Therefore, this geographic study of the Miskito settlement landscape fills a void in scholarly research by examining an important topic that has yet to receive adequate attention, while shedding light on the rarely studied Honduran portion of the Mosquito Coast.

Finally, proponents of the growing effort to preserve Miskito lands may also benefit from this research. According to Fernando Cruz-Sandoval (1984), the Miskito do not hold land titles, and therefore the state officially controls their land and natural resources. In recent years a growing self-awareness by native peoples resulted in demands for ancestral land rights as well as in a growing interest in autonomy by various indigenous groups around the world (Bodley 1982; Houseal et al. 1985; Nietschmann 1987; Herlihy 1995). As one of these groups, the Miskito mapped their settlements and adjacent areas they utilize for subsistence (including offshore islands and reefs) to document their claim to ancestral lands (Herlihy and Leake 1992, 1997; Nietschmann 1995a, 1995b; Herlihy and Knapp 2003; Offen 2003; Cochran 2005). I propose that an additional method the Miskito and other indigenous peoples can employ to document their claim to land and prove their distinctiveness is to identify elements of their created ethnic landscape. Therefore, in the future, scholars may use this study's identification and mapping of material culture elements as a methodology to help the Miskito and other groups document and strengthen their territorial claims. When used in this manner, this study is part of a broadly defined effort Davidson (1992:190) termed "applied ethnogeography."

The research methods I used are part of a long and storied tradition in cultural-historical geography associated with Carl Sauer. These methods, centered on field observation of cultural landscapes and archival research, are commonly practiced among Latin Americanist geographers. Cultural landscape studies in American geography began with Carl Sauer's (1925) essay entitled "The Morphology of Landscape," wherein he set forth his vision of landscape study within academic geography. Sauer (1927, 186) later defined the cultural landscape as "the forms superimposed on the physical landscape by the activities of man." More recently, other geographers defined the cultural landscape as "the natural landscape as modified by human activities and bearing the imprint of a culture group or society; the built environment" (Fellmann et al. 1995: 503). Lewis (1979, 1983) believed that "one can read the landscape as we do a book," and Meinig (1979) emphasized the usefulness of studying common, ordinary landscapes. The landscape reveals cultural messages and reflects past patterns of cultural origin and diffusion (Kniffen 1965; Richardson 1994; Rowntree 1996). Therefore, the cultural landscape is the visible, material expression of culture.

A significant reason scholars seldom study the Honduran portion of the Mosquito Coast is the region's relative isolation. No roads link the Honduran capital, Tegucigalpa, to the Coast. To arrive, one must fly from the north coast city of La Ceiba in a small turbo-prop plane over mountains and rain forest, to dirt landing strips in one of the four largest settlements. The only alternative is to travel several days by cargo ship from La Ceiba to Puerto Lempira. The Mosquitia has no running water and almost no electricity. Some residents, mainly in Puerto Lempira and other large settlements, have access to intermittent electricity powered by diesel generators. Dr. Bill Davidson, my advisor at Louisiana State University, was one of the few scholars actively conducting research in the region during the 1990s. In one of our first discussions, he talked about the "impressive [Moravian] church compounds" on the Coast and declared that "something interesting is going on down there" (Tillman 2008, 177). As a student curious about cultural landscapes, the geography of religion, and indigenous groups, I was fascinated by the opportunity to combine those topics in a study of Moravian influence on the Miskito settlement landscape for my doctoral dissertation.

I conducted field research in May 1996 and again from January through April 1998. I began the first trip in Palacios (Black River), a village in the northwestern portion of the Honduran Mosquitia, and boated and walked to the southeast, collecting data in villages along the coast, eventually reaching the village of Brus Lagoon. On the second trip, my wife and children accompanied me, and we stationed ourselves in Puerto Lempira, because I could reach the largest number of Miskito villages from that location. From Puerto Lempira I went on treks lasting from one to five days to outlying villages: by truck on pothole-marked gravel roads; by canoe across lagoons, up rivers, and through narrow canals; by small aircraft; and on foot through water-filled depressions, across sun-baked savannas, on bright, sandy beaches, and along shady village paths. I often used more than one of the above methods of travel on each journey. In all, I collected data in sixty-four villages (fig. 1.2; table 1.1; see appendix A for village populations).

In each of these settlements, I took photographs and, using a checklist, recorded information on the cultural landscape under the categories of settlement form, churches, housing, agriculture, and cemeteries. I sketched maps of each settlement, augmented with topographic maps from the Instituto Geográfico Nacional de Honduras, which included the layout and orientation of walking paths, houses, churches, and cemeteries. I also sketched maps of Moravian Church property, including buildings, grounds, and fruit trees, and made notes of building construction material and compass orientation. I toured Moravian church interiors, recorded types of adornments, and spoke with pastors when possible. For house types, I observed common dwelling forms and construction materials the Miskito use for roofs and walls. In cemeteries I made a checklist of the multiple ways the Miskito mark and decorate their graves. Data from these observations yielded a list of material culture traits

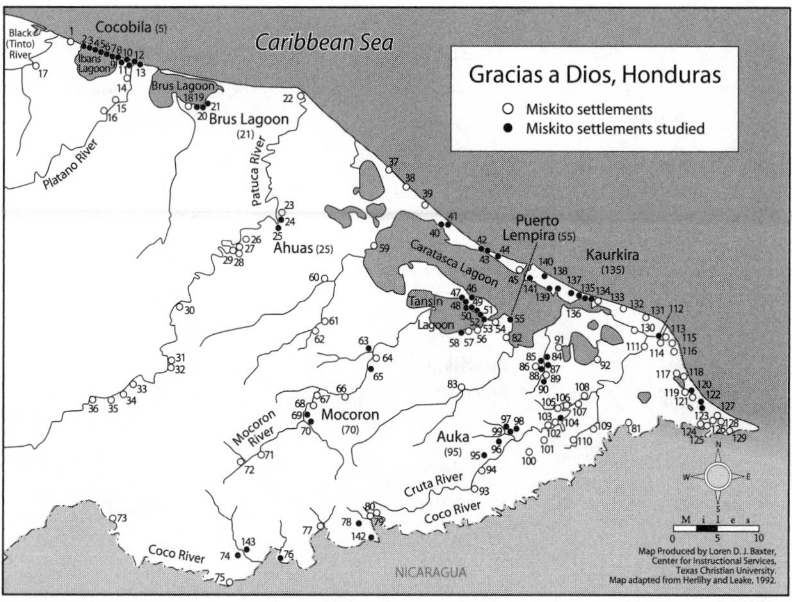

1.2 Miskito settlements studied in the Department of Gracias a Dios, Honduras, 1998 (see table 1.1 for settlement names).

TABLE 1.1. Settlement name and number as shown on fig. 1.2

1. Plaplaya
2. Piñales
3. Betania
4. Ibans
5. Cocobila
6. Raista
7. Belén
8. Payabila
9. Nueva Jerusalén
10. Kuri
11. Utla Almuk
12. Tasbapauni
13. Río Plátano
14. Sisinaylanhkan
15. Wapniyari
16. Las Marías Vieja
17. El Limonal
18. Klauhban
19. Twitanta
20. Kusua Apaika
21. Brus Lagoon
22. Barra Patuka
23. Kropunta
24. Paptalaya
25. Ahuas
26. Waksma
27. Usupun Pura
28. Kwihira
29. Wawina
30. Bilalmuk
31. Wampusirpi
32. Raya
33. Kurhpa
34. Tukrun
35. Arenas Blancas
36. Pimienta
37. Uhumbila
38. Ibatiwan
39. Ratlaya
40. Landin
41. Uhi
42. Krata
43. Puswaia
44. Yahurabila
45. Katski
46. Palkaka
47. Tawanta
48. Rupalia
49. Uhunuya
50. Tasbaraya (Tansin)
51. Kokota Almuk
52. Kokota
53. Walpata
54. Parada
55. Puerto Lempira
56. Priaka
57. Ahuaspahni
58. Mistruk
59. Aurata
60. Warunta
61. Coco
62. Wisplini
63. Wauplaya
64. Sudin
65. Sirsirtara
66. Rumdin
67. Sikia Ahuia
68. Walpa Kiakira
69. Dump
70. Mocorón
71. Waha Bisban
72. Limitara
73. Awasbila
74. Rus Rus
75. Saupani
76. Suhi
77. Pranza
78. Saulala
79. Wis Wis
80. Corinto
81. Rancho Escondido
82. Uhnuya
83. Tapamlaya
84. Laka Tabila
85. Tailiyari
86. Lur
87. Dakratara
88. Lakatara
89. Ahuas Luhpia
90. Tumtumtara
91. Ahuastingni
92. Kohunta
93. Srumlaya
94. Warbantara
95. Auka
96. Cayo Sirpi
97. Tipimunatara
98. Tipi Lalma
99. Lisangnipura
100. Lakunka
101. Baikan
102. Umro
103. Siakwalaya
104. Tikiuraya
105. Kuri
106. Liwa
107. Tuburus
108. Saubila
109. Turhalaya
110. Uhsan
111. Kalpu
112. Kruta
113. Kokotingni
114. Nueva Guinea

TABLE 1.1. (continued)

115. Uhsibila	127. Klubkimuna	139. Prumnitara
116. Tasbaraya	128. Kasautara	140. Katski Almuk
117. Pakwi	129. Irlaya	141. Kiaskira
118. Tusidaksa	130. Kanko	142. Leimus
119. Karaswatla	131. Yamanta	143. Mabita
120. Benk	132. Twimawala	144. Refugee cemetery
121. Titi	133. Tailibila	145. Daiwras cemetery
122. Raya	134. Kinankan	
123. Rayamuna	135. Kaurkira	
124. Mangotara	136. Halavar	
125. Wangkiawala	137. Dapat	
126. Klubki	138. Cocal	

common to Miskito settlements that, when compared to archival and published descriptions, produced evidence of Moravian modification of the settlement landscape.

Upon my arrival at a village, I asked to speak with the oldest person there to find out as much of the village's oral history as possible, including when the site was first settled, by whom, and changes influenced by Moravian missionaries. On one such occasion a group of young boys led me to an elderly man who was slowly moving along a footpath with the assistance of a walking stick. When I told him that I was looking for the oldest person in the village (I was trying to be polite by not assuming it was he), he unexpectedly responded, "They're all dead! We are the only ones who are left, just us, the kids, and the grandkids." His reply reminded me that Nietschmann (1973) recorded a similar experience in Nicaragua decades earlier.

Some residents, especially children, occasionally expressed surprise that a *meriki* (the Miskito term for an American that also applies to all white, non-Hispanic outsiders) was visiting their small village. Accustomed to foreigners in mainly the largest settlements, residents sometimes asked, "Why are you here, and not in Puerto Lempira?" My presence in villages usually attracted little noticeable attention other than friendly greetings. On one occasion, however, a visit to Cocal, it seemed the entire village came to meet me. The visit began with the help of a young girl, perhaps ten years old, who skillfully paddled a dug-out canoe fifty yards across a lagoon with me and her younger sister (who pretended to paddle with a thin piece of bamboo) as passengers. Upon arrival, the two girls, of their own accord, walked through the village and gathered approximately twenty-five people. Once I began talking, it was obvious from the group's facial expressions that they expected to hear something more exciting from me than questions about village history, house construction, fruit trees, and cemeteries.

My interviews with Miskito villagers, typically in the form of informal conversations held in Spanish but sometimes in English, confirmed and augmented information reported in written materials. These conversations were especially revealing, because the Moravians began their Honduran work in 1930, and many older Miskito, who witnessed first-hand the changes brought about by the missionaries, were able to describe village life before and after their arrival. Villagers provided particularly valuable information relating to missionary influences on housing and agriculture. The interviews gave the Miskito a "voice" in the study as they explained from their point of view the impact of Moravian missionaries on their settlements.

I conducted archival research at the Moravian Archives and Moravian College library in Bethlehem, Pennsylvania, during June and July of 1998. The Moravian Archives contain such vital records as mission reports, informal missionary letters, diaries, membership statistics, and other primary documents. The Moravian College library holds several missionary publications, including monthly and annual serials that contained official reports, descriptions of local conditions, and statistics from the various mission fields. A product of their era, missionary writings from the nineteenth and early twentieth centuries exhibited bias and ethnocentrism toward indigenous people that we would consider "politically incorrect" today. But one should not discredit the reports for that reason; after all, missionary attempts to convert the "heathen" required them to live in Miskito villages for multiple years, sometimes decades, where they observed everyday cultural practices. Some missionaries were diligent observers, and their reports contain valuable ethnographic commentary (von Oertzen, Rossbach, and Wunderich 1990). Although the missionaries opposed religious aspects of Miskito culture, they sometimes admired Miskito skills. For example, George Heath, founder of the Moravian church in Honduras, wrote diary entries critical of shamanic prophesy and the Miskito shamans' role in burial customs, but he also respected the shamans' knowledge of herbal medicine and used that knowledge to treat his own patients.

I invite the reader to accompany me as I seek to answer three questions in the following chapters: What is the distinctive Miskito settlement landscape? Which elements of the Miskito settlement landscape are the products of Moravian missionary influence? What were the primary factors in creating such landscapes? Chapter 2 begins with a brief historical geography of the Mosquito Coast and then moves to a short history of the Moravian Church. I explain why this small Protestant group, based in Germany and encouraged by political leaders interested in colonization, established a mission in Central America. The chapter concludes with an examination of the geographic spread of the church throughout the Coast. Chapter 3 examines Miskito interaction with their physical environment—particularly as it relates to settlement location and morphology, place names, and fruit trees planted in villages. The chapter concludes with brief descriptions of twelve representative settlements.

In chapter 4, I discuss the overt Moravian landscape, including church location and orientation, architecture, and adornments. I show how missionaries modified Miskito settlement morphology by implementing a distinctive settlement type based on their original settlement in Germany whereby church buildings were located on a central square bisected by the principal village road. Chapter 5 examines the complete change in Miskito housing resulting from missionary influence. Chapter 6 outlines Moravian modifications of Miskito agriculture that included the introduction of new seed crops and the pelipita banana, increased fruit tree cultivation, and the expansion of traditional dooryard gardens. Chapter 7 describes the material culture of Miskito cemeteries and shows how Moravians discouraged certain traditional Miskito burial practices while introducing one of their own, known as the Moravian Easter Dawn Service.

CHAPTER 2

The Setting

Mosquito Coast Geography and the Moravian Missionary Impetus

THE MISKITO OF EASTERN HONDURAS occupy the northern portion of the Mosquito Coast known as La Mosquitia, an area roughly equivalent to the modern Honduran political unit of the Department of Gracias a Dios. Both the Miskito and the Hispanic population of the "interior" recognize La Mosquitia to be a region distinct from the rest of Honduras. Honduran Mosquitia is part of the larger Mosquito Coast region, which includes the eastern lowlands of Nicaragua and is often referred to in that country as the Costa Atlántica (Atlantic Coast).

Augelli (1962) classified the Mosquito Coast as part of Middle America's "Rimland" because of its non-Mestizo and significant Euro-African populations, and because of its English-speaking, Protestant communities. The Rimland differs from the interior "Mainland" in landscape and material culture. These Rimland conditions exist because rugged, mountainous terrain and lack of interest by the Spanish combined to create a region isolated from colonial centers. As the region was outside the effective national territory of the Spanish, it became first a buccaneer refuge and later a foothold for colonial powers (first the British, then the United States) seeking to trade with the Miskito for New World resources and to establish other economic interests, such as banana plantations, gold mining, and timber extraction. The following statement by Parsons (1955, 63) illustrates the Coast's sustained isolation from the Hispanic cultural realm: "Until the establishment of regular airline service from Managua to Bluefields, Puerto Cabezas and the gold camps, it was easier to reach the Miskito Shore from New Orleans than from the interior capitals."

The Coast is part of a larger strip of historically non-Hispanic, often disconnected, territories along the east coast of Central America stretching from Belize to Panama (Parsons 1954; West and Augelli 1989; Jones

1970; Davidson 1984). Accordingly, the anthropologist Mary Helms (1971), who conducted field research on the Coast in the mid-1960s, reported that the Miskito and English languages were much more prominent than Spanish, and Protestant missions were more common than Catholic parishes.

Currently, however, the Mosquitia of Honduras is becoming increasingly Hispanicized. Miskito is still the dominant language, but Spanish (which is taught in schools) is widely spoken and replaced English as the lingua franca used to communicate between indigenous groups, *Ladinos* (non-indigenous Hondurans), and foreigners. English is still spoken by many individuals. The significant inroads made by the Catholic Church in recent decades are also indicative of the ongoing Hispanicization of the region.

Mosquito Coast Environments and Subsistence Activities

The Mosquito Coast is a humid lowland situated perpendicular to the moisture-laden trade winds. Annual rainfall increases from about 100 inches in the northern portion of the Coast to 155 inches just south of Bluefields (Parsons 1955). Few stations gather climatic data in the Honduran Mosquitia, but Ahuas, a village in the central area of the Department of Gracias a Dios, reported an annual mean rainfall of 108 inches and relative humidity ranging from 70 percent or higher in March to 90 percent or more in September (Dodds 1994). A distinct wet season occurs from early June through December, with the heaviest rains falling June through August. The five-month dry season occurs January through May. The yearly mean temperature for Ahuas is 78 degrees Fahrenheit.

The region is a land-and-water environment of pine savannas, saltwater and freshwater lagoons, rivers, creeks, gallery forest, mangrove swamps, and coastal waters. Within these microenvironments, the Miskito hunt and fish for a variety of fauna, primarily turtle, shrimp, manatee, tapir, deer, peccary, iguana, wild turkey, Muscovy duck, and a large variety of freshwater and saltwater fish. The Miskito practice slash-and-burn agriculture, also known as shifting cultivation, along rivers. Main food cultigens include a variety of bananas, manioc, corn, beans, and rice. Other important plant foods include sweet potato, sugar cane, coconut, mango, breadfruit, cashew, guayaba, rose apple, pejibaye, and papaya (Nietschmann 1973; Helms 1976; Dodds 1994).

The "Miskito pine savanna"—an extensive grassland interspersed with pine trees—is perhaps the most extensive of these environments (see appendix B for scientific names of vegetation). The savanna stretches over three hundred miles, from Cape Camarón, Honduras, in the north to a point just north of Bluefields where the southern-most stand of pine trees in the Americas occurs. Its territorial limits are roughly equal to those of the Miskito. Rivers flanked by tropical gallery rain forest frequently dissect the savanna, which people occasionally burn during the dry season to improve cattle grazing and hunting (Parsons 1955; Helbig 1965; Herlihy and Leake 1992).

The economic history of the Mosquito Coast includes a series of boom-and-bust cycles created when foreign companies sought to procure such resources as rubber, mahogany, gold, bananas, pine, and turtle. During the boom periods, Miskito men, and at times whole villages, relocated to areas of resource exploitation that provided wage labor. In times of bust, the Miskito normally returned to traditional villages and to subsistence activities (Helms 1971). But Nietschmann (1979) found that during the 1970s many Miskito men migrated out of the region in search of wage labor during the last economic downturn, instead of returning to traditional subsistence activities. In addition, the Miskitos' heightened dependency on outside goods purchased with cash received from wage labor increased their vulnerability to inflationary trends as traditional subsistence food items increased in market value and resources were depleted.

The Ethnogenesis Debate

Scholars do not agree on Miskito origins. Helms (1969:76) classified the Miskito as a "colonial tribe," which she defined as a "society which originated as a recognizable entity as a direct result of colonial policies." According to Helms, the ethnogenesis of the Miskito began in the mid-1600s when Amerindians near Cape Gracias a Dios intermarried with shipwrecked Africans and buccaneers. Conzemius (1932) thought that a Sumu (Mayangna) group, whom he called the Bawihka, was the forerunner of the Miskito, because of their location near Cape Gracias a Dios, and because of close similarities between the Bawihka and Miskito languages. Helms (1971) later supported this view. However, Offen (2002) reported that the term *Bawihka* does not appear in historical documents. He argued that Spaniards called the proto-Miskito group the Guabas or Guaian Indians in the early historical record, and that these terms were Spanish adaptations of the words *Wayah* and *Wayanh*, the Sumu terms for the Miskito.

Contact between the Guabas and Spaniards occurred by the 1620s, when Catholic priests made three separate attempts to Christianize the Amerindians in the vicinity of Cape Gracias a Dios. During each of the first two attempts, the ships carrying the priests and other Spaniards wrecked on reefs near Cape Gracias a Dios, and some of the survivors intermarried with the Guabas, producing a mestizo caste. The Tawahka reportedly killed the priests in 1623 (Davidson 2002; Offen 2002). The Guabas interacted with other Europeans by the early 1630s, when a colony of English Puritans on Providence Island, located east of the Nicaraguan mainland, traded with the group (Newton 1914; Floyd 1967; Davidson 2002).

In 1641, a slave ship wrecked off the Miskito Cays near Cape Gracias a Dios. The African survivors who reached the mainland intermarried with the Amerindians, and they and their offspring adopted the language and customs of the indigenous group (Conzemius 1932). Offen's research (2002) shows that the Miskito's absorption of Africans divided the population into two subgroups: an Amerindian-African racial hybrid known as the *Sambo* Miskito, and a mainly Amerindian group known as the *Tawira* (straight hair) Miskito.

By the mid-1600s, Cape Gracias a Dios became a refuge for buccaneers who raided Spanish possessions in the western Caribbean. Friendly exchange occurred between the buccaneers and the coastal inhabitants of the cape. Pirates traded iron tools for the services of Miskito women, and Miskito men traveled on pirate ships to provide food for the voyagers (Esquemelin [1684] 1951; Helms 1971). The Miskito were so skilled at procuring food that only one was needed to catch enough fish, turtle, and manatee to provide for a crew of one hundred. The Miskito's friendly relationship with the buccaneers eventually led to the infusion of additional European blood into the already mixed population. A 1963 study by Matson and Swanson verified the historical record by analyzing the blood of 150 Miskito from three different villages to determine the degree of racial admixture. The results showed a 16.59 percent of African admixture as well as blood antigens characteristic of Amerindians and Europeans.

Helms (1971, 1983) believed that the Miskito's desire to be like the English was also an important factor in their ethnogenesis. Not only did they learn English customs, but through trade they acquired English manufactured goods and clothing. English settlements along the coast, usually near river mouths or lagoons, acted as posts where the Miskito traded natural resources, including cacao, sarsaparilla, skins, and tortoise shell, to the English for cloth, guns, machetes, and rum. Part of their desire to obtain foreign goods was to live in "right English gentlemen fashion" (Roberts [1827] 1965:132). The Miskito spoke a pidgin English with their trading partners, and as early as 1699 they claimed to be different from the "wild Indians" of the interior because they traded with the British (W. [1699] 1732; Holm 1978). For Helms, "the existence of the Miskito as an identifiable ethnic group with a distinctive way of life is a direct result of trade with the West" (Helms 1971:228).

Although commonly cited, Helms's view of Miskito ethnogenesis has not won the agreement of all scholars. For Nietschmann (1973:25), "the Miskito did not 'originate' a new culture or go through a cultural metamorphosis as a result of trade with the West. They did, however, make extensive cultural adaptations. . . . The Miskito of the early seventeenth century had a well-defined, sea-oriented culture with a subsistence system focused on fishing, hunting, and a lowland tropical forest agricultural system." Part of Helms's and Nietschmann's disagreement is based on the number of adaptations a group can absorb before evolving into a separate ethnic identity (Holm 1978).

More recently, Offen (2002, 329) contributed to the Miskito ethnogenesis debate, stating that the "assumption that an entire Miskitu cultural way of life emerged historically after the mid-seventeenth century, and in direct response to a colonial political economy," is "unfounded," because the Miskito "maintained strong cultural traditions which included shamanic prophecy in hunting and raiding, marine turtling, social obligations, matrilocality, rules regulating ownership and exchange, and gendered subsistence activities." Offen strengthened his position by noting that the Miskito language, a Misumalpan language within the

Macro-Chibcha family, existed four hundred years before European contact. Herlihy (2002, 2008) reported that residents of Río Plátano, Honduras, considered themselves to be a racially and culturally mixed group formed through intermarriage with other coastal populations and united by the Miskito language. These same residents viewed themselves distinct from "Nicaraguan Miskitu who are more pure, more like their 'original' ancestors" (Herlihy 2008:140).

Origin of Name

Scholars dispute the origin of the Miskito's name, which, though probably from a foreign source, is unknown. More than fifteen different spellings of the word *Miskito* in historical documents led to confusion and speculation as to the reason the Amerindians acquired the name (Holm 1978). For example, Helms (1971) suggested that the term might have originated from the word *musket*, because the Miskito acquired guns from the buccaneers and English. However, as both Davidson (2002) and Offen (2002) argue, it is more likely that the term *Miskito* was first used as a toponym and then later employed by Europeans to refer to the local indigenous group. Maps dated as early as 1536 and 1540 variously label a river near Cape Gracias a Dios as "rio de Moschitos," and "Rio de Mosconitos" (Holm 1978; Offen 2002). In addition, a French map published during the reign of Louis XIII (1617–43) contained a river labeled "Rio de Mosquitos." During the mid-1600s, the British used the term to refer to a small group of islands off the coast of Cape Gracias a Dios known as the Mosquito Cays, while at the same time they referred to the Miskito people as the Indians of the Cape. But Europeans eventually used the term to refer to the Miskito population, first only the Sambo Miskito, and then the Tawira Miskito (Offen 2002). According to Holm (1978), the first time Europeans used the word *Miskito* to refer to the Amerindians in historical writing occurred in 1670, when Governor Modyford of Jamaica wrote of the "Darien and Muskueto Indians."

Territorial Expansion

The Miskito conducted friendly trade with neighboring indigenous groups during the late 1600s. In addition to trade, however, these groups also raided each other, capturing the children and young women for use as slaves or wives. But once the Miskito obtained firearms from the buccaneers, they dominated neighboring tribes (W. [1699] 1732; Helms 1983). As a result of their successful raids, Miskito males commonly had more than one wife. The stealing of women and children from other indigenous groups aided in the demographic expansion of the Miskito. Escaped slaves occasionally augmented the growing Miskito population. In one particular case, nine hundred freed slaves from Costa Rica joined the Miskito in 1710 (Holm 1978).[1]

In response to Miskito raids, neighboring indigenous groups, including the Kukra, Panamahka, Tawahka, Tungla, and Ulwa, retreated to the interior for protection. As these interior groups decreased in population and territory, they banded together and became collectively known as the Sumu after the mid-nineteenth century (Helms 1971). Meanwhile, the Miskito expanded territorially from their point of origin near Cape Gracias a Dios, following a regional pattern based on Sambo-Tawira geography. By 1740 the Sambo Miskito domain extended from Black River (Palacios), Honduras, in the north to Awastara, Nicaragua, in the south, and inland to the confluence of the Waspuk and Coco (Segovia, Wangki) rivers. The Tawira Miskito domain extended south from Krukira, Nicaragua, to Pearl Lagoon (Offen 2002). The Miskito are the only indigenous group in Central America that expanded territorially between 1500 and the present (Davidson 1993).

The Miskito traveled long distances in canoes, conducting raids on various indigenous groups outside the region to acquire more slaves to trade with the British (McSweeney 2004). The Miskito raided the Matina Valley of Costa Rica, as well as the Bocas del Toro, Chiriqui Lagoon, and the Darien regions in Panama. They also raided indigenous groups to the north and west, reaching as far as the Guatemalan–Honduran border. The Miskito sold the Amerindians they captured to traders who shipped them to British plantation owners in Jamaica (Olien 1988a). The height of the Miskito slave raids occurred between 1685 and 1740, corresponding to the labor demands of the Jamaican planters. After 1741, demand for Indian slaves declined because Indian slavery was officially banned in British colonies and Jamaican planters were established well enough economically to import large numbers of African slaves (Helms 1983; Offen 2002).

Miskito journeys to distant indigenous villages did not end, however, because a new economic incentive, tribute to the Miskito king, replaced the slave trade. Representatives traveled as far away as Costa Rica and the Chiriqui Lagoon in Panama to collect annual tribute in the name of the king. The tribute system began by the end of the 1700s and continued into the second half of the 1800s (Conzemius 1932; Olien 1988b).

The Miskito Kings

A general line of succession of Miskito kings and "hereditary chiefs" crowned by the British lasted from 1631 to 1894 (Olien 1983; Dennis and Olien 1984; Offen 2002). The British took the kings to Jamaica or England to be crowned. By the late 1600s the Miskito king Jeremy I declared the Miskito to be English subjects. The Miskito kingdom consisted of four districts, with the Sambo Miskito controlling the two northern districts located in eastern Honduras and northeastern Nicaragua, and the Tawira Miskito controlling the two southern districts that were located along the eastern coast of Nicaragua between Pahra and Pearl lagoons (Offen 2002).

Scholars have debated the king's role. In Helms's view (1969, 1971) the English used the position of king to gain an economic foothold in the Spanish New World that was outside the effective national control of any government. To establish that a "Miskito kingdom" existed separate from Spanish-controlled territory, the English singled out a Miskito village leader to be commissioned as "king." Once the English fostered a Miskito kingdom that desired trade with England, they were able to legitimize their presence on the Mosquito Coast to the rest of Europe. While to Helms the king was merely a figurehead who possessed little power, Dennis and Olien (1984) argued that the kings wielded considerable authority over their subjects. Offen (2002) found that the king and district leaders levied taxes, regulated contraband trade, and granted land and resource concessions. During the reign of the kings, the Mosquito Coast was a Superintendency of Great Britain, a political designation that lasted from 1749 until 1787, when England agreed to leave the Coast. The English returned to the Coast in the first half of the nineteenth century but left again in 1860, when they signed the Treaty of Managua establishing a Miskito reservation. The reservation lasted until 1897, when Nicaragua "reincorporated" the area (Dennis and Olien 1984; Olien 1987, 1988b).

Moravian Church Origins and Methods

The Moravian Church, officially named the Unitas Fratrum (United Brethren), traces its beginnings to the Czech reformer John Hus, a popular priest in Prague who criticized the Catholic Church for its practice of selling forgiveness of sins. The practice called for individuals to purchase forgiveness by paying for slips of paper called indulgences (De Schweinitz 1901; Schattschneider 1956). He also rebelled against Catholicism by preaching his sermons in the Czech language, rather than the required Latin, because, he believed, "the Czech tongue is as precious to God as the Latin" (Schattschneider 1956, 18). In addition, Hus asserted that Christ was the head of the church, and therefore the church did not need the pope or the cardinals, because they were human and could be tempted and led astray. The Catholic Church eventually excommunicated Hus, tried him for heresy, and burned him at the stake on July 6, 1415 (Schattschneider 1956). His death initiated the Hussite Wars and the rise of Protestantism in Bohemia and Moravia. In 1457, a small group of Hus's followers officially organized themselves into a church named the Unitas Fratrum. All Protestants in the region suffered a series of persecutions during the following centuries, at which time many members of the Unitas Fratrum either were killed, fled to Poland and joined other Protestant denominations, or remained in Bohemia and Moravia as a secret society. In 1722, a small number of the surviving United Brethren in Moravia fled to a safe haven in the Saxony region of Germany, on the estate of Count Nicholas Louis Von Zinzendorf, where they established a communal settlement named Herrnhut ("the place God will guard") (Schattschneider 1956).

Under the direction of Zinzendorf, the group appointed twelve men as elders who served as a town council, administering to both the secular and the spiritual needs of the community. Herrnhuters also organized themselves into groups called choirs that were based on age, sex, and marital status to create a stronger sense of community and allow a spiritual experience appropriate to one's stage in life (Gollin 1967). Herrnhut's economy was based on communal commercial endeavors such as a general store, credit union, brewery, and several crafts, but individuals, not the community, owned private property. Using the Herrnhut model, Moravians established several economically self-sufficient settlements in Europe and North America (Adams 1992; Murtagh 1967).

The Moravian missionary impetus resulted largely from the efforts of Count Zinzendorf. When he was fifteen, Zinzendorf and a few of his classmates established The Order of the Grain of Mustard Seed. Members made "a pledge of loyalty to Christ and promised to speak no slander, honor a promise made, [and] live clean lives" (Schattschneider 1956, 49). He later met a Danish missionary whose experiences had a profound effect on him. Zinzendorf decided that he would use the money that he would soon inherit to fund missionaries. While attending the coronation of the king of Denmark, Zinzendorf met an African slave from the West Indies named Anthony, who told him about the hardships of slave life. Both Anthony and Zinzendorf returned to Herrnhut to tell the slave's story, prompting two young men to volunteer to go to the West Indies as missionaries. They arrived in St. Thomas on December 13, 1732 (Hamilton 1901; Highfield 1994).

The Moravian Church was one of the earliest Protestant groups to support an organized international missionary effort. Indeed, one Moravian historian claimed that his church was the first international Protestant denomination (Hamilton 1900). Moravians established most of their missions during the eighteenth and nineteenth centuries, in Jamaica and several other islands in the West Indies, British and Dutch Guiana, California, Alaska, Labrador, South Africa, Tanzania, leper colonies in Tibet and Jordan, and, of course, Nicaragua (Helms 1971). Unsuccessful attempts to establish missions occurred in Lapland, Guinea, Algiers, Ceylon, Persia, Egypt, the Nicobar Islands, and southeast Australia. The Moravians typically abandoned work in the latter areas because of local political strife, high costs, and missionary deaths. Helms thought the church established missions in remote locales among minority populations because Moravians themselves were a minority religion seeking to avoid encounters with larger state churches, and because the temptations of European "worldly pleasures" were less prominent in these areas.

The Moravian missionary effort on the Mosquito Coast exhibited a trinity of purpose: preaching the gospel, education, and medical work.

The Moravian Church built hospitals and schools in Nicaragua and Honduras where government equivalents were nonexistent (Breckel 1975; Marx 1980). A Moravian historian explained his church's methods in this manner:

> Preaching in public and in private, heralding and the dispensation of the sacraments are held to be primary work, with well-organized stations as centers of itinerancy. A translated Bible is placed in the hands of the people. A Christian literature is created and scattered. The value of education is justly appreciated. . . . [Alms], the services of the medical missionary, the hospital, the dispensary and the orphanage, and the home for incurables are employed. Since the silent forces of example and of character ever prove influential, Christian artisans demonstrate to heathen and new converts the dignity of industry, the blessings of a consistent life and the sweetness of a Christian home. But all these agencies are supplemented by a most scrupulous attention to the care of individual souls. (Hamilton 1901: 210)

Unlike the Catholic Church, which practiced mass baptisms, Moravians emphasized what they called "heart" conversions on a personal level. This practice essentially required the missionaries to live among the Miskito, where they could have sustained contact with individuals and build up congregations. Missionaries benefited from the Miskito tradition of village gatherings—a custom that provided willing audiences when missionaries visited settlements. In addition, their previous exposure to Europeans meant that the Miskito were less apprehensive about listening to foreigners (von Oertzen, Rossbach, and Wunderich 1990).

Most Moravian missionaries were married couples. Each couple lived in a "mission station" consisting of the chapel and the missionaries' home. Moravian couples regularly taught school, treated the sick, and visited neighboring villages to build up additional congregations. Once missionaries deemed the membership in an outlying village large enough, a Miskito lay pastor was located there permanently, allowing the church to reach people beyond the settlements where foreign missionaries lived. The total number of foreign missionaries working at any given time in Nicaragua was at least as high as the thirty-two (including spouses) working in sixteen stations in 1905 (Proceedings of the Society for Propagating the Gospel Among the Heathen 1906:145, 1941:65). Local lay pastors filled the void when the number of foreign missionaries declined during subsequent years, falling to as low as fifteen by 1945. The Honduras mission's smaller area and population required fewer missionaries, with five working in three stations by 1945, and nine working in four stations by 1958 (Proceedings of the Society for Propagating the Gospel Among the Heathen 1945:70; Kortz 1958).

Missionaries overcame communication barriers and cultural differences by holding meetings in the Miskito language and by translating the Bible and hymns. (The Miskito pastors delivering sermons attended by the author in Brus Lagoon in 1996, and Puerto Lempira in 1998, alternated between Miskito and Spanish.) They successfully taught doctrine by relating biblical stories to everyday aspects of Miskito life. The practice of teaching with biblical accounts is now apparently so prevalent in Miskito culture that they use it even in nonreligious education, including workshops that teach mapping techniques to document land claims (Offen 2003).

Although the church eventually obtained a large following, the Miskito were not passive listeners who readily accepted Moravian instruction. For example, the Miskito demonstrated their agency by refusing to follow Moravian guidelines prohibiting alcohol consumption (von Oertzen, Rossbach, and Wunderich 1990). Missionary writings often expressed frustration at the reluctance of some Miskito to adopt Moravian teachings regarding house construction, agricultural methods, and burial practices.

Many Miskito initially rejected Moravian doctrine in favor of their own religion that centered on a belief in a great spirit—a mother deity known as Yapti Misri. The Miskito also believed in *lasas*, or evil spirits. These evil spirits were responsible for illness and death, drought and crop failures, poor fishing, hurricanes, drownings, and all manner of accidents. The Miskito relied on a *sukia*, the village shaman, to control the lasas. The sukia was an exorciser, a diviner, and a healer (Helms 1971). Although the Moravian Church discouraged belief in sukias, a few still exist, practicing in secret. Current sukias focus on curing illnesses by using natural remedies, such as medicinal herbs, and by casting spells in behalf of others to get revenge, or to win the love of another. Moravian doctrine largely supplanted traditional Miskito beliefs. Still, Herlihy (2002, 2006:143) reported that women in Kuri use "plant-based, supernatural potions in an attempt to control men and their money." Both men and women believe these secretive potions, the knowledge of which is passed down from mother to daughter, have the ability to manipulate the emotions of others.

The majority of Moravian missionaries sent to Nicaragua before the First World War came from Germany. During the war, the church transferred administrative oversight from Herrnhut to Bethlehem, Pennsylvania, after which most missionaries originated from England, Jamaica, the United States, and Canada. The first missionaries were craftsman with little formal education, but by the 1870s most missionaries in Nicaragua were "mission school" graduates. After 1900, many Mosquito Coast missionaries were highly educated and multiskilled (von Oertzen, Rossbach, and Wunderich 1990).

George R. Heath, the missionary who founded the Moravian mission in Honduras, was an exceptional member of this multitalented group. Heath was born in Jamaica in 1879 and raised in Barbados. His parents (and grandparents) were Moravian missionaries from England. Heath's parents sent him to a Moravian school in England at age eight, and he completed his formal education at the Moravian Mission Training College in Niesky, Germany. Beginning in 1901, he lived with his wife in Nicaragua and Honduras for over forty years, becoming an expert in Miskito language and culture. Fluent in twelve languages, Heath was an accomplished linguist, publishing articles on Miskito grammar in the *International Journal of American Linguists* and *American Anthropologist*, a book on Miskito grammar, and a Miskito–Spanish dictionary. He also translated the New Testament from the original Greek and Aramaic into Miskito. In addition, Heath had extensive medical training that he frequently used. For example, in 1935 he attended to 1,420 medical and minor surgical cases in his dispensary at the Kaurkira, Honduras, station (Marx 1942).

The Moravian Church wanted missions to eventually become national churches, ecclesiastically and financially independent of the missionaries and congregations of other countries. Hamilton (1901, 210) stated, "Therefore contemporaneous with the effecting of heart-conversions, the organization and development of native congregations, self-dependent alike in financial support, in the dispensation of the word and the sacraments, in the administration of discipline and in effective prosecution of a policy of organized extension and of self-multiplication, has long been enunciated as the aim of missionary endeavor on the part of the Moravian Church." The Nicaragua mission achieved independent status in 1974, and the Honduran mission did so in 1995. However, the church transferred the Honduran mission administration to Miskito leadership in 1977. North American missionaries sent after 1977 were not primarily ecclesiastical leaders but instead served in medical, development, and agricultural programs.

The Moravian Role in German Colonization Attempts on the Mosquito Coast

Although relatively isolated, the Mosquito Coast was nevertheless a potentially strategic location during the mid-nineteenth century, because of the growing interest in constructing a canal across Central America. Foreign powers viewed the San Juan River as one of the better locations for constructing a canal across the Central American isthmus, because it connected to Lake Nicaragua from where access to the Pacific Ocean would be relatively easy, and its mouth opened into the Caribbean Sea at San Juan del Norte (Greytown), located near the southern edge of the Mosquito Coast. The British claimed a "protectorate" over the region, but Nicaragua also claimed the territory as its own. In addition, the United States relied on the Monroe Doctrine to maintain its influence in the area (Henderson 1944).

It is within this context that Prince Karl (Charles) of Prussia and Prince Schönburg-Waldenburg turned their attention to the Mosquito Coast. In 1844, Prince Karl dispatched a three-man commission to survey the Mosquito Coast and ascertain its potential for colonization. The group determined that the Coast was suitable for colonization and published a report of their findings upon their return to Germany (Fellechner 1845). Interested parties created organizations in Berlin and Konigsberg to promote and carry out the colonization effort, while both princes attempted to purchase a suitable tract of land. However, the German leaders were repeatedly thwarted in their attempts, because individuals on the Coast attempting to sell the land did not possess legitimate title, and also because they had to deal with sovereignty issues (Henderson 1944). The organizations recruiting colonists in Berlin and Konigsberg were later dismantled because of a law that prohibited the promotion of colonization, and the German leaders eventually disassociated themselves from colonization activities (Hansen 1940).

Although the recruitment of potential colonists officially ended, a small group of individuals in Konigsberg persevered and purchased land located near Bluefields from English traders (Hansen 1940). Unfortunately, upon their arrival to Bluefields in September 1846, the 107-member group learned the traders' claims were illegal. To make matters worse, the ship that they arrived on slipped out of the bay without paying port taxes and left the immigrants stranded. Even though several members of the group died from illness, the failed colony avoided total disaster, because Patrick Walker, a British diplomat on the Mosquito Coast, assisted the landless colonists in obtaining medicine and shelter (von Oertzen, Rossbach, and Wunderich 1990). Baron Freiherr von Bulow, a German businessman who visited the Mosquito Coast in 1847, attempted another colonization project. Bulow's project never developed, because his plan called for the protection of the Prussian government—a requirement that was unacceptable to the British consul (von Oertzen, Rossbach, and Wunderich 1990; Henderson 1944).

The Moravian Church, whose interest in establishing a mission on the Mosquito Coast began with the encouragement of Prince Schönburg-Waldenburg, also played a role in the German attempt to colonize the Mosquito Coast (Potthast-Jutkeit 1994). In addition to information pertaining to colonization, the 1845 Fellechner report described "the appalling spiritual and moral destitution of the country and the tremendous need for an agency to counteract these conditions." At this point Schönburg-Waldenburg, whom a Moravian historian described as a "warm friend of the Moravian Church" and its missionary work, petitioned the church's missionary board to establish a mission on the Mosquito Coast (Mueller 1932:8).

In 1847 the board sent two missionaries located in Jamaica to Bluefields to assess the possibilities of starting a mission there. While their purpose was primarily to obtain information regarding the establishment of a mission, they also participated in the advancement of colonization by aiding Schönburg-Waldenburg. The missionaries, on behalf of the prince, requested information from the British consul in Bluefields about the validity of various land grants that were for sale and the possibility of purchasing other tracts of land for colonization if local leaders deemed the grants invalid. These grants were indeed false, but the Council of State of the Mosquitia offered legal grants to the duke. The council, under the direction of the British consul, also offered land for the construction of a church and formally requested that the Moravians send missionaries to the Coast (Henderson 1944; von Oertzen, Rossbach, and Wunderich 1990).

During the 1848 General Synod at Herrnhut, the mission board submitted the requests by Prince Schönburg-Waldenburg and the Council of State of the Mosquitia to open a mission on the Mosquito Coast, as well as information from the Fellechner report and information acquired by the missionaries who visited the region during the previous year, to church officials. After assessing the available information, the church decided to establish a mission on the Coast (Mueller 1932).

Clearly, the context of German colonization prompted the Moravian decision to begin missionary work on the Mosquito Coast. But their arrival to the Coast was also partially a result of the actions of Patrick Walker, the British consul in Bluefields. Walker attempted to "modernize and civilize" all aspects of life on the Mosquito Coast (von Oertzen, Rossbach, and Wunderich 1990). One of his main goals was to change the focus of agricultural production from subsistence to market. To effect this change, Walker sought European immigrants, and he therefore encouraged German colonization as long as it did not threaten the sovereignty of the Coast. For example, when the previously mentioned Konigsberger colonists arrived on the Coast in 1846, he made several attempts to keep them there.

Another way Walker attempted to "civilize" the Coast was through the use of Protestant missionaries. He initially solicited missionaries from the Anglican Church to establish a mission in Bluefields, but when their efforts did not produce the desired results, he quickly seized upon the opportunity to bring Moravian missionaries to the Coast by offering them land for a church and by formally petitioning the Moravian Church to begin a mission there. Although Walker died before a Moravian mission was founded, Moravian missionaries, whose profound and lasting influence we see in the region's cultural landscape today, had a greater impact on the Mosquito Coast than all other aspects of his "civilization project" (von Oertzen, Rossbach, and Wunderich 1990).

Therefore, the reasons leading to the creation of a Moravian mission on the Mosquito Coast consisted of a combination of factors, including German colonization attempts, British political leadership that supported the missionary effort, and the ever-present willingness of Moravians to establish missions in remote locations. Henderson (1944, 259–60) aptly described the entire course of events:

> No one at this date took Prussia or her emigration problems seriously; but if she had, at this date, secured a foothold on this strategically important territory, it might have proved an event of world importance . . . . All the elements of an early stage of colonial activity are illustrated: the royal prince, Charles of Prussia, who is interested in colonial projects; the business man (in this case a baron) of doubtful commercial, or other, probity; the rascally sea captain who deposits a band of poverty-stricken emigrants on a fever-ridden shore and departs without paying his bills, but with an emigrant young woman still in his cabin; the pious Prince Schönburg-Waldenburg, who is interested in missionary endeavor, and the Moravian Brethren who propose to save the souls of the Mosquito Indians. These are all familiar figures in early colonial history; and they are all to be found, operating from Germany, and in the narrow strip of the Mosquito shore, within the space of four years. Given slightly different circumstances, this activity might well have resulted in a German colony forty years before the first was founded—and in the Americas instead of in Africa.

It is important to note that the Moravians themselves were not colonists; they did not seek to create a Central American colony for their European membership. Moravians therefore exhibited different motivations and methods than the numerous foreign agricultural colonies in Latin America. Though some of these colonies were nonreligious in nature, such as the Italians in Costa Rica and Japanese in Argentina (Eidt 1968; Dixon 1993), others, such as the Mennonites in Mexico, Belize, Bolivia, and Paraguay, originated precisely because of religious practices. The Mennonites, whose religion prohibited some modern technologies, often founded new colonies when group members disagreed on whether to adopt certain agricultural innovations (C. Minkel 1967; T. Minkel 1967; Sawatzky 1971; Everitt 1983; Cornebise 1990). By contrast, the Moravians encouraged the Miskito to use new techniques, emphasizing those they could adapt to the Mosquito Coast environment.

Diffusion of the Church on the Coast

A Moravian mission was formally established on the Mosquito Coast at Bluefields, Nicaragua, on March 14, 1849 (Wilson 1990). The Moravian missionaries found their first converts among the Creole population of Bluefields. On June 10, 1855, the first Moravian church on the Mosquito Coast was dedicated in Bluefields. At the dedication, Princess Matilde, sister of the king, became the first Miskito Indian baptized into the Moravian Church (Wilson 1990; Mueller 1932).

At first, the missionaries attempted to teach the Miskito by encouraging them to settle in Bluefields, where their children would go to a Moravian school. This idea was unsuccessful, however, because the Miskito returned to the savanna after only a short stay in Bluefields. The church's conversion strategy changed in 1856, when church leaders determined that missionaries should live among the Miskito instead of encouraging them to settle in Bluefields and that missionaries should communicate with the Miskito in their own language (Mueller 1932).

Church membership grew slowly for the next few decades, expanding mainly northward along the coast, beginning with a mission station established at Pearl Lagoon in 1855 (fig. 2.1) (Hamilton 1901). From 1858 through 1859, Moravian missionaries made three unsuccessful attempts at establishing a mission station at Cape Gracias a Dios near the mouth of the Coco River. Although these efforts were unsuccessful, the missionaries were able to explore other possible locations for mission stations along the coast. As a result, the church established stations at Wounta Haulover in 1860, Tasbapauni in 1864, and both Kukallaya and Quamwatla in 1871 (Wilson 1990). The Moravians also located a station among the Rama Indians on their cay south of Bluefields in 1858, and a station on Corn Island in 1860. By the end of 1879, thirty years after the Moravians first became established in Bluefields, there were seven mission stations, fourteen missionaries, and 1,080 members on the Mosquito Coast (Moravian Church 1849–87,31:338).

A stage of rapid membership growth took place between 1881 and 1891. During this period, known as the "great awakening," membership grew from around 1,080 to 3,294, with the establishment of mission stations at Yulu and Quamwatla, in 1884, and, at Little Sandy Bay and Twappi in 1886 (Wilson 1990). The "great awakening" occurred at a time when the British contemplated leaving the Coast, Nicaragua threatened to invade Miskito lands, and American business established itself in the region. Rossbach (1987) and Potthast-Jutkeit (1994) believed the Miskito responded to this period of political, economic, and social upheaval by seeking out the stability of the Moravian Church.

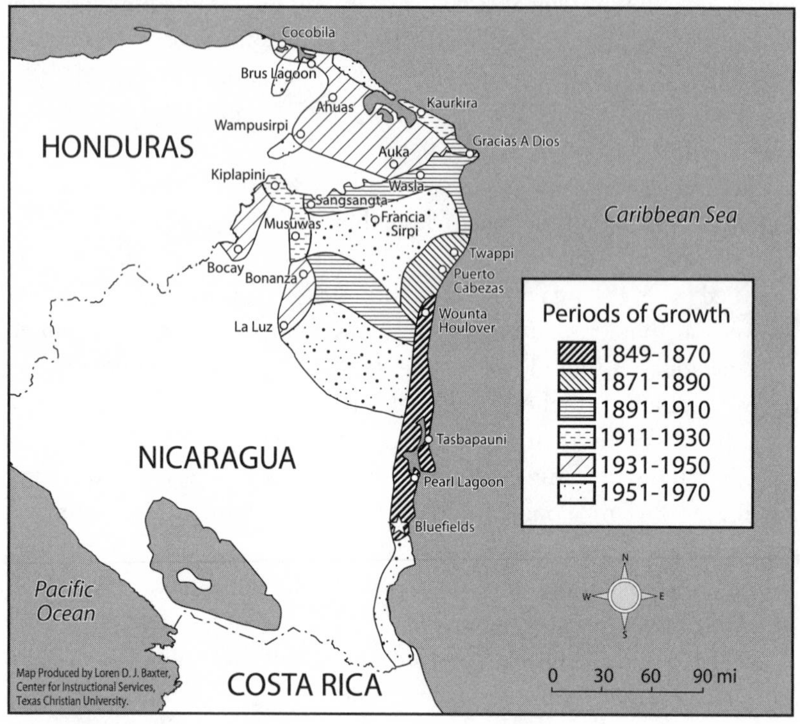

2.1 Diffusion of the Moravian Church on the Mosquito Coast, 1849–1970.

The missionaries began a new initiative in the 1890s with the organization of the Sumu station at Karawala. The village of Karawala was formed in 1894 when a Moravian missionary gathered a group of Sumu followers located higher up the Rio Grande and encourage them to settle near the coast. This event marked the Moravians' first serious attempt to convert the Sumu people (Mueller 1932).

By 1900, the Moravians reached the Coco River, the present border between Nicaragua and Honduras, establishing stations at Wasla in 1895, and Cape Gracias a Dios in 1900 (Mueller 1932). Wasla was an important starting point for Moravian Church growth up the Coco River. In 1895, two missionaries made an exploratory trip up the river, reaching as far as Kiplapini. Missionaries conducted exploratory trips up the Coco again in 1902 and 1907. This time the missionaries traveled as far as the village of Bocay. These explorations eventually led to the establishment of several mission stations, the first of these being Sangsanta in 1907. Other early stations included Kiplapini (1923), and Musawas, a Sumu settlement on the Waspuk River (1922). In addition to their geographic expansion west along the Coco River, the missionaries continued to travel north along the coast from the station at Cape Gracias a Dios to the mouth of the Kruta River, where by 1910 they baptized several Miskito (Wilson 1990; Mueller 1932).

By the late 1920s the geographical expansion of the Moravian Church had extended northward along the coast to the Kruta River, expanded westward along the Coco River to Kiplapini, and up the Waspuk, a tributary of the Coco, to Musawas. In 1930 the Moravian Church reported a membership on the Mosquito Coast of 13,243, with fourteen stations and nineteen missionaries (Mueller 1932). The Moravians expanded farther into the Nicaraguan interior during the 1930s, following Miskito men who moved to the mining district in search of employment. The continued growth in mining town population led the missionaries to establish stations at Bonanza in 1938, and La Luz and Siuna in 1939. Next, church influence continued to expand up the Coco River reaching the Sumu village of Bocay in 1949. The Moravians then looked south of Bluefields, reaching El Cocal in 1954, and Barra del Colorado (Costa Rica) in 1958 (Wilson 1990).

A new area of expansion opened in northeast Nicaragua after 1960, when the World Court ruled that the long-disputed territory between the Kruta River and the Coco River belonged to Honduras. Many Miskito living in the disputed area, called the *zona recuperada* (recuperated zone) by Hondurans, relocated to the pine savanna of northeast Nicaragua. During the relocation period, known as the *traslado* (transfer), the Miskito created new villages, such as Francia Sirpi. Miskito workers and their families founded additional savanna villages in northeast Nicaragua during the 1960s when they migrated to labor in foreign-owned pine-lumber and turpentine (pine resin solvent) industries. The Moravian Church established mission stations in these new villages a short time after their creation. During the 1970s, the church continued its expansion up the Coco River, reaching the village of Wiwili in 1974; in 1973 it established a congregation southwest of Bluefields, in Rama (Wilson 1990).

Beginning at Bluefields, the Moravian Church in Nicaragua first spread northward along the coast and inland along rivers. This pattern follows what geographers call contagious diffusion (the wavelike spread of ideas across geographic space) and reflects growth along the most efficient transportation routes. Water routes were not a factor in the establishment of mission stations in the mining district and on the savanna of northeast Nicaragua when the church followed the Miskito who moved to these areas in search of work. I do not categorize all station growth as contagious diffusion, because site selection also involved factors such as dry locations along transportation routes, perceived receptiveness of the villagers, settlement size, and the number of other villages within easy reach. Moreover, one missionary stated that he selected Sangsangta "because it was the wickedest place on the river" (Hutton 1922:343). In most cases, including the first station at Bluefields, missionaries made one or more exploratory trips before establishing a mission station in a new area. Because of these fact-finding journeys, one can best describe Moravian expansion on the Mosquito Coast as planned contagious diffusion that later evolved into planned hierarchical diffusion; that is, Moravians often established stations in large settlements first, before "trickling down" to smaller villages.

Moravian Expansion into Honduras

The Moravian Church first opened a Honduran mission in 1930. The church's expansion was preceded by an initial trip by missionaries, who traveled northwest along the coast to the mouth of the Black River. Upon returning to Nicaragua, the missionaries recommended that the church establish stations at Brus Lagoon, Kruta, and Tansin. Eventually, missionaries founded stations at Kaurkira in 1930, Brus Lagoon in 1933, Auka in 1935, and Cocobila and Ahuas in 1936 (Heath 1939a, 1949; Marx 1980). Missionaries chose these locations because of their sizable populations, centrality, and strategic locations near transportation routes. Referring to the selection of the sites, a missionary explained, "We have planted out five centers so that all our Indians are within reach of the Gospel, and so that with hard work they can in some measure be shepherded" (Heath 1939b, 56). The missionaries diligently proselytized during the following decades, and by the 1990s there were Moravian chapels in over forty Miskito villages in Honduras (table 2.1).[2]

The Moravian Church in Honduras entered a new era of geographical expansion during the 1990s, one that took it outside of the Mosquito

TABLE 2.1. Moravian Church expansion in the Honduran Mosquitia, 1930—1999

1940s	1950s	1960s	1970s	1980s	1990s
Río Plátano	Palkaka	Tukrung	Tasbaraya	Belén	Sambo Creek
Yahurabila	Waksma	Uhi	Pimienta	Tapamlaya	Trujillo
Wampusirpe	Mistruk	Ohumbila	Paptalaya	Tuburus	Cusuna
Tocamacho Klaura	Barra Patuka	Puerto Lempira	Ibans	Nueva Jerusalén	San José de la Punta
Mocorón	Wauplaya	Prumnitara	Sico	Kuri	Sangrelaya
Laka	Wauplaya	Usibila	Dapat		Ciriboya
Wawina		Batiltuk	Ocotales		Tocamacho
		Krausirpe	Sambita		Iriona Viejo
		Sirsirtara			Batalla
					Limón
					Aguan
					Katski
					Cocal
					Rumdin

Sources: Marx (1980); Housman (1972); Platino (1996)

Coast and among a different indigenous group of Central America. In 1992, the Moravian Church began missionary activity among the Garifuna, who live along the north coast of Honduras adjacent to and just west of the Miskito. By 1996, the Moravians organized congregations in the Garifuna communities of Sambo Creek, Trujillo, Cusuna, San José de la Punta, Sangrelaya, Ciriboya, Tocamacho, Iriona Viejo, Batalla, Limón, and Aguan (Platino 1996). The Moravians did not proselytize earlier among the Garifuna because the Garifuna were already being visited by Catholic priests as well as a missionary from a different Protestant religion, and in part due to lack of resources. The missionary Heath explained, "For the present we have thought it best to make no definite move among the Caribs [Garifuna] beyond taking every opportunity for personal conversation and distribution of evangelical literature. The

Caribs have had good government schools among them, and many can read well, and speak several languages" (Heath 1939b, 56).

In addition to its expansion among the Garifuna, the church has also begun a new initiative among the Tawahka living along the upper Patuka River (less successful attempts were made in the 1960s), placing pastors in Krausirpi, Krautara, and Yapuwas. The church had already sought converts among the Pech decades earlier, constructing a chapel in Batiltuk in 1967. Moravians also proselytized among Spanish-speaking Hondurans in the region, establishing congregations in Sico, Ocotales, and Sambita during the 1970s (Marx 1980).

As in Nicaragua, Moravian growth in Honduras followed a pattern of planned hierarchical diffusion. Growth in Honduras differed from growth in Nicaragua because missionaries initially selected five strategic centers to reach the greatest number of Miskito possible. One hundred sixty years after Moravians reached Central America, they have successfully diffused throughout the Mosquito Coast region and beyond, proselytizing primarily among the Miskito, but also the Creole, Rama, Sumu, Ladino, Pech, and Garifuna populations. The Moravian Church reported a total Nicaraguan membership of 73,140 in 1994 and a total Honduran membership of 8,896 in 1995 (fig. 2.2) (Moravian Church 1994; Iglesia Morava, Nicaragua 1997).

The Honduran Moravian Church split into two factions in 1998, because of disputes over worship styles. In the years leading up to 1998, some congregations adopted a "Pentecostal" style of worship emphasizing "gifts of the spirit," including speaking in tongues. A smaller number of conservative congregations eventually broke off from the church. Disputes between the two groups over church property ownership are ongoing. According to Rev. William C. Sibert Jr. (e-mail message, November 29, 2007), the executive director of the Moravian Board of World Mission, the Moravian Church recognizes the larger Pentecostal-like group as the official Moravian Church in Honduras, because it was the conservative group that broke off and tried to form its own leadership structure. According to Julian Platino (e-mail message, December 12, 2007), chair of the Honduran Provincial Board of the official Moravian Church, Gracias a Dios membership now numbers 26,000 in seventy-five congregations, with an additional 6,000 belonging to the splinter group. There are now 960 Garifuna members in sixteen congregations, 3,000 Ladinos

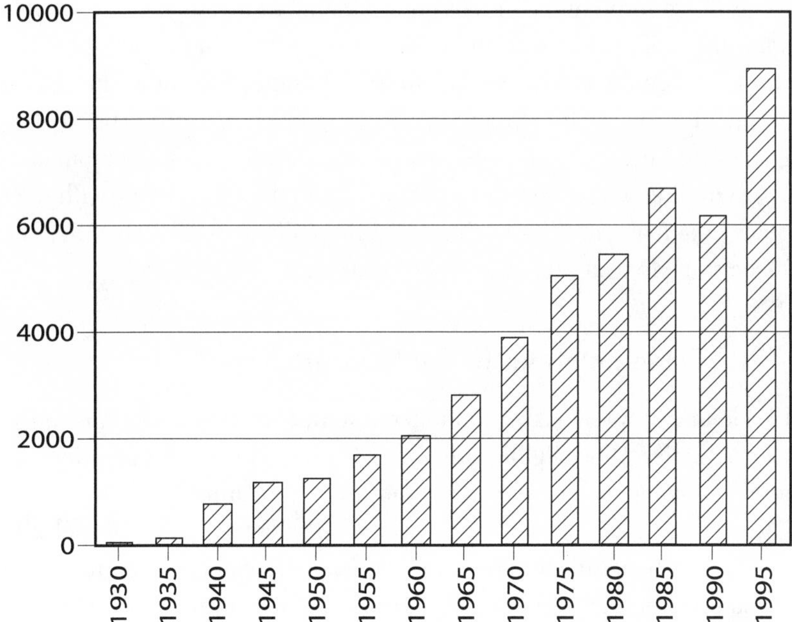

2.2 Moravian membership growth in Honduras, 1930-1995.

in nineteen congregations, and a mission in Belize with 300 members. Nicaraguan Moravian Church membership numbered 83,686 in 1998 (William C. Sibert Jr., e-mail message, November 30, 2007). Based on these figures provided by Moravian officials, and the 2001 census that reported 47,120 Miskito living in the Department of Gracias a Dios, approximately 68 percent of Miskito in the department are also Moravian.

When considering the growth of the Moravian Church among the Miskito, one must ask the obvious question: why were the Moravians successful in converting the Miskito, while other religions were not? Helms suggested that the Miskito accepted Moravian missionaries because of cultural similarities between the two groups, including "egalitarianism balanced by a strong sense of personal individuality" and "their mutual emphasis on 'kinship' organized society" (Helms 1971, 214–15). Helms also hypothesized that the Miskito accepted Moravians because they (unlike Catholic missionaries) were not Spanish, and therefore not automatically rejected, and because the Miskito culture had already experienced several forms of western contact, predisposing them "to investigate the possible advantages of dealing with the newcomers." Although correct, these last two points could also be applied to earlier attempts by other Protestant groups. I consider the Moravian missionaries' use of the Miskito language for church services, everyday communication, and written materials, including school curriculum, hymns, and the Bible, along with their practice of living in Miskito villages, as more likely factors explaining the success of Moravian missionaries in Honduras.

Other Denominations in the Mosquitia

In addition to previously mentioned attempts to establish a mission at Cape Gracias a Dios in the early 1600s, Catholic priests temporarily conducted missionary activities at the mouth of the Patuka River during the late 1600s (Marx 1980). The Society for Propagating the Gospel also made several significant attempts at missionary work in the Honduran Mosquitia, including baptizing Miskito kings and royal family members. A Moravian named Christian Frederick Post, who worked as a missionary for the Schwenkfelder society (not the Moravian Church) in Black River, Honduras, from 1768 to 1775, conducted the most successful of these attempts (Klingberg 1940; Berky 1953; Marx 1980; Offen 2002). When Moravian Church representatives first visited the Coast at Bluefields in 1847, they found that an English-speaking Jamaican catechist of the Anglican Church read sermons on Sunday and that Anglican missionaries periodically visited but had little success in gaining converts. Locals also described the previous efforts to the Moravians by a Methodist missionary located in Bluefields (Hamilton 1901; Wilson 1990).

The first permanent establishment of the Catholic Church on the Mosquito Coast occurred in 1915, when Capuchin Friars arrived in Bluefields and Cape Gracias a Dios. Based in Cape Gracias a Dios, Friar Melchor of the Capuchin order visited several villages in the zona recuperada while it was still under Nicaraguan control. He built churches in Kruta (1932), Suhi (1936), and Awasbila (1938). During the 1940s and 1950s, Capuchin friars regularly visited twelve villages in the zona recuperada (Smutko 1996). Meanwhile, the first permanent establishment of the Catholic Church in the Honduran Mosquitia occurred when the church installed a priest at the mouth of the Patuka River in 1935. Not until 1961 did the Catholic Church permanently station a priest in Puerto Lempira, the present-day capital of Gracias a Dios. Since 1976, four nuns have also been located in Puerto Lempira, where they dispense low-cost medicines to the community, in addition to other duties.

The Catholic Church in the Honduran Mosquitia does not record official membership statistics, but Smutko (1996:158) estimated "twelve thousand or more" practitioners in fifty-one villages (appendix C). The priest located in Puerto Lempira during my fieldwork in 1998 did not know the total number of Catholics in the Honduran Mosquitia but estimated that about 40 percent of his parish was Catholic,[3] 40 percent was Moravian, and the remaining 20 percent belonged to other denominations or to no church at all. However, when the total 1995 Moravian membership of 8,896 and the Honduran census figures for the Mosquitia of 31,478 in 1988, and 47,120 in 2001, are taken into account, the figures estimated by Catholic leaders do not agree. Unfortunately, precise statistics on church membership in the Honduran Mosquitia do not exist at this time.

The Baptist Church and the Church of God are the only other denominations in the Honduran Mosquitia with large followings. The Baptist Church is headquartered in Puerto Lempira, where a North American introduced it in 1967. Baptist leaders estimated their church's membership was about three thousand people in forty-four villages. The Church of God headquarters is also located in Puerto Lempira, across the soccer field from the Catholic church. According to the church's leader in Puerto Lempira, the Church of God entered the Honduran Mosquitia during the 1980s, when several of its members living in Nicaraguan Miskito villages along the Coco River crossed the border as refugees during the Sandinista revolution. The Church of God's congregations continued functioning in the refugee camps and also established congregations in local Honduran Miskito villages. By 1998, there were eighteen Church of God congregations (total membership unknown) in the Honduran Mosquitia. Finally, small numbers of Pentecostals (Cocobila, Piñales, Kuri), Seventh-Day Adventist (Kaurkira), and Assemblies of God (Puerto Lempira) were also present, and the Jehovah's Witness regularly flew into the Mosquitia from La Ceiba to distribute their literature.

CHAPTER 3

Miskito Settlements
Change and Continuity

GEOGRAPHERS STUDY SETTLEMENT PATTERNS because they are a significant part of the cultural landscape and because they represent a fundamental type of human–environment interaction (Jordan 1966; Stouse 1970; Roberts 1996). Physical geography and culture combine to affect a settlement's morphology (form). Though nature may draw the first line in human settlement, culture adds detail to the sketch, influencing where a group situates its dwellings and other structures (Floyd 1967; Davidson 1976, 2002). A culture's settlement morphology shows how that particular group organizes and uses geographic space within its physical environment. Therefore, each culture group tends to have its own distinctive settlement morphology.

Locational Aspects of Miskito Settlements

The most consistent aspect of Miskito settlement location is that such settlements are always situated on relatively high ground. Because much of the Honduran Mosquitia is low-lying, high ground in the region is often only one to three feet above the surrounding terrain. Therefore, I define "high ground" as it relates to Miskito settlements as the highest land available or as locations that do not flood during the rainy season.

All villages are located within a short distance of a water source such as the sea coast, a lagoon, a river, a creek, or an artificial canal. Those settlements located in the savanna are in close proximity to creeks or rivers. As Nietschmann (1973) pointed out, settlement location near bodies of water allows access not only for domestic use, but also for transportation and food procurement. The Miskito typically locate their settlements near more than one water source to maximize such opportunities.

The majority of villages I visited near the Caribbean coast have a lagoon to the interior, and it is to the lagoon, not the sea, that houses and stores are oriented. Lagoon-oriented villages are usually separated from the ocean by dense coastal vegetation and sand dunes breached by an occasional footpath. Coastal villages with especially strong lagoon orientation include Ibans, Cocobila, Raista, Belén, Landin, Uhi, Krata, Pusuaia, Yauhurabila, Kiaskira, Prumnitara, Cocal, Dapat, Halaver, Kaurkira, Kinankan, and Tailibila. Sea-oriented villages include Katski Almuk, Utla Almuk, Tasbapauni, Río Plátano, and Kuri. Canals connect the last three villages to Ibans Lagoon.

Villages in the zona recuperada such as Benk, Raya, and Rayamuna were located next to canals connected to the Kruta River. A dredged, manmade canal connects the Kruta River to the Kaurkira Lagoon (and subsequently the Caratasca Lagoon), allowing villagers in the zona recuperada much easier access to Kaurkira and Puerto Lempira. Before the canal was dredged, travelers had to drag their canoes overland for several hours.

Several interior savanna villages are located in areas where creeks join larger rivers. Of these, Mocorón, Sirsirtara, and Suhi are situated at the confluence, while Ahuas, Auka, Cayo Sirpe, Lisangnipura, Tipimuna, and Warunta are located along or near creeks, several hundred yards upstream from the creeks' intersection with a river. Villages located on riverbanks, such as Paptalaya, on the Patuka River, Mocorón and Sirsirtara on the Mocorón River, and Tikiuraya, Kuri, Tuburus, Saubila, and Kalpo on the Kruta River are all located on the cut-bank side (the outer bank of a meander), to take advantage of the higher elevation.

The highest ground near the Caribbean coast is found on beach ridges (relict sand dunes made stationary by vegetation). Of the coastal settlements studied, most are situated on beach ridges. In these villages, houses are aligned along the tops of beach ridges, parallel to both lagoon and ocean shorelines. The number of parallel rows of houses varies, depending on the population size of the settlement and number of ridges, and ranges from two rows in Cocobila to seven rows in Krata. Other villages, including Brus Lagoon, Twitanta, all villages on Tansin Island, and Puerto Lempira, are located on the interior shores of lagoons where the pine savanna meets the lagoon at relatively high points.

The most unusual type of village location with respect to topography occurs in the Laka region, where villages are atop small, rounded elevations that from a distance appear to be floating in a sea of low-lying, swampy grassland. Even in the dry season, these savannas become inundated during brief rains. These villages are located along the navigable Laka Maya Creek that helps drain an expansive low-lying savanna extending from Tipimuna to the southeastern edge of the Caratasca Lagoon. Helbig (1965) called it the largest swamp in the Mosquitia. Like the Laka villages, Tipimuna and Tipilalma are located on dry "islands" in the southwest corner of the savanna. Although not in the same area, Wauplaya has the same situation and appearance as the Laka and Tipi villages—it is located on a low, rounded hill in a part of the savanna that the Mocorón River floods during the rainy season.

The Kruta Exception

The settlement currently known as Kruta is the only exception to the high-ground rule. Formerly known as Walpatara, Kruta is located in a low-lying area a few miles from the mouth of the Kruta River. The settlement begins on a small patch of relatively high ground at the bank and runs perpendicular from the river. Its layout is elongated, with houses on both sides of a raised dirt footpath, five feet wide and two feet high, supported by retention walls made of boards and stakes (fig. 3.1). During the seasonal rise of the river, most houses in Kruta stand over the water. For this reason, residents of Kruta raise their houses on stilts five to seven feet above the ground—a few feet higher than the three-to-four-foot norm for most of the Mosquitia. Kruta's location presents the following questions: Why did so many Miskito locate uncharacteristically in a low area? What led to its name change?

Kruta's location, name change, and large size are due mainly to a hurricane that devastated the area in 1941 (Marx 1980). Originally the name Kruta referred not to a village but to a promontory known as False Cape by English-speakers, to a river, to a sandbar on the north side of the mouth of the Kruta River where a seasonal fishing village was located, and to the entire region in the vicinity of these locations. A Moravian missionary explained, "The Indians are hardly acquainted with the name 'False Cape'; they call this promontory and the whole surrounding district 'Kruta.' Nature itself has suggested the name. For a certain kind of fruit called 'Kru' grows there which the Indians are very fond of eating. 'Ta' means 'point' or 'cape.' Accordingly, there can be no other name for

3.1 Raised footpath and stilt dwellings in Kruta, 1998.

this cape, where their favorite fruit, 'kru,' grows, than 'kru-ta' or Kruta" (Zollhofer 1911:191).

For the Moravians, Kruta was an area that included several villages in the vicinity of the Kruta River and the zona recuperada. Perhaps the largest of these villages, named Wahamlaya, was located on the coast next to a lighthouse (Danneberger 1919). Photos of Wahamlaya indicate that, as in other villages along the coast, houses were situated in parallel rows on top of beach ridges with at least one elongated pond or large puddle filling a depression (swale) between elevated ridges (Mueller 1932). Grazing cattle and several coconut palm trees were visible in the photographs. The houses were also typical for the period and the coastal location, with the majority having saw cabbage palm trunks placed vertically for walls, saw cabbage palm fronds used as roof thatch, and dirt floors. A statement in the mission's annual report gives additional insight about the region: "At Wahamlaya where our station is located are perhaps more Indians than in any other place along the coast. It is very centrally situated. Also the people are entirely different from the inhabitants of the lower coast. They eat different food and earn their living from the soil. Almost all of our Kruta people are wealthy in cattle, but money is an almost unknown thing among them" (Annual Report of the Province, Nicaragua 1919). The Moravians stationed a registered nurse at Wahamlaya, and Miskito lay pastors stationed there made regular visits to nearby villages, including Benk, Raya, Klupki, and Walpatara (Old Cape Annual Report 1930, 3–4).

Long before the 1941 hurricane, beach erosion was threatening Wahamlaya. In 1926, a missionary reported the church needed to be replaced, because "the sea is eating in to the land. In perhaps four years at the outset it will have reached the site of the house" (Hamilton 1926a). The erosion continued and in 1933 a missionary reported that "on account of the encroachments of the sea her [Moravian nurse's] house had to be taken down and rebuilt on a new site" (Kruta and Raya Station Report 1933). Hurricanes then struck the area in 1935, 1940, and 1941 (Hamilton and Hamilton 1967). Storm surge from the 1935 hurricane covered Wahamlaya under seven feet of water and left only one house standing, but the 1941 hurricane devastated the area even more (Kaurkira Station Diary 1935:87).

A 1943 missionary report stated that most of the Miskito had returned to the area and that a new church had already been built, but the report did not specify the location within the Kruta region (Proceedings of the Society for Propagating the Gospel Among the Heathen 1943:53). The details are lacking, but at some point the site at Wahamlaya was completely abandoned, perhaps due to further erosion. Heath's 1947 dictionary of the Miskito language identifies Wahamlaya as "a name of a former village a mile and a half south of Kruta Bar, now destroyed by winds and waves and submerged" (Heath 1947:453).

An elderly Moravian pastor I spoke with in present-day Kruta, a long-time resident of the area, explained that after the 1941 hurricane most of the former inhabitants of Wahamlaya relocated to the nearby villages of Usibila and Walpatara (present-day Kruta). Before this event, Walpatara was probably small, with all its houses located on the high patch of ground at the bank of the Kruta River. It is not known exactly when Walpatara became known as Kruta. Heath's dictionary (1947) identifies Kruta as the name of a cape and of a river, but not of a village. The seven-and-a-half-minute topographic map produced by the National Geographical Institute of Honduras, for which data were collected between 1966 and 1970, designates the current Kruta settlement as Kruta-Walpatara. Probably, Walpatara became known as Kruta between the late 1940s and early 1960s, after residents of the destroyed Wahamlaya relocated there.

The present Kruta maintains a relatively large population (708 in the 2001 census) in a low-lying location in part because it has become an important stop in the canoe traffic between the villages in the zona recuperada, Kruta River, Puerto Lempira, and Kaurkira. Kruta is located near the intersection of main transportation routes that have become more heavily traveled due to the increase in outboard motor use, and the new canal dredged to link the Kruta River with Kanko and Kaurkira, and subsequently Puerto Lempira. Kruta is now a secondary economic center, with small stores selling gas, food, and other manufactured items brought from Puerto Lempira and Kaurkira.

Other Settlements Affected by Natural Hazards

The village of Prumnitara was also formed as a result of the 1941 hurricane. The tidal surge drowned twelve inhabitants of a small, no-longer-existing village on the Island of Tansin. Heath reported that "the survivors, along with some others, have made a new settlement at Prumnitara, an attractive location between Kaurkira and Yahurabila" (Heath 1941a:64).

Natural events altered the settlements of Tasbapauni, on the west side of the mouth of the Plátano River, and Río Plátano, on the east side of the mouth of the Plátano River. According to Tasbapauni villagers, several years ago houses had to be moved inland from the eroding shore. In addition, the Moravians built a new church several yards farther inland from the previous site, because of beach encroachment. In Río Plátano, the threat came in the form of migrating sand dunes. The dunes completely engulfed a concrete-block Pentecostal church, which its congregation had to abandon. The migrating dunes also surrounded several houses. In one instance a family temporarily solved the problem by placing new posts behind their house and sliding the house backward onto the new posts away from the dunes. The same family also reduced the size of the dune by moving sand from in front of the house and placing it in the water-filled depression behind the house.

Settlement Agglomeration

Most of the sixty-four Miskito settlements included in this study follow a pattern geographers classify as an irregular clustered village, but a few settlements have grid-street patterns or are elongated. Houses were typically interspersed approximately 10–40 yards apart, depending on the degree of agglomeration (proximity of dwellings). As part of a matrilocal society, married Miskito women locate their homes near their mother and sisters, forming a neighborhood within a village (Herlihy 2006). Settlement population size and available dry land are the most important factors determining the distance between houses. For example, some villages, such as Kruta, had little available high ground and are therefore more compact. Others, such as Cocobila, are elongated because of their location on narrow necks of land. Still other villages, newer ones such as Nueva Jerusalén, have plenty of available land and are therefore more dispersed. The traditional Miskito settlement morphology, with no overt center, was often altered significantly by the establishment of a Moravian church compound, with its spacious, open green, creating a central place that would frequently become the focus of the settlement. In some cases Moravian missionaries also influenced settlement agglomeration, especially in their earlier years in Nicaragua.

Shortly after their arrival to the Nicaraguan Mosquito Coast, Moravians unsuccessfully attempted to settle the Miskito in Bluefields (Moravian Church 1849–87, 20:381; Mueller 1932). Earlier Moravian missions, particularly those in South Africa and North America, successfully gathered indigenous populations into planned settlements (Kruger 1966; Danker 1971). Even after the 1856 mission strategy change requiring missionaries to live in Miskito villages, Moravians still, on occasion, attempted to resettle the Miskito in larger villages and in more accessible locations. The missionaries sought the Miskito king's help, asking him to "explain to his people the importance of the instruction which we impart, and to induce them to settle in larger villages, and in more healthy and accessible localities" (Feurig 1858:347).

There are indications that the presence of missionaries may have attracted the Miskito to villages. According to one missionary, the Quamwatla village grew in anticipation of the arrival of a Moravian missionary. He reported, "Our people at Quamwatla are very much troubled that a missionary has not yet been appointed for them. . . . Eight years ago the place was quite forsaken by its inhabitants. Now there are again twenty houses there, and more are to be built in the expectation that a missionary will be sent" (Sieborger 1884:175).

In some cases, the missionaries changed the layout of villages and created streets. The residents of Wounta Haulover realigned their homes along a new road (Lundberg 1872), and in Kukalaya, the villagers "under Br. Blair's direction . . . made a proper street in the village" (Lundberg 1870:197). Helms (1971:47) attributed Asang's street arrangement of "more or less parallel rows" to Moravian influence. Evidence of this influence is found in a missionary's statement concerning Asang's changed appearance years after the church was established there: "Now they have neat houses, built in a row, street fashion, with the church and the home of the evangelist in the midst" (Moravian Church 1890–1956, 10:407). Perhaps the most striking example of settlement modification occurred when a Moravian missionary relocated an entire village belonging to the neighboring Sumu in Nicaragua. Reminiscent of Spanish *reducciónes,*

> He persuaded them to move farther down river and settled them on land obtained from the government on one of the side arms of the Rio Grande. The settlement was named Karawala. Bro. Lewis laid out a regular plan for it: a central square, with church and mission house; streets running in two directions on the height of land, and he lined these streets with orange and lemon trees. He settled the twakkas on one side of the square, and the Uluas (Woolwas) on the other, these being sub-divisions of the Sumos. Bro. Lewis also made rules for an orderly communal life and saw to their observance. It was an entirely new plan and to judge from all appearances, it worked splendidly, for Karawala is to this day one of the cleanest and finest Sumo towns, with good homes, all kinds of fruit trees, good plantations and a well-ordered life. (Mueller 1932, 117)

Although missionaries in Honduras made no major attempts at agglomeration (such as those made in Nicaragua), Moravians did influence settlement morphology in important ways. For example, Moravian missionary Werner Marx constructed at least two streets in Brus Lagoon (Werner Marx, pers. comm., July 16, 1998). The first of these was the main street that extends from the lagoon, past the Moravian church and public school, to the airport. The other street Marx made no longer exists, due to the grid street pattern laid out by the Honduran government. In other instances, residents in several villages cleared landing strips under the direction of the Moravian church to facilitate travel between these villages and the Moravian hospital in Ahuas. In the most significant example, Moravian missionaries altered Miskito settlement morphology by implementing a settlement type patterned after Herrnhut and other planned Moravian communities in Europe and North America (Tillman

2005). The type, consisting of a fenced compound that was bisected by the principal village road, a spacious central square, and buildings that served various church functions, was most fully developed in Kaurkira, Cocobila, and Brus Lagoon. Moravians altered the morphology of twenty-five additional villages to a lesser extent by constructing smaller, less elaborate church compounds within those settlements. Moravian compounds are examined in further detail in chapter 4.

Vegetation Canopy

Fruit-bearing trees are an integral part of Miskito settlements. Besides the obvious purpose of providing food, planting trees often marks property lines. The trees also provide shade and are so numerous in many settlements that they block nearby houses from view. Because fruit trees always occur in conjunction with settlements, the Miskito used them to locate villages from a distance (Bell 1862). For example, during my travels, Miskito frequently referred to groves of fruit trees as village sites, saying, "See those mangos over there [on the horizon]? That's Auka." They would say, "See those breadfruits? That's Laka." The Miskito also use fruit trees as landmarks when giving directions: "Walk down the beach until you get to the coconut grove, then follow the path [inland] to Kaurkira."

Certain species are consistently present in Honduran Miskito villages, resulting in a Miskito "fruit tree complex." This complex includes coconut, breadfruit, mango, cashew, orange, lemon, grapefruit, nance, lime, and rose apple. Of these, coconut, breadfruit, and mango are the primary trees, because they are the most common, and the most prominent in size. Fruit trees of secondary importance (because they were typically planted in fewer numbers) include avocado, papaya, soursop, peach palm (pejibaye), mamey, and guayaba.

The Miskito vegetation canopy is most noticeable in savanna settlements where villages appeared as islands or domes of trees in a sea of grass. Vegetation canopies expand with the village. When the Miskito build new houses outside of the canopy, they plant several types of fruit trees around the home, and these trees eventually become part of the already existing canopy (fig. 3.2). Examples are easily detectable in several savanna settlements, including Palkaka, Walpata, Laka, Sirsirtara, Tipilalma, Puerto Lempira, and Brus Lagoon. Villagers fence newly

3.2 Sticks protecting newly planted fruit trees from cattle in Walpata, 1998.

planted trees off from roaming cattle with trunks of small cabbage palm trees, barbed wire, or sticks placed in the shape of a cone.

While savanna settlements have vegetation domes, one can best describe most coastal villages as "cleared-forest settlements." Unlike the domed settlements of the savanna, cleared-forest settlements are located in formerly forested areas cleared of unwanted vegetation. Villagers then plant new fruit trees, creating a vegetation canopy. Differences between the two types of villages are clearly discernible from aerial photographs taken in 1961.[1] Coastal villages are located in areas cleared of most vegetation and surrounded by thick brush and other secondary growth. A vegetation canopy exists, but it does not appear as thick as the secondary vegetation surrounding the village. Savanna settlements, on the other hand, appear as thick stands of trees in open grasslands.

One of the best examples can be seen from a comparison of air photos taken of Puerto Lempira in 1961 and 1980. In 1961, Puerto Lempira had an airstrip and a curved road connecting the airstrip with the pier. The only trees in the photo are the mango trees in the main plaza and the mango trees a short distance south of the pier, along the lagoon. The photo also shows six houses unevenly distributed in a field. There is no grid street pattern. The 1980 air photo shows Puerto Lempira with a grid street pattern of three north–south-running streets and seven east–west-running streets. The area within the grid contains dense stands of fruit trees forming a vegetation canopy. In another example, Moravian missionaries located their Brus Lagoon compound on the open savanna in the 1930s, but it was eventually enveloped by the vegetation canopy as the town grew up around it (Housman 1958).

The distribution and concentration of fruit trees are not uniform in the Mosquitia. Frequently villages seem to specialize in certain trees: coconut trees in Kaurkira; plum trees in Belén; breadfruit in Laka Tabila; and rose apple in Ahuas. Particular fruit trees are sometimes underrepresented, because they do not grow well in a given location. For example, one explanation for the small number of rose apple trees in many coastal settlements is that rose apples grow poorly in sandy soil.

Roads and Paths

Four main types of roads exist in Mosquitia. The most widely used are the simple footpaths that connect houses and villages, and in some smaller villages serve as the main road. The second type is the raised footpath. The Miskito raise footpaths in low areas by digging a shallow trench on each side of the path and piling the dirt on top of the path. Raised paths exist in many villages, but most notably in Belén, Tasbapauni, Benk, Raya, Yahurabila, Palkaka, and Walpata. The third type is a dirt road, ten to twenty feet wide, that is essentially a widened footpath. This type of road is typically fenced off from adjacent property with barbed wire. The fourth type is a gravel road made with the aid of at least some heavy machinery. This type of road is found only in a few villages, including Brus Lagoon, with roads connecting Brus Lagoon to Kusuapaika and Twitanta, and Ahuas, Paptalaya, Mocorón, and Puerto Lempira. This gravel road type also connects Puerto Lempira with other villages such as Mocorón, Sirsirtara, Suhi, Rus Rus, Lemuis, Saulala, Auka, Tipimuna, and Lisangnipura. Gravel roads are typically constructed by the Honduran government, international relief organizations, and foreign oil and logging companies.

Settlement Names

The study of place names, or toponyms, is inherently geographical. For Sauer (1966, 59), "place name is location in cultural connotation." Toponyms offer clues to a region's cultural history because they often survive longer than the culture group that first placed them on the land. Place names also provide insights into cultures' "habitats, and spatial and environmental perception" (Jett 1997:481). When individuals or groups assign names to places, they reveal their desires to claim those places as their own.

The vast majority of Miskito settlement names describe resources or features of the natural environment (appendix D). The Miskito frequently assign plant or animal names, as well as terms describing physical geography, to their settlements. A small number of settlements are also named for people or events. Several names reflect the influence of the English and Spanish languages, and a handful of names do not fit into any particular category.

Examples of settlement names describing physical geography include Prumnitara (big hill), Tasbapauni (red earth), Suhi (flat stone), and Wapniyari (straight river channel). Some village names, including Rayamuna (new settlement inland) and Tipi Lalma (east Tipi), specify directions. Plant names are the most popular terms used to identify settlements. Examples include Yauhurabila (place of much manioc), Cocobila (place of many coconut trees), Mangotara (large mango tree), Sirsirtara (large tree used for charcoal), Kanko (trunk of the saw cabbage palm tree), Kruta (palm fruit point), and Auka (gold trumpet tree). The Miskito also assign animal names to their settlements, including Limitara (large tiger) and Warunta (white-collared peccary). The villages of Rupalia, Mabita, Brus Lagoon, and Alexandra (Cocal) are all named for individuals, while Kinankan and Rumdin are named for events. According to Heath (1947, 135), Kiangkan was the "name of a Kaurkira hamlet which was burned ('angkan') by the [Miskito] king to punish the insubordination of its chief man, Kupias." Rumdin (drunk rum) was reportedly named for a woman who drank an excessive amount of alcohol and then seriously injured herself.

Settlement names have also originated from other languages, including Landin (landing), Halaver (haul over—a narrow neck of land used for hauling a canoe over from one body of water to another), Benk (river bank—a remnant of the mahogany trade [Revels 2008]), and Bilalmuk (old bell)—all from English. Spanish place names include Puerto Lempira (port of Lempira), Las Marias Vieja (older Las Marias), Río Plátano (Plantain River), Nueva Jerusalén (New Jerusalem), Belén (Bethlehem),

Corinto (Corinth), and Rancho Escondido (hidden ranch). In addition, names of settlements such as Kukubila and Mukrung have been Hispanized such that their names have changed to Cocobila and Mocorón. A handful of village names do not fall into any of the above categories, including Utla Almuk (old house), Priaka (widow), and Kwihra (pregnant).

Only Liwa, Sisinaylanhkan, Belén, Nueva Jerusalén, Betania, and Corinto can be considered religious place names. Liwa (water spirits) and Sisinaylanhkan (silk cotton tree spirit) are reminders of the Miskito's pre-Christian belief in spirits, while both Belén and Nueva Jerusalén were named by members of the Moravian Church who originally settled those locations. Betania (Bethany) and Corinto are both New Testament place names, but they could be used as personal names. It is unknown whether these sites were named for religious or other reasons. Another religious place name may soon appear on the landscape. The Moravian Church attempted to change the name of Rumdin (drunk rum) to Monte Olivo (Mount of Olives). The Moravians are encouraging the name change because, explained a Miskito-Moravian pastor I spoke with, "the drunk rum Moravian church sounds ugly." The complete lack of saint names and other religious place names related to Catholicism is impressive evidence of the region's distinctiveness from the rest of Honduras.

Settlement Descriptions

Brief descriptions of twelve Honduran Miskito settlements follow. I chose to illustrate these particular villages because they are either representative of various aspects present in many settlements or, as I specify in a few cases, they are anomalous or otherwise outstanding. A sketch map based on my field notes accompanies each description. I did not draw the sketch maps to scale and intend them only to show the general layout of paths and streets, dwellings, and churches.

Cocobila

Cocobila is located on the narrowest portion of the spit of land separating Ibans Lagoon from the Caribbean (figs. 3.3 and 3.4). A main footpath

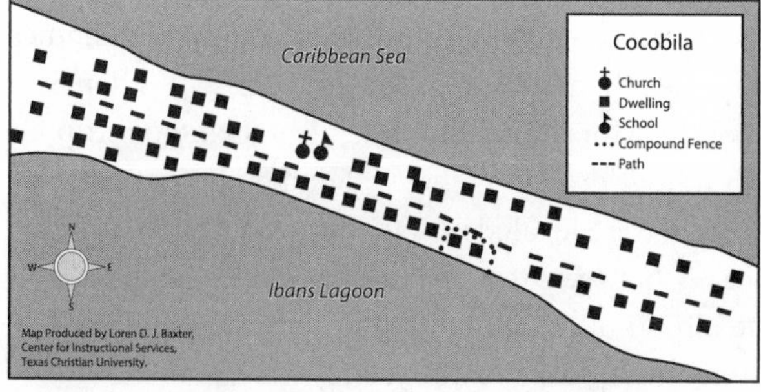

3.3 Sketch of Cocobila, 1998 (adapted from Tillman 2005).

3.4 Cocobila, 1996. The Caribbean Sea is at the top of the photograph, and Iban's Lagoon is at the bottom.

that connects all villages on the spit bisects the settlement. Due to the narrowness of the land, approximately fifty to seventy yards at its narrowest point, Cocobila is elongated and consists of a single row of houses on either side of the path for a significant distance. In areas where space permits there are two rows of houses on either side of the footpath. Cocobila's central area is also elongated and extends from stores just west of the Moravian church to the open area located next to the Moravian reverend's home.

Belén

Belén is located southeast of Cocobila, on the wide end of the spit separating Ibans Lagoon from the Caribbean. A family from Cocobila founded the settlement in 1947 (Dodds 1994). Because space is available, homes in Belén are more dispersed than homes in Cocobila (fig. 3.5). There was also enough terrain for the Moravian Church to clear a landing strip for small aircraft. The church is located on the west end of the runway, and the school and airline office are located next to the middle of the runway. Most homes are located between the runway and the lagoon. Belén's center consists of the airport office (important because of its radio communication with other villages) and nearby school and store.

Krata

Village tradition maintains that Juan Mendez first settled Krata in the 1880s. He came from Laka to raise cattle, and his family members later joined him. His descendants now live near Krata's main boat landing,

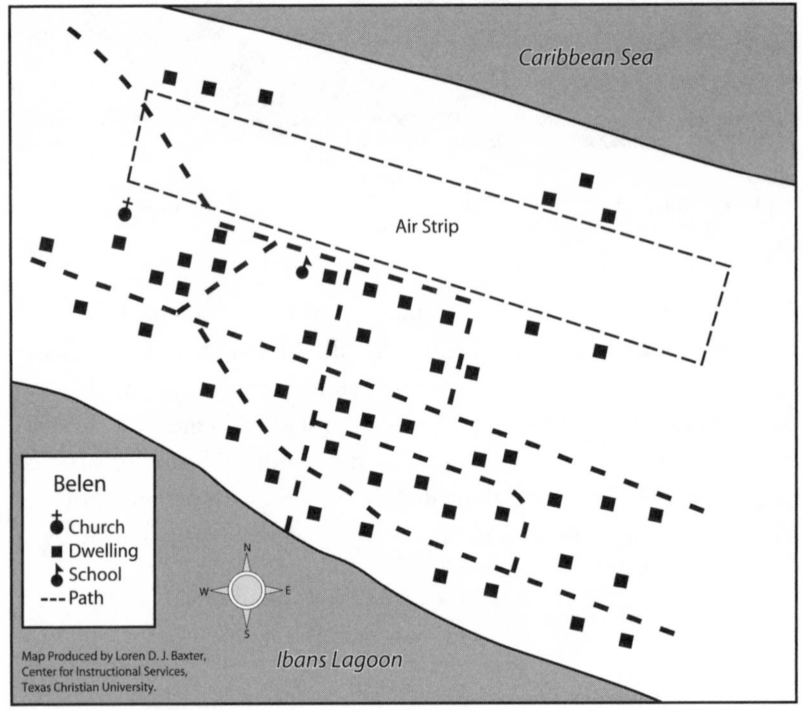

3.5 Sketch of Belén, 1998.

which they believe is the same area where he first settled. Located on a narrow section of a spit that separates the Caratasca Lagoon from the Caribbean Sea, Krata is the epitome of a beach ridge settlement (fig. 3.6). Seven roughly parallel rows of houses on five tall beach ridges occupy the spit's widest point. Three to five rows of houses on three to four beach ridges occupy the narrower sections of the spit. The beach ridges are relatively high, ranging from three to five feet. The depression between beach ridges nearest the lagoon is the largest and contains water year-round (fig. 3.7). Bridges constructed of saw cabbage palm trunks periodically spanned the elongated pond. Krata has no obvious center, because there are no large stores (there are several stores in nearby Yahurabila), and due to a lack of high ground there is no large plaza area. The school, the Catholic church, and the main boat landing are all separated from each other, inhibiting the formation of a true center.

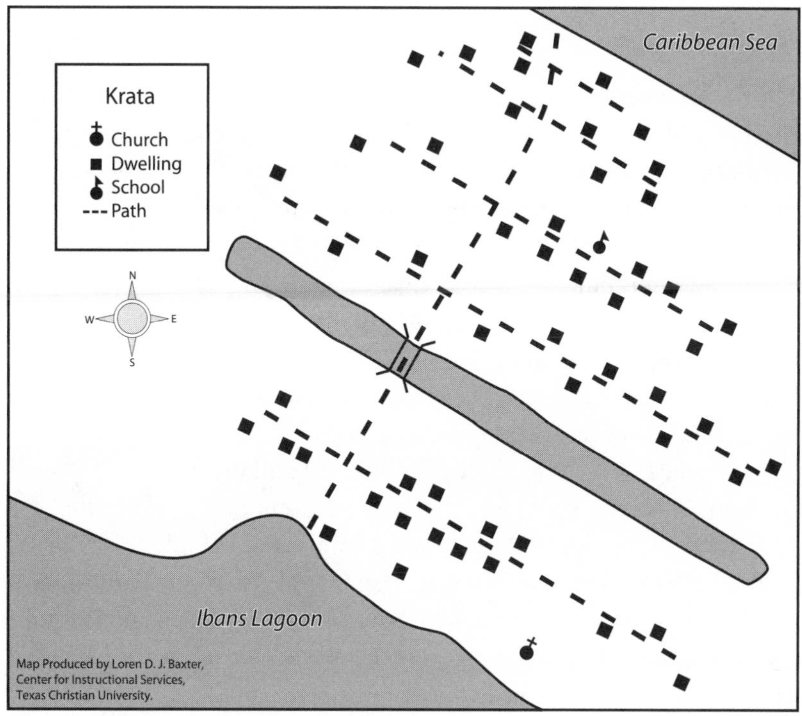

3.6 Sketch of Krata, 1998.

3.7 Houses on beach ridges, and elongated ponds, are significant components of Krata's settlement landscape, 1998.

Kaurkira

Kaurkira (Cauquira and Kaukira are Spanish adaptations of this Miskito place name) is a very large linear beach ridge settlement located on a narrow spit between the ocean and the lagoon. The street pattern consists of a single street that is fenced on each side with barbed wire and extends over five miles. The path links the villages of Dapat, Halaver, Kaurkira, Kinankan, and Tailibila. These villages have grown together, forming one long, continuous settlement. Many Miskito now refer to the whole group of villages as Kaurkira. Houses in Kaurkira are built closer together near the center of the settlement (fig. 3.8). Generally, there is only one row of houses between the lagoon and the street, and one to two rows on the other side of the street between the street and the ocean.

Kaurkira's center is elongated and consists of several stores that sell clothes, food, hardware, electronics, and a variety of additional items. It also includes docks for incoming cargo and passenger boats, a large warehouse, school, and plaza area. Seventh-Day Adventist and Catholic churches are located near the west end of the center, while the Moravian compound is located at the east end of the center and includes a church, homes for church leaders and doctors, a medical clinic, dock, landing strip, and cemetery.

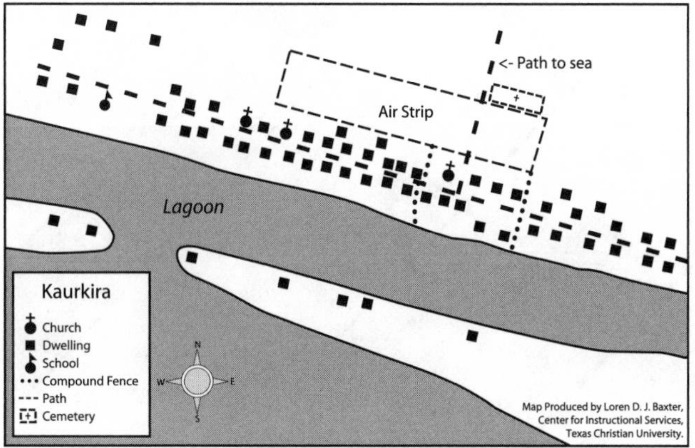

3.8 Sketch of Kaurkira's center, 1998 (adapted from Tillman 2005).

Raya

Raya is centered on the landing strip built by members of the community under the direction of the Moravian Church (fig. 3.9). Of all the settlements whose form has been altered by landing strips, Raya had its morphology impacted the most. The landing strip is the literal center of town, with the Moravian church and government-run health clinic located on the southeast side, and a school, principal stores, a restaurant, and a hotel on the southwest side. Homes are also situated along each side of the runway. A canal that leads to the sea forms the east border of Raya, and another canal, which connects to other villages in the area and to the Kruta River, forms the southwest border.

Tikiuraya

Tikiuraya is located on a narrow portion of high ground between the cut banks of two advancing meanders of the Kruta River (fig. 3.10). Tikiuraya's center is located at the narrowest point between meanders and contains a Catholic church, school, and government-run health center. Houses are mainly located along the river in a single row, and the main footpath follows the riverbank.

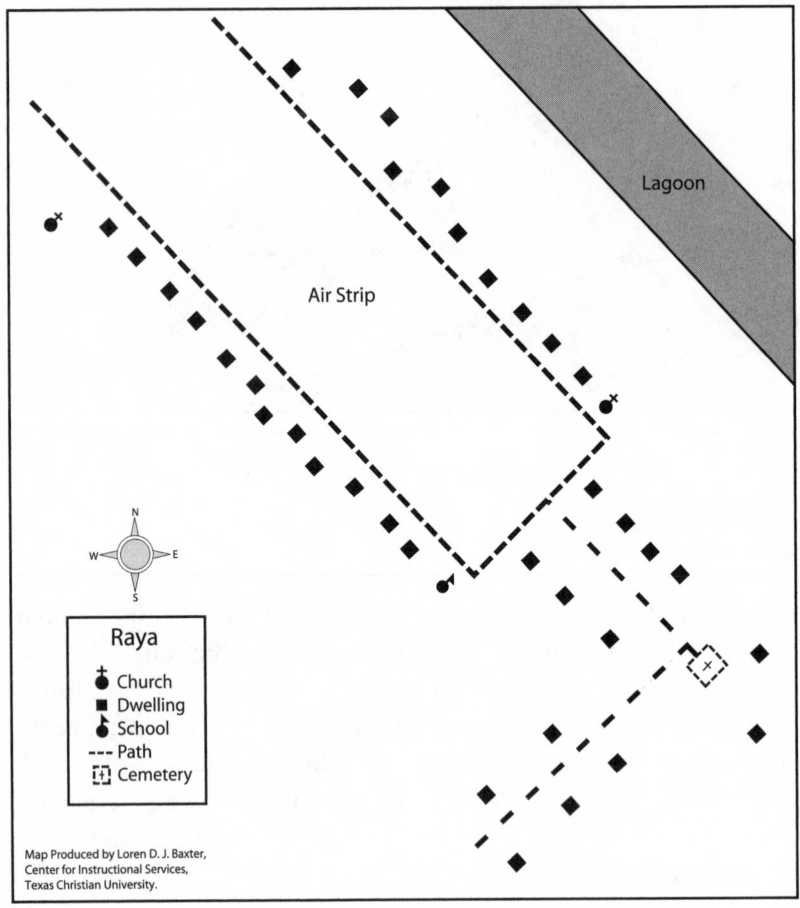

3.9 Sketch of Raya, 1998 (adapted from Tillman 2005).

Laka Tabila

Laka Tabila is one of several villages located on elevated mounds in an extensive savanna that is partially submerged during the rainy season (fig. 3.11). Villages in the area tend to be somewhat rounded, following the shape of the high ground they occupy. Laka Tabila outgrew its original area and abandoned its rounded shape. Homes in the Laka-area villages tend to be spread randomly at large distances, averaging forty yards apart as available high ground allows. Because of the randomness of house placement and the large distances between housing units, these villages

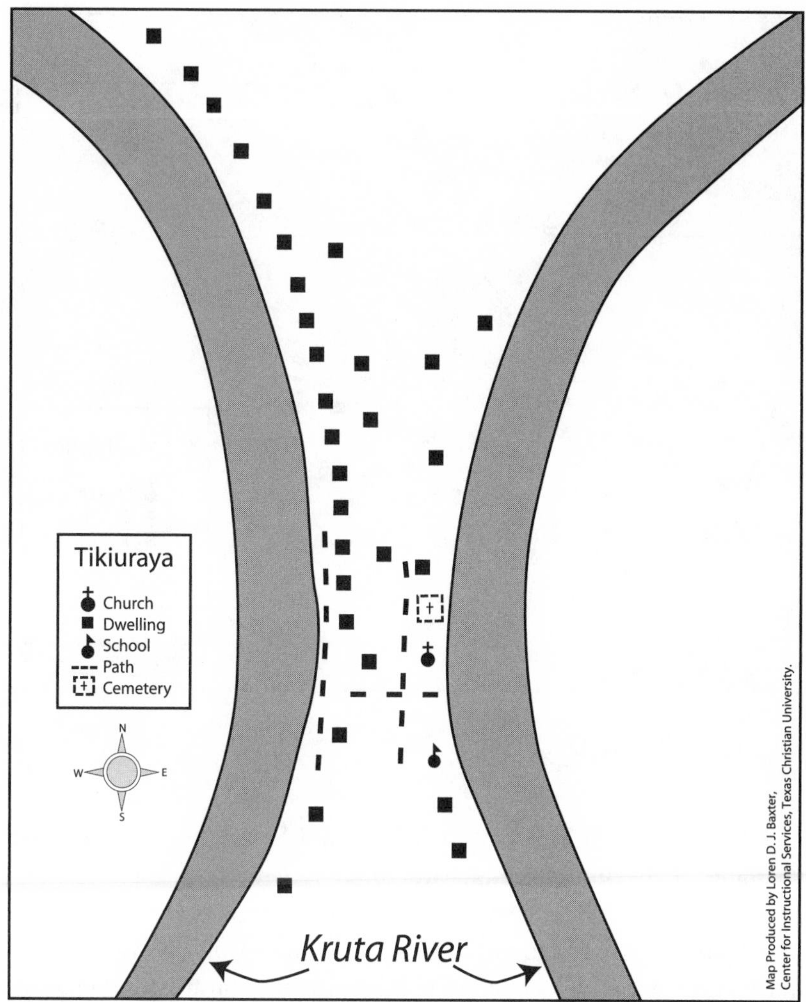

3.10 Sketch of Tikiuraya, 1998.

do not have concentrated centers, but boat landings, churches, and schools act as individual "centers of activity."

Lisangnipura

The United Nations created the village of Lisangnipura, named for the crystal-clear water of the adjacent creek, as a new settlement for the

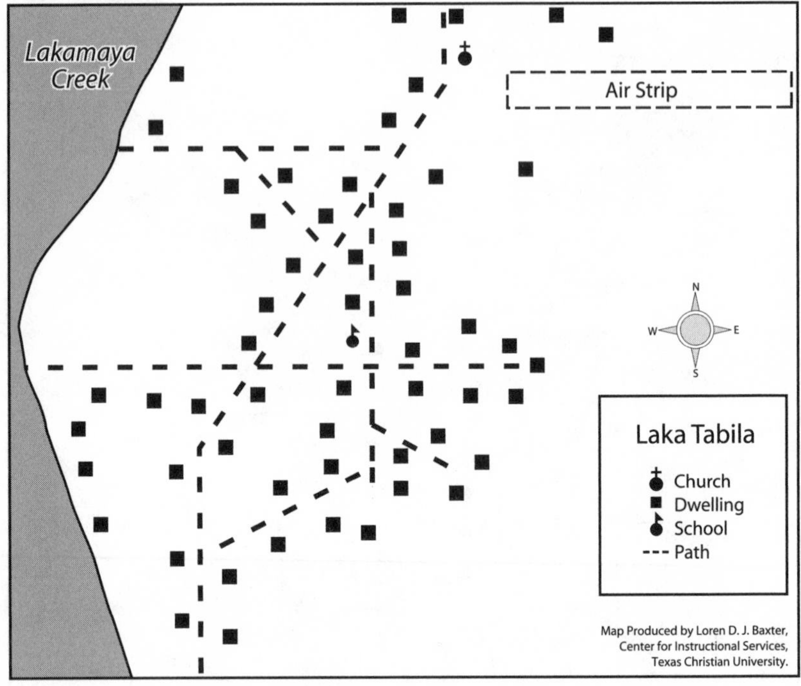

3.11 Sketch of Laka Tabila, 1998.

inhabitants of Lakunka, Baikan, Umro, and Siakwalaya, after massive flooding of the upper Kruta River in 1993 devastated these villages. Lisangnipura residents reportedly chose the location of the new settlement, and with the help of the United Nations, which provided trucks for hauling wood, zinc roofing, nails, and tools, constructed their own homes from pine trees cut in the savanna. The UN did not provide enough wood and supplies to make separate kitchens, so many houses in Lisangnipura have clay ovens located on their front porches.

Planned by the United Nations, Lisangnipura's layout was the most unusual of all Miskito villages, consisting of a regular grid pattern eight rows wide and eight rows deep (fig. 3.12). The layout also provided space for a soccer field and a community meeting hall. Inhabitants later constructed a new school east of the grid, and Baptist and Catholic churches are also present in the village. Occasionally, there are empty spaces in the rows of houses, because villagers never constructed houses, or they

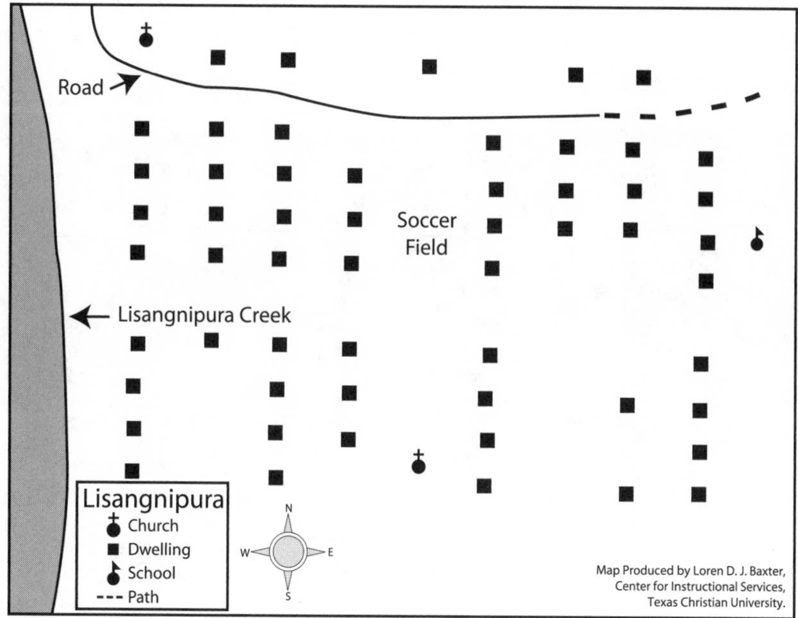

3.12 Sketch of Lisangnipura, 1998.

dismantled their houses and reconstructed them elsewhere. Some families returned to live in their previous villages, but most remain in Lisangnipura, returning only to farm their crops along the Kruta River.

Mocorón

Mocorón is located at the intersection of the coffee-colored Mocorón River and the crystal-clear spring-water run called Dursuna (fig. 3.13). Village tradition maintains the first individuals to settle Mocorón were two men: a Honduran Miskito named Armundo Garcia and a Nicaraguan Miskito named Sico Flores. These men lived on the Island of Tansin and frequently traveled up the Mocorón River to hunt; they eventually decided to settle at the site now called Mocorón. Like Mocorón, many river villages, such as Wauplaya, Suding, and Sirsirtara, were initially temporary encampments for people who lived in downstream villages but came upstream to work in their farming plots. These temporary encampments often grew into permanent settlements (Kaurkira Station

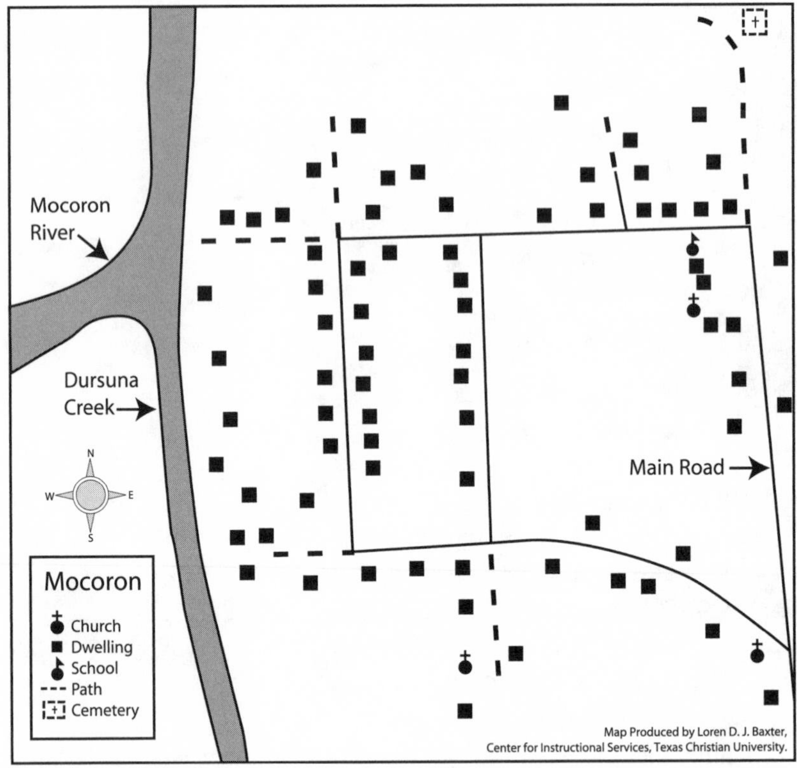

3.13 Sketch of Mocorón, 1998.

Report 1935:3). Mocorón also grew because of its relative proximity to villages on the Coco River where salt and other goods were available (Kaurkira Station Report 1935:3).

In 1981, Mocorón became a camp for ten thousand Nicaraguan Miskito refugees of the Sandinista–Contra war, funded primarily by the United Nations High Commissioner for Refugees (UNHCR) (Davidson 2009; Dodds 1989). While Mocorón was a refugee camp, its layout changed considerably as the UN constructed new streets in a gridlike pattern. A new settlement center was also created farther away from the river, surrounded by buildings constructed by relief agencies. After the refugee camp disbanded, the Moravian church reportedly relocated from a site closer to the river next to the current pastor's house, a building constructed by relief organizations at the new center of the settlement.

Puerto Lempira

Puerto Lempira is located on a short peninsula in the Caratasca Lagoon, at a point where the pine savanna extends to the shore. Originally known as Ayayeri, Puerto Lempira contained only one house in 1931 (Kaurkira Station Diary 1931:41). The Honduran government selected the site for a military base in 1937 during the dispute between Honduras and Nicaragua over ownership of the territory between the Kruta and Coco rivers. But Puerto Lempira did not grow significantly until oil companies began searching for deposits in the 1950s and 1960s (Helbig 1965). It eventually became the largest settlement in the Mosquitia, and capital of the Department of Gracias a Dios.

Puerto Lempira has become the Mosquitia's main government and economic center, connected to major Honduran cities by airplane and cargo ship. The town is also connected to Ahuas, Brus Lagoon, and Belén by small aircraft. In addition, regular overland trips by trucks connect Sirsirtara, Mocorón, and Leimus with Puerto Lempira. However, the use of small watercraft is by far the most common method of transportation within the Honduran Mosquitia. On any morning except Sunday, and especially after the arrival of a cargo ship, the pier at Puerto Lempira appears to be a floating parking lot, accommodating twenty to thirty small boats from various villages. Most boats are *cayucos*—dugout canoes with outboard motors, or *tuktuks*—dugout canoes with inboard motors. Most outboard motors range in size between fifteen and twenty-five horsepower, but the Miskito use a few forty- and eighty-horsepower motors. Tuktuk motors are normally smaller: three- to seven-horsepower Briggs and Stratton engines. However, a Datsun car engine powers a large tuktuk that makes the run between Kaurkira and Puerto Lempira.

Typically, boats arrive in Puerto Lempira from outlying villages between six and nine in the morning. Passengers either continue travel by air or boat to another location or stay in Puerto Lempira to conduct business or to purchase food, fuel, and other goods. After passengers complete their business and shopping, they return to the pier to wait. Once a given boat is full or nearly full of passengers, it will return to its village. Boats leave the pier anywhere from ten a.m. to two p.m. By three p.m. the pier is nearly empty. In 1998, most fares ranged between $2.00 and $2.50, but fares fluctuated depending on the availability of gasoline.

Puerto Lempira's main street runs northeast–southwest between the pier and the Catholic church and contains the main plaza, hotels, and stores selling a variety of items, including construction materials, outboard motors, food, and clothes (fig. 3.14). It also contains an airline office, a cargo freight office, bars, restaurants, a hair salon, a bank, and a government hospital and health center. The uniform portion of the grid, which was reportedly constructed in the 1960s, has four northwest–southeast streets and nine northeast–southwest streets. Beyond this area, main streets running north–south become footpaths, but some northeast–southwest streets continue to the airport. There are several areas where villagers built new homes outside the grid, but subsequent roads or dirt paths do not follow a grid pattern.

Ahuas

Ahuas is located on a pine ridge in the savanna near the Patuca River. In 1932, a Moravian missionary reported Ahuas contained twenty houses and had plenty of food because "good provision grounds [were] within easy reach" (Kaurkira Station Diary 1932:72). Ahuas has become a large and important settlement in the Honduran Mosquitia, in part because it is the site of the Honduran Moravian Church headquarters and the Moravian hospital. Moravians established a church in Ahuas in 1937, a clinic in 1946, and a landing strip in 1948 (Marx 1980).

Apparently, Moravians made no significant attempts to create a grid pattern or to change the street layout of Ahuas. American missionaries lived in Kaurkira, Cocobila, and Brus Lagoon, but not in Ahuas, except for Samuel Marx, who was the first doctor-pastor in the clinic beginning in 1952 (Marx 1980). Although the Moravians did not create a grid, they did construct a substantial number of large buildings that visually dominate the town.

Ahuas is a binodal settlement (fig. 3.15). The primary node includes the airport office, police station, airplane hangar, Moravian hospital complex, and nearby stores. The secondary node is closer to the geographic center of Ahuas and includes the local Moravian chapel and the Moravian Church headquarters. Ahuas's main road begins at the airport and runs along the east side of the village to the Paptalaya landing on the Patuka River. Residents I spoke with stated that most of the houses were

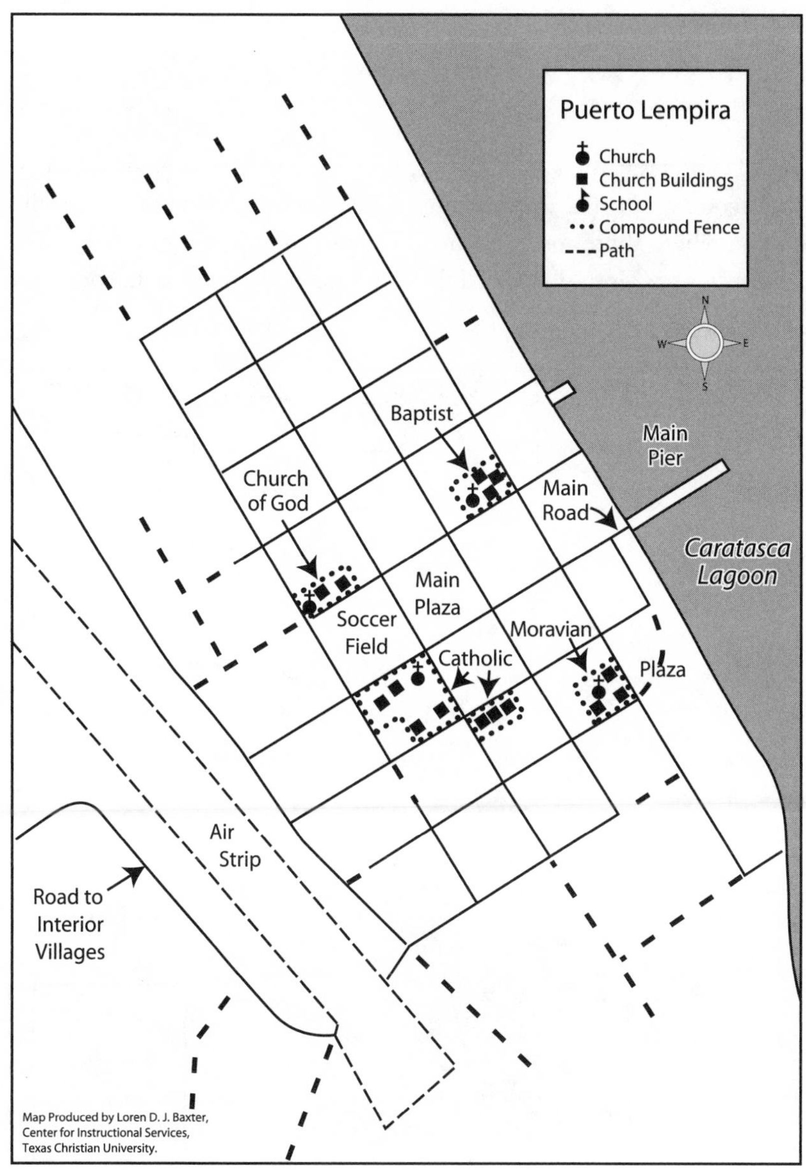

3.14 Sketch of Puerto Lempira, 1998.

initially located closer to the river, in the vicinity of the Moravian church, but that over the years the settlement grew toward the hospital and airport.

Brus Lagoon

Brus Lagoon is named after "Bloody Brewer," a pirate who took refuge in the lagoon during the 1650s (Helbig 1965). Located on the interior of the lagoon where shore meets savanna, Brus Lagoon is one of a few settlements in the Mosquitia that follows a grid pattern. Brus Lagoon is a

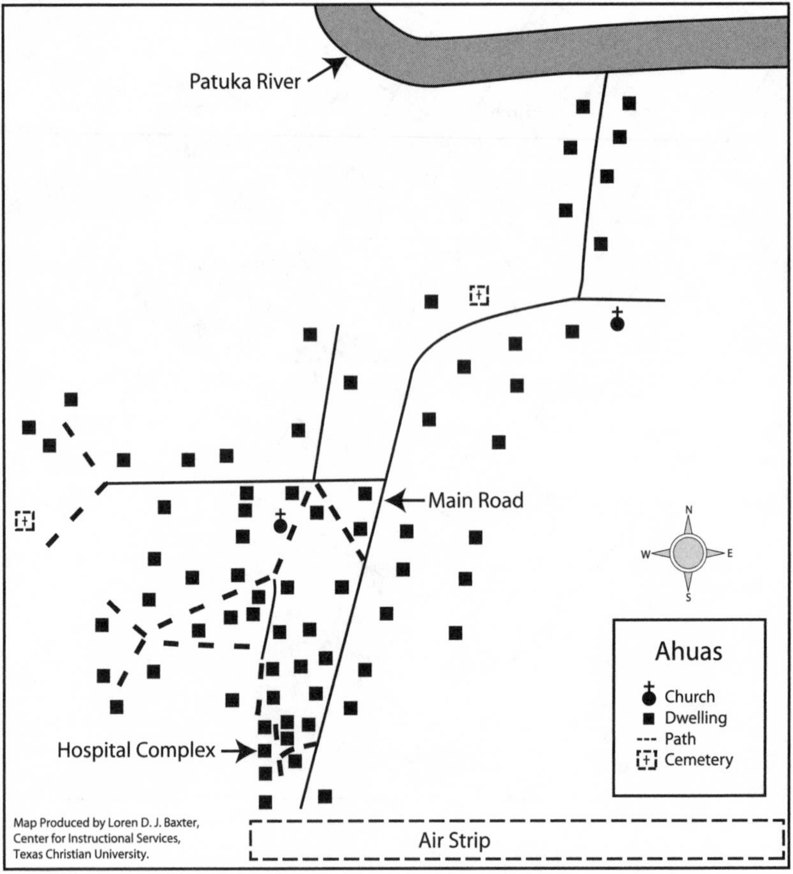

3.15 Sketch of Ahuas, 1998.

cabecera municipal (municipal head), a government center similar to a county seat, and during the 1950s the government constructed its gravel roads in a gridiron pattern (fig. 3.16). Air photos taken in 1961 reveal that the grid was superimposed on the existing village and new residents placed their dwellings to match the pattern. Today, a few streets continue past the original grid, but most homes constructed beyond the grid were not built to match an organized street pattern.

A Moravian missionary directed construction of the principal street before the Honduran government laid out the current grid. It runs from the lagoon through the Moravian compound, which is the center of the settlement, and continues on to a field that serves as a landing strip for small planes (larger, twelve-passenger turbo-prop airplanes arriving from

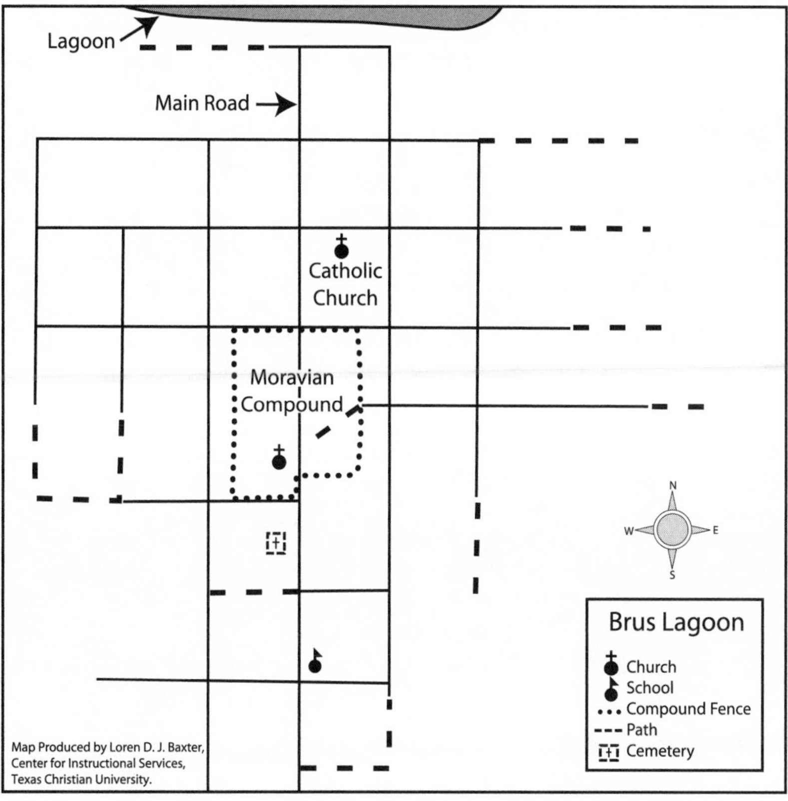

3.16 Sketch of Brus Lagoon, 1998 (adapted from Tillman 2005).

La Ceiba use a longer landing strip located farther outside the settlement). A handful of businesses are located along this street, with perhaps the most prominent being a store and hotel adjacent to the lagoon, and a large business situated next to the Moravian compound that houses a general store, an airline ticket office, and a small hotel.

Brus Lagoon is a significant settlement because it served as Moravian Church headquarters from the late 1940s to the early 1960s and is the best example of the German settlement type Moravians introduced into the Honduran Mosquitia. This settlement type and the overt Moravian landscape consisting of churches and compounds are discussed in chapter 4.

CHAPTER 4

The Overt Moravian Landscape

Churches and Compounds

THE GEOGRAPHY OF RELIGION encompasses a variety of cultural–geographic themes (Sopher 1967; Kong 1990). For example, geographers study religious regions and map the distribution and spatial diffusion of religious groups over time (Zelinsky 1961; Meinig 1965; Shortridge 1976; Stump 1984). Geographers also examine religion's influence on the cultural landscape, including Black Christ pilgrimage shrines in Central America (Horst 1998), fruit tree dispersal in the Mediterranean (Isaac 1959), settlement form in the mountain west (Jackson and Layton 1976), and domestic architecture in North America (Francaviglia 1971a, 1978; Noble 1986; Kent and Neugebauer 1990). For Park (1994, 244), "the impacts of religion on landscape represent without doubt the most visible link between geography and religion."

Geographers designate houses of worship as significant components of the cultural landscape because, as sacred space, houses of worship are distinct from other structures. Jackson and Henrie defined sacred space as "that portion of the earth's surface which is recognized by individuals or groups as worthy of devotion, loyalty or esteem. Sacred space is sharply discriminated from the non-sacred or profane world around it" (Jackson and Henrie 1983, 94). Geographers also examine why church form and building materials may change over time, and they investigate how believers orient and situate their sacred edifices within settlements (Fuson 1969; Shilhav 1983; Prorok 1988, 1991).

Church Orientation and Location within Settlements

Unlike in the rest of Honduras, where one can almost always find an east–west-oriented church on the east side of the plaza (Tillman 2008), churches in Mosquitia are usually not oriented to specific compass headings or cardinal directions, but instead are commonly oriented to natural or manmade features (table 4.1). For example, churches in Cocobila, Twitanta, Dapat, and Puerto Lempira face lagoons; the Tasabapauni church faces the sea; and the Dakratara church faces toward Lacamaya Creek—the main transportation route in that area. Main paths or roads commonly serve as orientation points for churches, including those in Brus Lagoon, Katski, Kusua Apaika, and Mocorón. Churches in Belén, Kaurkira, Raya, and Tumtumtara are located parallel to adjacent airstrips.

In coastal settlements, the ridge lines of churches often parallel the ridge lines of houses. This type of orientation occurs most often in seaside villages, including Ibans, Belén, Nueva Jerusalén, Uhi, Yahurabila, Katski, Pumnitara, Kaurkira, Benk, and Raya. Residents of these villages place the ridge lines of their structures perpendicular to the trade winds, allowing maximum breezes to flow through the windows. The Miskito often oriented their churches to more than one feature. For example, churches with ridgepole or lagoon orientation often face or are adjacent to main paths as well.

Of course, church orientation can change through time. For example, new chapels constructed in Ahuas, Brus Lagoon, Kaurkira, Kruta, Mistruk, and Mocorón, face different directions than the previous buildings. Reasons given for the change in orientation reflected congregational preferences and practical decision making. In one settlement, residents told me that local church leaders changed the church's position ninety degrees so that the prevailing breeze would flow better through the windows. In another case, the residents reoriented a chapel by ninety degrees so that passing pedestrians would not distract worshippers sitting by windows. Lack of space was the most common reason church orientation changed. New churches were always larger and were often constructed adjacent to the old church. The new building often had to be pivoted to fit on the lot.

Murtagh (1967) found that chapels "visually dominated" Moravian settlements in Germany and North America. Moravian missionaries in Nicaragua thought it important to locate churches on high ground. For the village of Twappi, they selected a site "above the village and commanding a good view over the sea which [was] about a mile distant" (Moravian Church 1849–1887, 34:109). Helms (1971:46) reported the Moravian church in Asang, Nicaragua, was visually prominent and

TABLE 4.1. Moravian churches in Mosquitia: Orientation and construction materials (adapted from Tillman 2005)

Settlement*	Compass Heading	Feature Orientation	Floor/Walls/Roof
Ahuas (25)	10°	north/road	concrete/concrete/asbestos
Auka (95)	220°	dwelling ridgepoles	posts/boards/zinc**
Belén (7)	100°	dwelling ridgepoles	concrete/concrete/asbestos
Benk (120)	330°	dwelling ridgepoles	posts/boards/zinc
Brus Lagoon (21)	100°	main street	concrete/concrete/zinc
Cocal (138)	300°	plaza	posts/boards/zinc
Cocobila (5)	200°	lagoon	concrete/concrete/zinc
Dakratara (87)	80°	creek	concrete/concrete/zinc
Dapat (137)	~SW	lagoon	concrete/concrete/asbestos
Ibans (4)	115°	dwelling ridgepoles	posts/boards/zinc**
Katski Almuk (140)	140°	main path	dirt/kanko/thatch
Kaurkira (135)	110°	dwelling ridgepoles	concrete/concrete/asbestos
Kruta (112)	~N	path/river	concrete/concrete/zinc
Kusua apaika (20)	20°	road	posts/boards/zinc
Mistruk (58)	~N	path	posts/boards/zinc**
Mocorón (70)	40°	plaza	posts/boards/zinc**
Nueva Jerusalén (9)	100°	dwelling ridgepoles	posts/boards/zinc
Palkaka (46)	70°	lagoon	concrete/concrete/zinc
Paptalya (24)	~N	north/road/river	concrete/concrete/asbestos
Prumnitara (139)	140°	main path	concrete/concrete/zinc
Puerto Lempira (55)	~NE	lagoon	concrete/concrete/zinc
Raya (122)	140°	runway	concrete/concrete/zinc
Sirsirtara (65)	320°	creek/river	posts/boards/zinc
Tasbapauni (12)	20°	ocean	concrete/concrete/asbestos
Tasbaraya (50)	230°	main path/lagoon	posts/boards/zinc**
Tumtumtara (90)	90°	runway/main path	posts/boards/zinc
Twitanta (19)	20°	lagoon/main path	posts/boards/zinc
Uhi (41)	~NNW	main path	posts/boards/zinc
Wauplaya (63)	270°	none	posts/boards/zinc**
Yahurabila (44)	300°	lagoon	concrete/concrete/asbestos

* Parenthetical numbers are to be used in conjunction with the designations in fig. 1.2.

** A concrete church was under construction at the time of the study.

could "be seen several miles down river." Moravian missionaries in Honduras also located their churches in visually prominent places. Several factors cause this visual prominence. First, churches are usually located on high ground and in open areas. Second, churches are almost always the largest buildings in their communities. Third, while most Miskito dwellings are unpainted, Moravians typically paint their church walls white and their churches' metal roofs with a red-colored rust inhibitor. Because of the above factors, one can often spot a settlement's Moravian church from a significant distance. For example, one can see the unpainted, shiny zinc roof of Prumnitara's church glimmering in the sun from across the lagoon in Puerto Lempira, a distance of approximately thirteen miles. In another outstanding example, the Dakratara church rests on some of the highest ground in the Laka savanna, and its white walls and red roof can be seen from other villages in the area. One can also see churches in Cocobila, Dapat, Palkaka, and Puerto Lempira from a distance when approaching from the lagoon.

The missionaries placed churches in settlements that they considered strategic locations based on accessibility, future population, and membership growth (Reinke 1913). For example, in Honduras, missionaries chose to place their first churches in Kaurkira, Brus Lagoon, Cocobila, Auka, and Ahuas, with the hope of reaching the entire Miskito population from those locations (Heath 1939b). Once the Moravians established primary congregations, missionaries traveled to neighboring villages to organize new congregations (Heath 1941b).

Missionaries also deliberated carefully before determining where to locate a church within a given settlement. They typically considered such factors as high ground, centrality within settlements, and locations central to several nearby villages. For example, Heath selected the Kaurkira church's site because it was the available land most central to surrounding settlements, but in Brus Lagoon, Moravians "erected [the church] on the highest point of the savanna, not far from the grave yard" (Kaurkira Station Diary 1930:1933).

Moravian Church Architecture

Moravian church architecture in Herrnhut and other locations, such as Bethlehem, Pennsylvania, consisted of large, three-to-four-storey edifices typically constructed of brick or stone. In distinctive Moravian style, architects positioned belfries in the center of the roof rather than at one of the gabled ends. Unlike common church architecture, where the main entrance and pulpit are located on opposing gabled ends, with pews running the width of the building, early Moravian chapels had the pulpit and main entrance on the longer, non-gabled walls, with pews running the length of the building (Kalfus 1957; Moravian Church 1972).

This type of architecture was not always feasible in Moravian missions abroad. Moravians adopted a style common among Protestant groups, consisting of the entrance and pulpit being located on opposite gabled ends, with the belfry located at one of the ends (usually at the entrance); they propagated this style throughout their missions. Moravians adopted this style not only because it was popular among many Protestant groups during the period, but also because it was functional, less expensive, and simple, and therefore easy to learn and replicate. During the 1800s, and into the 1900s, Moravians used this style of church architecture so widely throughout their missions that it effectively became "standard" Moravian church architecture.

Honduran Stages of Construction Material

Honduran Moravian church architecture changed over time, beginning with local forms and materials, continuing with European forms and both local and manufactured materials, and concluding with imported, manufactured materials. I classify churches into three stages, primarily by foundation and secondarily by roof and wall materials. In the first stage, churches were built of local materials and had dirt floors. On occasion, boards or split trunks of saw cabbage palm laid on the dirt served as flooring. The first buildings constructed by the Moravians in Honduras were stage-one structures. For example, Kaurkira's first church had a roof of saw cabbage palm thatch and walls of saw cabbage palm trunks placed vertically (Proceedings of the Society for Propagating the Gospel Among the Heathen 1937:63). Small, beginning congregations, such as the one in Katski Almuk, still use this type of church construction today (fig. 4.1).

Likewise, the first churches in Cocobila and Brus Lagoon had dirt floors and were built with local materials. Both churches were made of split bamboo walls (bamboo that is slit lengthwise and then pressed flat

4.1 A stage-one church in Katski Almuk, 1998.

like a board) and had thatched roofs made of suita palm fronds (Proceedings of the Society for Propagating the Gospel Among the Heathen, 1938:46). Although the missionaries approved of thatch as a roofing material, they did not like to use saw cabbage palm trunks for walls. Heath wrote, "Apart from good posts and thatched leaves, there are no satisfactory building materials in the neighborhood [Kaurkira]. Indians make a sort of wall to their houses of upright papta stems [saw cabbage palm trunks]; but the result is untidy and not durable" (Kaurkira Station Diary 1930:2). Furthermore, the missionaries preferred buildings raised above the ground on posts, and palm trunks were most easily used if the structure had a dirt floor. Missionaries only temporarily used saw cabbage palm trunks and split bamboo as wall material, until they could saw or purchase lumber (Kaurkira Station Report 1935:2).

In the second stage, Moravians constructed their churches with board floors raised three feet above the ground on posts. Sawed boards and zinc were the most common wall and roof materials employed in the construction of second-stage churches, but thatch and split bamboo were occasionally used. Moravian congregations often painted the board walls of stage-two churches white, and zinc roofs were painted with a red-colored rust inhibitor, causing the building to stand out from its generally brown-and-green surroundings (fig. 4.2). Stage-two churches were much larger than their predecessors, typically ranging in width from twenty feet to thirty feet, and in length from forty feet to sixty feet. They generally seated 150 to 250 people.

I classify Moravian churches constructed with concrete foundations and walls into stage three. An off-white corrugated material the Miskito called "asbestos" was most often used as roofing, but zinc was still common. Stage-three churches vary in size more than stage-two churches, but a width of forty feet and a length of eighty feet was a common size. The Moravians built their first stage-three church in Kaurkira in 1972 (Johnson 1972) and completed the largest stage-three church on April 19, 1998, in Ahuas (Marx 1998). Moravians claim this one-hundred-by-sixty-foot church is the largest church of any denomination in the Department of Gracias a Dios (fig. 4.3). Most stage-three churches are similar in form (rectangular) to stage-two churches, but Moravians built stage-three churches in Tasbaraya, Mistruk, and Mocorón in the form of a cross.

4.2 A stage-two church in Twitanta, 1996.

4.3 A stage-three church in Ahuas, 1998.

While the Katski Almuk chapel was the only stage-one church used in the villages I visited, several stage-two chapels were still in use, including those in Nueva Jerusalén, Twitanta, Kusu Apaika, Uhi, Cocal, Benk, Tumtumtara, and Sirsirtara. Stage-two churches in Ibans, Auka, Mocorón, Mistruk, and Wauplaya will eventually be replaced by concrete churches under construction in those villages. Concrete churches were in use in Ahuas, Belén, Brus Lagoon, Cocobila, Dakratara, Dapat, Kaurkira, Kruta, Palkaka, Paptalaya, Prumnitara, Puerto Lempira, Raya, Tasbapauni, and Yahuarabila. Moravian congregations used some stage-two buildings replaced by concrete structures for other church functions, such as Sunday school meeting rooms or as rooms for youth groups, but dismantled others and used their materials to construct pastors' homes.

Moravian leaders believe that the more-expensive concrete buildings will be cost-effective in the long run because they withstand the rain and termites for a longer period of time. In addition to making regular weekly financial contributions, some congregations operated small kitchens that sold lunch to raise money for building construction and other purposes. The first and most significant of these was probably located in Cocobila across the main path from the church. Built in 1980, this twenty-by-seventy-foot structure was known as *kisikin* and contained a kitchen and store. Local members used store profits to purchase a large canoe and an ice machine, and also to build a house for the resident pastor (Marx 1980). Some villagers stated that a few congregations, especially those along the coast, received donations from lobster divers (who make high wages in comparison to other jobs in the region) and lobster-boat owners. In some cases, Moravian congregations in the United States donated money and labor.

The Influence of European Moravian Town Planning on Honduran Compounds

Moravian communal settlements in Europe and North America were planned and exhibit at least three common characteristics. First, settlements contained a central square, often bisected by the principal road. Second, Moravians frequently constructed churches within the square, but at times chapels and church-owned buildings lined the sides of the square. In the latter case, the square contained gardens or was simply an open green. Third, churches were typically the largest structures in the settlement and therefore visually dominated their communities (Murtagh 1967; Büttner 1974). For example, a 1722 plan of Herrnhut shows that the Moravians planned the town around a central square. The church dominated the central square, which also contained a fire station and a formal garden (Murtagh 1967). In another example, a 1742 plan of Nisky illustrates that Moravians centered the town on a square that was bisected by the town's main road. Unlike Herrnhut, Nisky's central square was left void of buildings and was essentially a large garden divided into four sections.

The principal Moravian settlement in North America, Bethlehem, Pennsylvania, was also planned around a central square. Bethlehem's central square did not contain structures or a garden but was intended to remain an open green (Murtagh 1967). Other Moravian settlements in North America followed similar designs. For example, the North Carolina settlements of Bethania, founded in 1759, and Salem (Winston-Salem), founded in 1766, were planned around a central square that was bisected by the main road, with church buildings constructed around the square. Also the town of Lititz, Pennsylvania, consisted of a central square located on the south side of the principal road that was surrounded by church buildings. In all of these settlements, gardens and orchards were prominent (Murtagh 1967; Merian 1975; Brownlee 1977; Griffen 1985).

These examples make it clear that positioning a settlement's main road to run through the religious compound was a key aspect of Moravian town planning. This type of settlement morphology served practical purposes and conveyed symbolic meaning. Because of its central location, the compound not only served as the focal point of religious life but could also be a center for nonreligious community activities. In addition, just as the church was located in a prominent place within the settlement, it also played a prominent role in the lives of community members.

Moravian expansion on the Mosquito Coast centered on the establishment of "mission stations," which I refer to as compounds, because they are typically enclosed and fenced off from surrounding property. The following is an 1855 description of the first Moravian compound on the Mosquito Coast, located in Bluefields, Nicaragua: "About ten acres of land belong to the Mission, six or seven of which are inclosed with a fence, and these are again subdivided into smaller portions. In the garden, which is next to the dwelling-house, the esculent productions of the tropics grow in perfection, as is also the case with the cocoa-nut and other fruit-trees which have been planted there. A good deal of labour has been bestowed upon the ground. There are six cows and twenty pigs belonging to the Mission" (Wullschlagel 1856:33–36).

Similar to the central portion of Moravian communities in Europe and North America, Honduran compounds consisted of an open green that typically contained a church and a house for the missionary couple. In time, compounds with large congregations expanded to include several buildings, such as community kitchens, schools, and health clinics. In addition, small gardens and fruit trees were important compound features. Because Moravian missionaries consistently planted fruit trees in each new compound they established, Nietschmann (1973) credited them with aiding the dispersal of fruit trees, particularly breadfruit and rose apple, to various villages. Fruit tree species commonly cultivated in Honduran compounds I studied include coconut, breadfruit, mango, cashew, orange, lemon, grapefruit, lime, pelipita, and rose apple.

Hierarchy of Moravian Centers

I placed each of the thirty settlements studied with a Moravian church into a "hierarchy of Moravian centers" to determine where the overt Moravian landscape was most evident (table 4.2). I created a hierarchy based on the compound's number and function of buildings, the compound's prominence within a settlement (central or peripheral location), the compound's impact on settlement form, congregation size,[1] and the presence or lack of other denominations in the settlement. Level one consisted of fully developed compounds with large, open greens, fruit trees, gardens, and boundaries clearly demarcated by fencing. In addition to the church and pastor's or reverend's home (a reverend oversees several congregations), these compounds contained a Moravian school, clinic, or hospital, and/or followed the German-Moravian settlement type, whereby the main village road bisected the compound. I categorized villages with relatively large congregations and compounds, but without Moravian schools, medical facilities, and German-Moravian settlement

TABLE 4.2. Hierarchy of Moravian centers

Level 1	Level 2	Level 3
Ahuas (25)*	Auka (96)	Cocal (138)
Brus Lagoon (21)	Belén (7)	Dakratara (87)
Cocobila (5)	Benk (120)	Dapat (137)
Kaurkira (135)	Ibans (4)	Katski Almuk (140)
	Kusua apaika (20)	Kruta (112)
	Mocorón (70)	Mistruk (58)
	Nueva Jerusalén (9)	Sirsirtara (65)
	Palkaka (46)	Tasbaraya (50)
	Paptalaya (24)	Wauplaya (63)
	Prumnitara (139)	
	Puerto Lempira (55)	
	Raya (122)	
	Tasbapauni (12)	
	Tumtumtara (90)	
	Twitanta (19)	
	Uhi (41)	
	Yahurabila (44)	

* Parenthetical numbers are to be used in conjunction with the designations in fig. 1.2.

patterns, into level two. I placed settlements with only a church and no permanently stationed pastor, or settlements with small congregations and small, unfenced compounds, into level three. It is important to note that many Miskito-Moravians living in settlements without churches travel short distances to attend Moravian church services in nearby villages. In fact, some villages do not have their own Moravian church only because village population is too small or because they have access to a church in a neighboring settlement.

A map of the hierarchy highlights a reoccurring theme (fig. 4.4). The four major centers (Ahuas, Brus Lagoon, Cocobila, and Kaurkira) are also four of the five original sites where Moravian missionaries initially established congregations when they began their Honduran work in 1930. These four compounds exhibited the greatest overt Moravian influence on the Miskito settlement landscape, because they are the only sites where the church permanently stationed its foreign missionaries. In contrast, a Miskito pastor founded Auka, the fifth and most geographically isolated original congregation. The map also shows that the capital of

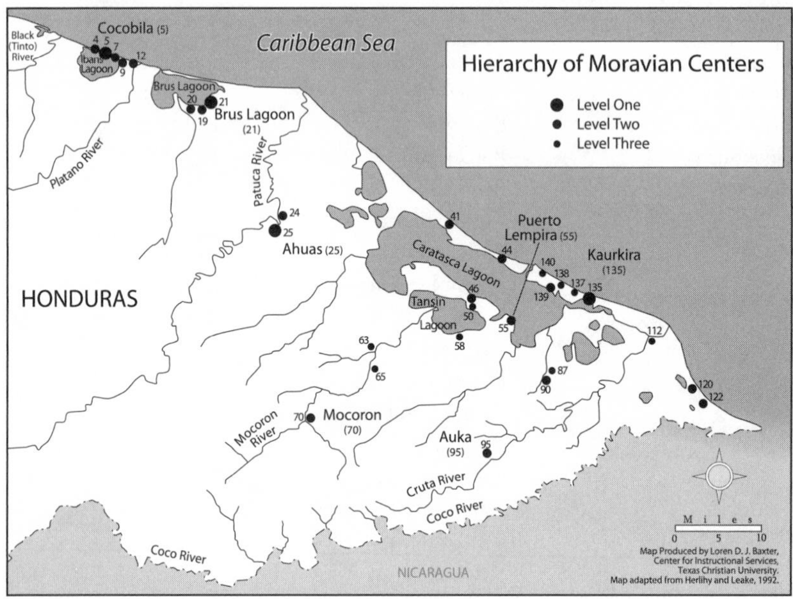

4.4 Hierarchy of Moravian centers, 1998 (see table 1.1 for settlement names).

the Department of Gracias a Dios, and its largest settlement—Puerto Lempira—is not a major Moravian center. Puerto Lempira's compound was not as large as compounds in the four major Moravian centers, it did not follow the German-Moravian settlement type, and the town was also the headquarters for the Catholic Church, the Baptist Church, and the Church of God.

The Four Major Centers

Excluding the special case of Ahuas, which I will discuss shortly, only three compounds—Kaurkira, Cocobila, and Brus Lagoon—were operated by foreign missionaries. Not coincidentally, these three locations contained the largest compounds and followed the settlement pattern Moravians used in their European and North American towns, consisting of buildings located within or around a main square that was bisected by the principal road in the settlement.

Kaurkira

George R. Heath (1958) founded the first Moravian mission station in Honduras at Kaurkira on November 18, 1930. At the time of my 1998 visit, the compound ran parallel to the lagoon and was bisected by Kaurkira's main road (fig. 4.5). The reverend's and pastor's homes, church kitchen, boat shed and dock, storage shed, and a house for patients' families are located between the lagoon and the main road. The church, clinic office and doctor's home, two clinic buildings which housed patients downstairs and doctors and other visitors upstairs, and a small utility building sheltering a large diesel-powered electric generator are all located on the other side of the street, away from the lagoon. Both sides are fenced off from the surrounding area, but the portion containing the clinic is also surrounded by shrubbery and includes a variety of fruit trees. A groundskeeper maintains the property, and its resulting appearance is radically different from the typical Miskito yard. The landing strip and cemetery, which formerly belonged exclusively to the mission, were located behind the clinic portion of the compound. Concrete construction now dominates the compound. Buildings and portions of buildings constructed of concrete include the posts of the reverend's home and the

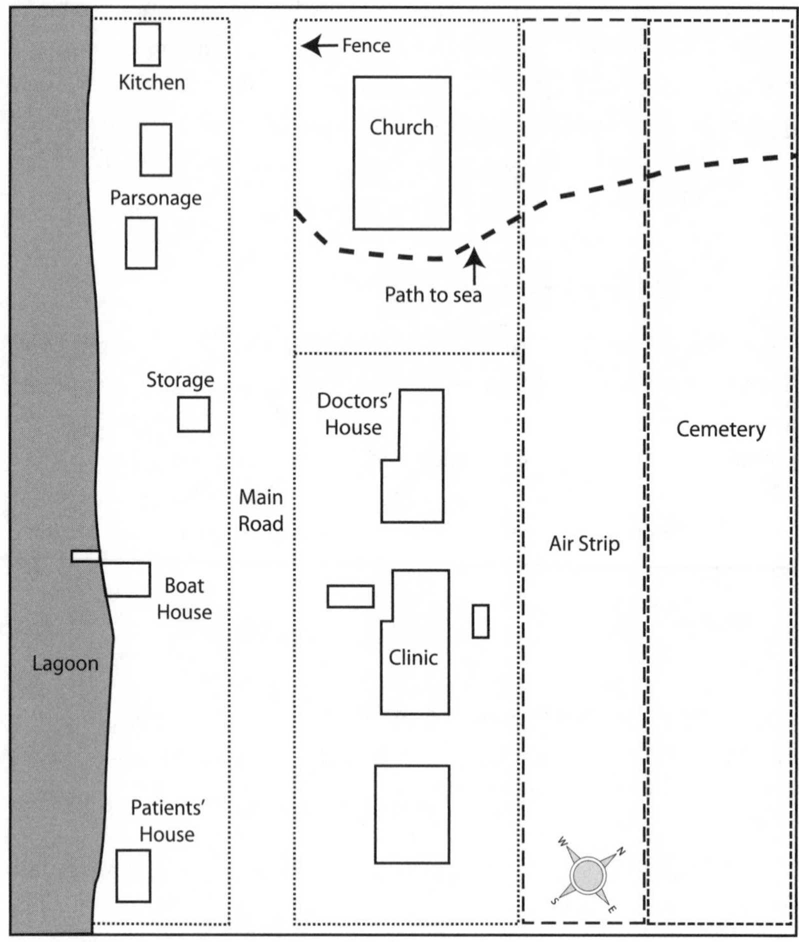

4.5 Sketch of the Kaurkira Moravian compound, 1998 (adapted from Tillman 2005).

clinic office and doctor's home, as well as the entire church, the bottom floors of the two clinic buildings, the boat shed, and utility buildings.

Cocobila

George Heath also constructed Cocobila's compound when permanently stationed there in 1938 (Marx 1937; Heath 1940a). According to

Cocobila residents I spoke with, Heath planted several breadfruit trees and coconut palms within the compound, but a hurricane later destroyed many of the trees. As in Kaurkira, the principal village road bisects the Cocobila compound (fig. 4.6). The first church, a twenty-by-forty-foot structure with dirt floor, split bamboo walls, and thatched roof, occupied a large open area on the east side of the main path across from the current reverend's home, but several years later the Moravians built a new church

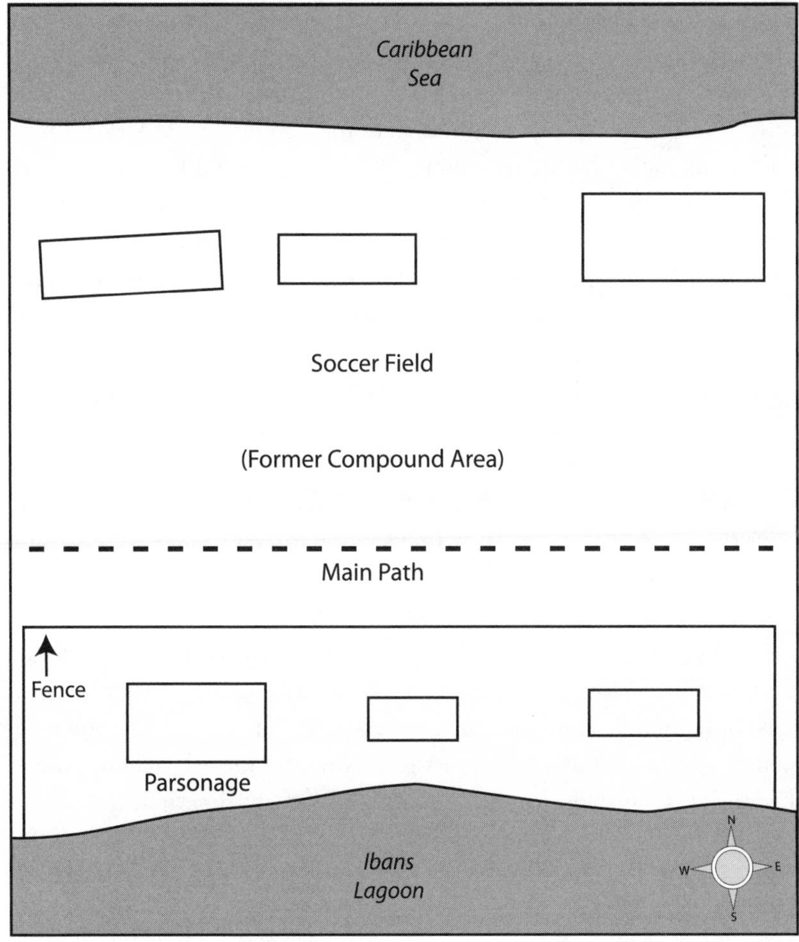

4.6 Sketch of the Cocobila Moravian compound, 1998 (adapted from Tillman 2005).

outside of the original compound area, in what has become a more central location. By 1978, the Moravian Church no longer owned half of the original square, and by the time I conducted fieldwork in 1996, a private residence and business were located on the side opposite the reverend's home (Dreger 1978; Wilford Dreger, pers. comm., July 15, 1998).

Brus Lagoon

Brus Lagoon is the best example of a Moravian compound in Honduras (fig. 4.7). Brus Lagoon served as Moravian Church headquarters in Mosquitia from the late 1940s to the early 1960s, and since 1951 the Moravian school *Renacimiento* (renaissance, rebirth) made the settlement one of Mosquitia's most important educational centers (Marx 1980). Originally constructed by the missionary Werner Marx, and bisected by Brus Lagoon's main road, the compound spans a spacious central square (Werner Marx, pers. comm., July 16, 1998). As in European and North American Moravian settlements, Moravians in Brus Lagoon utilized a large portion of the compound for growing fruit trees. Buildings located within the compound included a church, houses for the reverend and local pastor, classroom buildings, a carpentry school workshop, a small library, boys' and girls' dorms, and an auditorium. Brus Lagoon's Moravian congregation constructed their new church and carpentry school with concrete foundations and walls, but the rest of the buildings had construction consisting of wood floors raised three feet above the ground on posts, board walls, verandas, and gabled zinc roofs (fig. 4.8). German geographer Manfred Büttner described Moravian architecture as consisting of "large, long, barracklike buildings similar [to] and manifest[ing] the same spirit" of Moravian settlements located throughout the world (1974: 171–72). Although Moravian construction present in the Brus Lagoon compound may use different architectural forms and materials than those of Europe and other locales, it still matches Büttner's description.

Ahuas

Notwithstanding its importance as provincial headquarters for the Moravian Church, Ahuas did not possess a clearly demarcated compound like the above-mentioned sites. This was probably because a Miskito pastor,

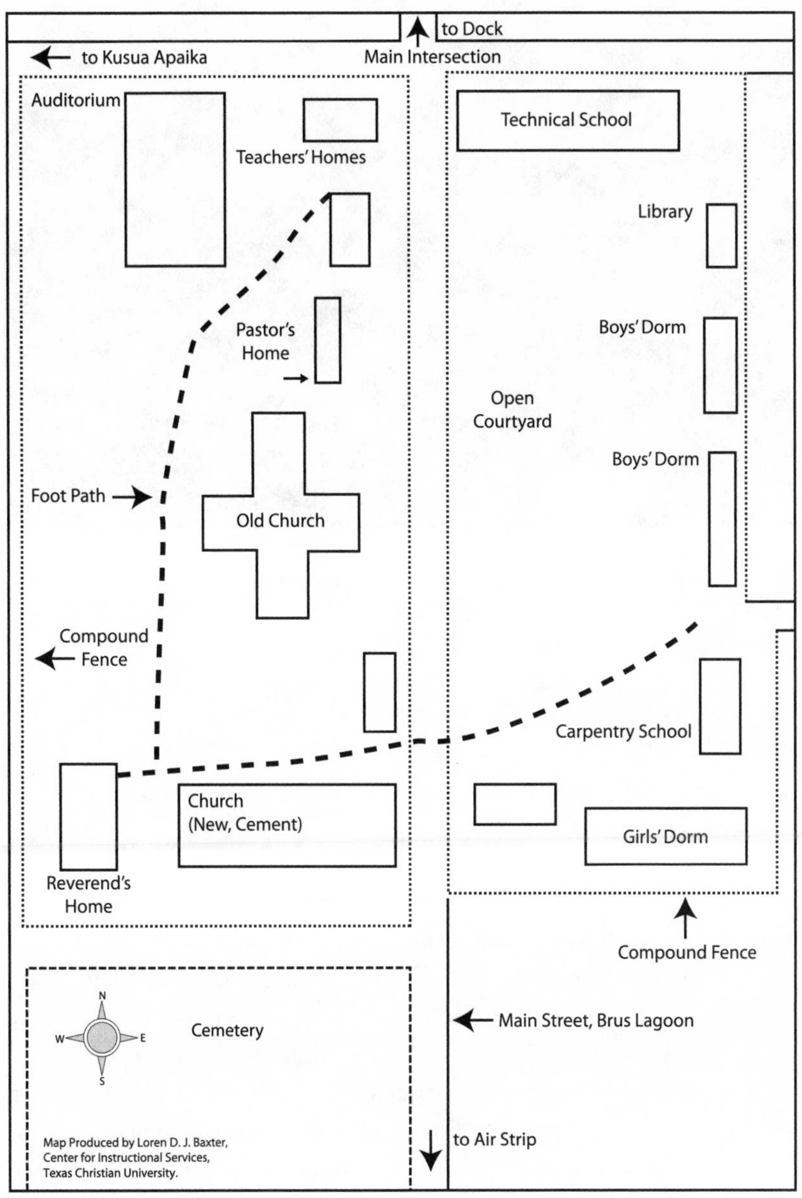

4.7 Sketch of the Brus Lagoon Moravian compound, 1998 (adapted from Tillman 2005).

4.8 A portion of Brus Lagoon's compound, located across the road from the church, 1998 (adapted from Tillman 2005).

not a foreign missionary, originally established the Moravian Church in Ahuas. Dr. Samuel Marx, who served as both a doctor in the clinic and local pastor from 1952 to 1964, and again from 1968 to 1974, was the first foreign missionary stationed in Ahuas (Marx 1980). Moreover, Ahuas did not become an important center until the 1950s. The missionaries were aware of Ahuas's potential future importance, however, as they judged it to be the population center of the Honduran Mosquitia (Proceedings of the Society for Propagating the Gospel Among the Heathen 1944:60). For this reason, Moravians selected it to be the site for the hospital and airplane that would bring patients from distant villages. Permanently staffed with two U.S.–trained physicians, a registered nurse, and a pilot, the Moravian hospital in Ahuas is now the largest medical facility in the Honduran Mosquitia. In addition to common medical services, the hospital provided a hyperbaric chamber to help the numerous lobster divers who routinely suffer from decompression sickness because they spend too much time underwater or surface too fast (the church also hired a consultant to train lobster divers in how to avoid decompression sickness).

Moravian buildings in Ahuas were located in two nodes; the first consisted of a medical node including the hospital complex and airport near the edge of the settlement, and the second was an ecclesiastical node that included the church and provincial offices in the center of town.

Church Names and Adornments

Miskito-Moravians typically name their churches after people or places found in the Bible. Examples include Cocobila's Getsemaní (Gethsemane), Ahuas's Ebenezer, Ibans's Rosa de Saraón (Rose of Sharon), Nueva Jerusalén's Immanuel, and Tasbapauni's Monte Olivo (Mount of Olives). The names are typically painted above the church doors. Newer churches often have large, varnished double doors that contain engraved decorations. Examples of engraved decorations include crosses on the Cocobila church doors, and diamonds and stars at Tasbapauni.

The Moravian seal is also a popular symbol engraved on church doors. The first known use of the seal among the Unitas Fratrum dates back to 1540 (Atcheson 1953). Variations exist, but the seal typically contains a lamb, representing Jesus Christ, holding a staff with a banner, and a cross representing victory. The words "Our Lamb has conquered, let us follow him" are written around the outside circumference. In Honduras, the motto is written in Miskito, in Spanish, and, in one instance, Puerto Lempira, in Latin (fig. 4.9). The seal appears on the doors of churches, on the outside front wall of churches, on the inside back wall of churches behind the pulpit, on the outside of the Moravian hospital, and on the new provincial office building in Ahuas.

The multipointed Christmas star is another important Moravian tradition in Honduras. Wide use of the star by Moravians did not begin until the 1880s. The star was popular enough that eventually the Herrnhut Star Factory in Saxony, Germany, was founded to keep up with demand (Atcheson 1953). While in some countries Moravians use multicolored glass stars with electric lights, Moravians in Honduras make their stars of white paper. Miskito Moravian congregations often leave their stars hanging from the church ceiling throughout the year. Other paper decorations hang from the ceiling for Christmas and weddings, and palm fronds are used for Palm Sunday.

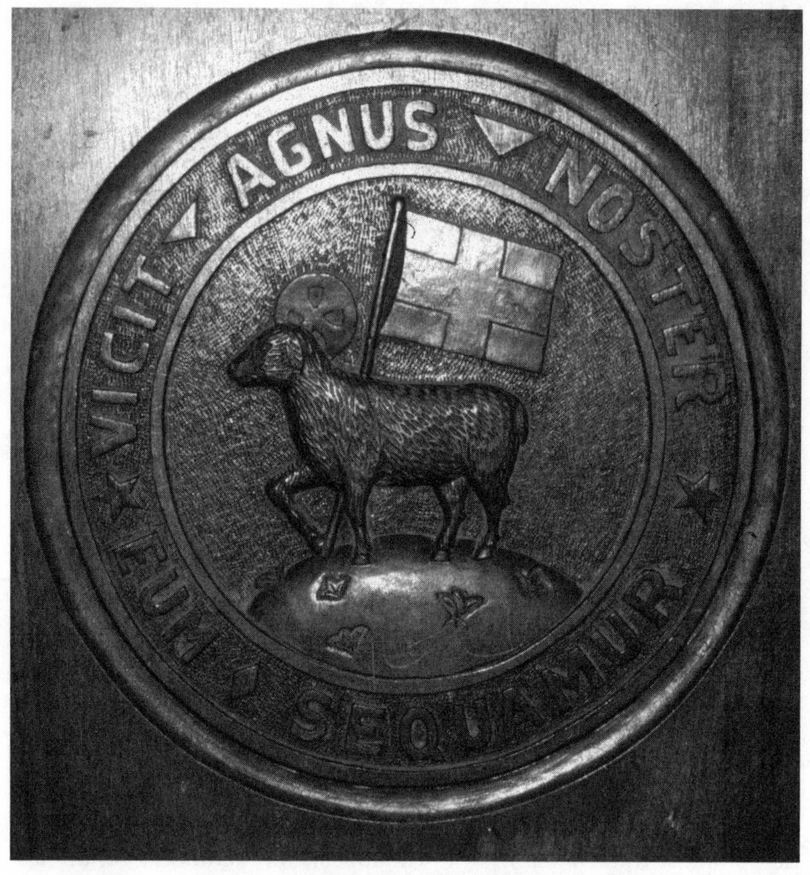

4.9 A Moravian seal with Latin lettering engraved on the Puerto Lempira church door, 1998.

Colored cloths also hang on the wall behind the pulpit or are placed on the pulpit. According to a Moravian pastor, the church uses black during Holy Week to represent the death of Christ. Used in March, red cloth represents the blood of Christ and his death on the cross. White symbolizes purity and is used for weddings and communion. Green represents spiritual growth and may be used throughout the year.

Though less commonly, congregations paint pictures of the Bible on the inside back wall behind the pulpit of a few chapels. These consist of particular verses of scripture or, as in the Cocobila and Tasbapauni churches, a picture of an open Bible pouring out water, accompanied

4.10 A map, a Moravian seal, and other decorations on display inside the Tasbapauni church, 1996.

by the words *aguas vivas* (living waters). Perhaps the most interesting decoration from a geographer's perspective is the map of the Mosquitia displayed in the Tasbapauni church with the words, "*El 18 de noviembre de 1930 fue la llegada del evangelio para el Reino de Dios en La Mosquitia de Honduras*" (the 18th of November, 1930, was the arrival of the gospel to the Kingdom of God in the Mosquitia of Honduras) (fig. 4.10).

CHAPTER 5

From Top to Bottom

Moravian Modification of Miskito Housing

FOLK HOUSING IS PERHAPS the most distinguishing and important feature of the cultural landscape. Folk house builders construct their preferred house types and floor plans from mental images, not blueprints. Their dwellings reflect a society's collective memory, values, and cultural history. The physical environment can influence dwelling types, but according to Rapoport (1969:47), folk houses are primarily a "consequence of a whole range of socio-cultural factors."

Geographers study folk housing because as "a basic fact of human geography . . . [i]t reflects cultural heritage, current fashion, functional needs," and human–environment interaction (Kniffen 1965, 549). J. B. Jackson (1952, 2) even went so far as to declare that "the primary study of the human geographer must be the dwelling and the establishing of dwelling types." Such studies often focus on origins, dispersals, and regional distributions, and emphasize diffusion of cultural traits from the Old World to the New World (West 1974; Winberry 1974; Jordan and Kaups 1989; Kniffen 1990; Brown 2005). While most scholars consider folk housing to be conservative, traditional, and slow to change, Steinberg (1996:87) reported that "there was little correlation between folk housing and traditional culture" among the Mopan Maya in Belize, because of Protestant missionary influence. Before I explain how Moravians modified Miskito dwellings, I must first describe traditional Miskito housing soon after European contact, using the few details mentioned by early travelers and other writers.

Traditional Miskito Dwellings

The Miskito formerly lived in long, communal houses (Kirchhoff 1948). The buccaneer known as M. W. probably saw this type of dwelling in

1699 when he described the village of Sandy Bay, Nicaragua, as having twelve houses and four hundred inhabitants (W. [1699] 1732). The Miskito later constructed smaller rectangular dwellings that had dirt floors, thatched roofs rounded on the ends, and four hardwood support posts. The posts used were generally cortes, ironwood, and sapodilla. These dwellings had palm-thatched roofs made of cohune, suita, caña danta, and saw cabbage palm (Romig 1891; Conzemius 1932). Cooking took place within the dwelling on the dirt floor, and many homes contained an attic created by laying split bamboo across the beams. These habitations did not contain walls, but the roof reached to within a few feet of the ground and effectively prevented rain from reaching the floor. The traditional dwelling was well suited for the Mosquito Coast environment. The high ceiling allowed hot air within the structure to rise, while the steeply pitched roof quickly shed the heavy rains, and the lack of walls and partitions allowed breezes to pass through the living area.

Moravian Modifications to Miskito Dwellings

During the eighteenth and nineteenth centuries, the Miskito were exposed to several dwelling types constructed by foreigners on the coast, including those by English colonists, European buccaneers, Africans, Creoles, Jamaicans, and Ladinos, as well as buildings constructed by foreign industries such as mining and lumber companies. However, foreign influence was most likely limited and geographically restricted to the coastal settlements with which the Miskito experienced the most contact. Also, though foreigners had a large impact, any changes they may have brought would still depend largely on local knowledge, materials, and technology. In many settlements, major changes in housing did not occur until the arrival of Moravian missionaries, because they enthusiastically taught and encouraged the Miskito to construct houses with nontraditional forms and materials (Smith 1872).

Many Miskito initially resisted adopting the missionaries' preferred house types. In fact, sometimes when Moravians moved to a new village, missionaries used indigenous house forms and construction materials, because Miskito villagers constructed temporary churches and parsonages. In this limited sense, the Moravians, even if only temporarily, were like the Spanish conquerors in Mexico who adopted some aspects of indigenous dwellings (Butzer and Butzer 2000). My research found that the Miskito eventually accepted the house types promoted by Moravian missionaries and continue to incorporate new forms and manufactured materials.

In addition to teaching their doctrine, the Moravians sought to improve living conditions, and housing was one of the first items that the missionaries attempted to change (Hamilton 1939). Houses without walls were common when the missionaries arrived on the Mosquito Coast, and one finds many such descriptions in their literature (Smith 1877; Romig 1891; Grossman 1988). The Moravians first altered Miskito dwellings by encouraging them to construct walls for privacy. The missionaries also credited changes in Miskito housing to their religious teachings (Mueller 1932; Hamilton 1939). A missionary's description of Wounta Haulover, Nicaragua, gives insight into the degree of village change as a result of missionary influence: "The civilising effects of the Gospel are very strikingly manifest at Ephrata [Wounta Haulover]. In 1860, a few huts were to be seen in wretched condition, now you find a double row of cottages, some of them with boarded floors, and all neatly kept, and clean. Some have gardens attached" (Lundberg 1870:405).

House type transformation correlated with the presence of the Moravians to such a degree that the missionaries later classified dwellings without walls as belonging to non-Christian Miskito. Moreover, the missionaries labeled entire villages and portions of villages as "uncivilized" and "un-Christian" based on house types. A missionary asserted, "One can usually tell what progress the gospel has made in a village or in a family by the appearance of the houses" (Romig 1891:395).

In Nicaragua, the missionaries first encouraged Miskito residents to build walls of saw cabbage palm trunks placed vertically, but soon after, missionaries asked residents to build walls with wickerwork of split saw cabbage palm trunks (Mueller 1932). Bell (1989:24) noted that some Mosquito Cost inhabitants used this type of wickerwork, in his description of the home of a former African slave that "was like all the houses of the common people at Blewfields." According to Heath (1904:101), "the trunks [of the wickerwork] are split longitudinally into laths, which, interlaced at right angles, keep out the rain, but let in plenty of fresh air." Mosquito Coast residents also made wickerworks of split bamboo in some cases (Pim and Seemann 1869; Lundberg 1872). Conzemius

(1932:31) reported that regional differences in wall materials eventually emerged. In the interior, side walls were made of a "wattlework" of split bamboo, while coastal inhabitants made walls with vertically placed trunks of saw cabbage palm. This regional difference was most likely a result of the availability of the two types of vegetation. Eventually, Moravians attempted to change the wall material from saw cabbage palm trunks to pieces of split bamboo placed vertically (Mueller 1932).

Another change to Mosquito Coast dwellings brought by the missionaries was a floor of split bamboo or sawed boards raised above the ground on posts (Mueller 1932; Grossman 1988). Though they did not introduce the use of posts to the Mosquito Coast, Moravian missionaries did encourage the geographic spread of post dwellings from Bluefields and small English settlements along the coast to indigenous communities, for several reasons. First, much of the ground near the coastal regions is continually wet during the rainy season. The floor's elevation above ground kept the house drier and cleaner. The raised floor also discouraged insects, small rodents, reptiles, and other animals from entering the house. In an attempt to cultivate privacy within the home, missionaries also encouraged villagers to partition their dwellings into two rooms. One room was used for sleeping, while the other room served as both a kitchen and a dining room. Other important modifications made by the missionaries included the introduction of an external kitchen and a full-length gallery (fig. 5.1) (Mueller 1932; Helms 1971).

Because the missionaries arrived in Honduras in the 1930s, many elderly Miskito with whom I spoke witnessed firsthand the changes to housing motivated by the missionaries. According to people from several villages, the majority of homes before the arrival of the missionaries had dirt floors, walls of saw cabbage palm trunks placed vertically, and thatched roofs (fig. 5.2). Heath's 1930 diary correlates with villager accounts. He recorded that Kaurkira residents walled their homes with trunks of saw cabbage palm—a material he disliked because it was "untidy' and "not durable" (Kaurkira Station Diary 1930:2). Missionaries preferred framed dwellings raised approximately three feet above the ground on posts, with board walls and zinc roofs, and they typically constructed their parsonages and churches in this manner.

As part of their efforts to improve living conditions, the missionaries encouraged the Miskito to construct similar homes. However, the

5.1 A split-bamboo-walled home raised above the ground on posts, with a suita thatched roof and gallery, in Piñales, 1996.

5.2 A Cocobila home with a suita thatch roof, the gabled end walled with saw cabbage palm trunks, and the front walled with split bamboo, 1998.

differences in the construction of a home with a dirt floor versus a framed dwelling on posts necessarily required different skills and tools that many Miskito apparently did not possess at that time. A great demand arose in the Honduran Mosquitia for individuals with carpentry skills, and Heath (1931, 1940a, 1940b) often noted in his reports whether a particular individual had such abilities. Some Miskito learned how to build frame homes on posts and developed other carpentry skills by assisting in the construction of parsonages and churches as apprentices. For example, an "Austrian carpenter with Indian assistants" constructed the first Kaurkira parsonage (Heath 1949:2).

Missionaries also directly assisted in the construction of Miskito dwellings. For example, the missionary Werner Marx assisted several Miskito who were attempting to build frame homes by demonstrating to them how to install corner braces (Werner Marx, pers. comm., July 16, 1998). Corner wind braces were an important part of wooden frame construction in the Honduran Mosquitia and were found in virtually all buildings, including homes, businesses, hospitals, parsonages, and churches. Without these braces, placed at forty-five-degree angles and nailed to corner posts, the structure would be too flimsy and could be easily pushed over by strong winds. Once frame homes on posts became common, saw cabbage palm trunks were not a practical wall material and were replaced by split bamboo or boards.

Moravians also introduced the double-handled ripsaw technique for sawing lumber that the Miskito still use today (Hamilton 1918; Kaurkira Station Diary 1932; Helms 1971; Grossman 1988; Werner Marx, pers. comm., July 16, 1998). The procedure requires that a log be situated on a six-foot stand. Two men, one standing on the ground and the other standing on the log, saw the log into boards (Helms 1971). Villagers I spoke with described how the missionaries brought saws with them when they began congregations in such places as Kaurkira, Brus Lagoon, Yahurabila, Cocobila, Ahuas, Dakratara, and Auka to begin immediate work on the church and parsonage. The same villagers recounted that before Moravians introduced the saw, some individuals would hew boards out of logs with axes. In this fashion they were able to hew only one inch-and-a-half-thick board per tree trunk (Haglund 1930; Hamilton 1939).

Missionaries also encouraged the Miskito to construct external kitchens. Although English settlers used external kitchens on the coast before the arrival of the Moravians, the Miskito did not widely use these kitchens until their houses were raised above the ground on posts. Once the Miskito placed their dwellings on posts, they moved their kitchens to a separate structure (Conzemius 1932; Dawson 1986). The Moravians encouraged the Miskito to build separate kitchens for sanitary reasons and to reduce the risk of fire (Mueller 1932; Werner Marx, pers. comm., July 16, 1998).

The component names of Miskito houses provide important evidence of foreign introductions. In general, components that existed in traditional Miskito dwellings have Miskito names, while more recent introductions have foreign names with Miskito pronunciations (appendix E). Original Miskito terms mainly describe parts of the roof and its supporting posts, while more recent introductions, including the wall, raised floor, room, door, stairs, gallery, separate kitchen, parts of the frame, and manufactured roofing materials have foreign names. Posts supporting framed houses have a Miskito name, even though they were a foreign introduction. Apparently, these posts were given the same name as the posts that supported the roof of traditional dwellings because their purpose was similar—posts planted in the ground to support the shelter.

House Type Surveys Illustrate Change

In 1953, over six months, the German geographer Karl Helbig (1965) traversed much of northeastern Honduras. The fact that Moravian influence on Miskito domestic architecture was ongoing during Helbig's visit is reflected in his description of two principal house types—one consisting of a dirt floor, saw cabbage palm trunk walls, and a thatched roof, and the other consisting of a floor on posts with board walls and a thatched roof. Helbig noted that some businesses and mission buildings had zinc roofs, but Miskito homes did not contain zinc roofs at that time. However, zinc soon began to replace thatch as a roof material—a trend that initially developed among those with close ties to the Moravian Church (Ligon 1968). Even though North American missionaries stopped serving as ecclesiastical leaders in Honduras by the late 1970s, Miskito housing continued to change, in part due to the increased use of manufactured materials that have become available in this relatively isolated region only in recent years. Helbig's observations documented Honduran Miskito house types that existed during the early 1950s and provide a benchmark to measure change over several decades.

Surveys I conducted of fifty-eight homes in Belén, fifty homes in Laka Tabila, and twenty-four homes in Brus Lagoon illustrate changes to Miskito housing since Helbig's study. Out of fifty-eight homes in Belén, forty-one (71%) were on posts (actually a much lower percentage than in most villages). With respect to wall materials, twenty-eight (48%) had *yagua* walls, sixteen (28%) had board walls, eight (14%) had split bamboo walls, and six (10%) had concrete walls. With respect to roofs, thirty-two (55%) were thatch, with twenty-two of those (38%) being suita, and ten (17%) being fronds of saw cabbage palm. Of the remaining roofs, nineteen (33%) were zinc, six (10%) were corrugated tarpaper, and one (2%) was white, corrugated asbestos.

Laka Tabila is a somewhat isolated village that Miskito from other places described as "very traditional." All dwellings surveyed in Lake Tabila were on posts. Thirty-eight out of fifty homes (76%) had board walls, while twelve (24%) had yagua walls. Thirty-five roofs (70%) were made of thatch (with the majority being of saw cabbage palm thatch), and fifteen (30%) were zinc.

In contrast to Laka Tabila, Brus Lagoon, a government and commercial center, is the second-largest settlement in the Mosquitia. Its importance as a commercial center, including its port and small airline connection with larger Honduran cities, results in a relatively high rate of movement of people and goods into the town. Brus's domestic architecture reflects its exposure to the outside world. Of the twenty-four homes surveyed in Brus Lagoon, seventeen (71%) were on posts, five (21%) had concrete foundations, and two (8%) had dirt floors. Fifteen homes (63%) had board walls, while four (17%) had cement walls, three (13%) had bamboo walls, and two (8%) had yagua walls. With respect to roofs, twenty (83%) were zinc, three (13%) were made of thatch, and one (4%) was of asbestos.

It is clear from these surveys that Miskito domestic architecture has changed since Helbig's 1953 description. Whereas Helbig stated that about half the homes had dirt floors, such homes occur with much less frequency today, while homes on posts are almost the rule. Likewise, homes with saw cabbage palm walls were nonexistent in the three-village surveys (although a few still exist in other locations), and walls of split bamboo were few, but homes with board or yagua walls were common. In addition, Helbig did not mention zinc roofing in any of his descriptions of Miskito housing. Today, however, it is common, especially in settlements such as Brus Lagoon that have many connections to the outside world. These data also indicate that concrete construction is a new trend occurring in Miskito domestic architecture, and one should expect that concrete homes with zinc or corrugated asbestos roofs would be even more common in the future. Observations I made in other villages shed additional light on the changes in Miskito domestic architecture during the past five decades and show some indication of regional variation.

Contemporary Domestic Architecture

Current homes consist of four main corner posts with secondary vertical members on the sides and ends (fig. 5.3). Corner wind braces, placed at forty-five-degree angles, support the main posts. The roof consists of beams and rafters of sawed pine two-by-fours or poles of cedro macho stripped of bark (Dodds 1994). Short king posts extend vertically from the tie beams to support the ridgepole that varies in height from fifteen

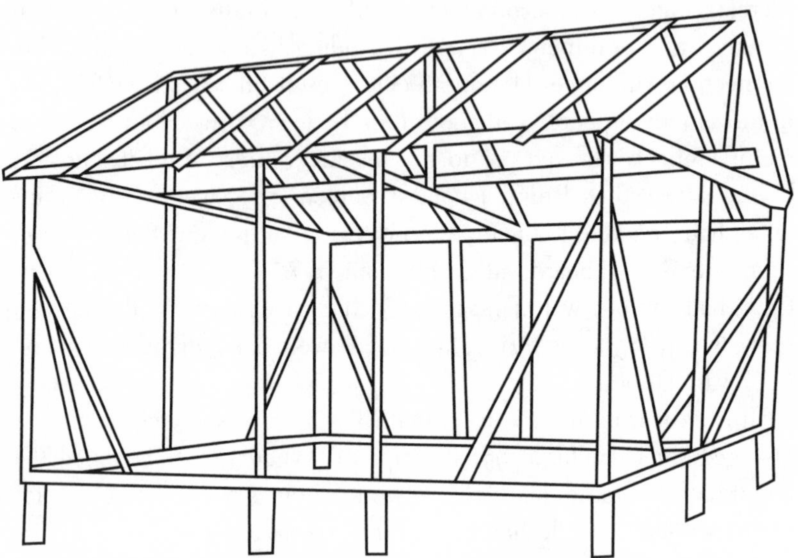

5.3 Sketch of a typical dwelling frame (based on Salinas 1991).

to twenty feet above the ground. Small rods are placed horizontally across the rafters to help support the thatch. Although a few Miskito homes have hipped roofs, the vast majority of dwellings have gabled roofs (Ligon 1968).

The floor of a Miskito dwelling consists of sawed boards raised three to five feet above the ground, and supported by four rows of three posts. The floor plan may consist of a single room that serves as a kitchen, main room, and bedroom, but most homes are rectangular structures of eighteen by twenty-two to twenty-four feet, divided into sleeping compartments and a larger main room by wood or bamboo partitions (fig. 5.4) (Helms 1971). The main room contains a table, benches, and chairs, while the bedrooms contain wooden sleeping platforms called *krikris*. Although the Miskito have traditionally slept directly on wood, mattresses are common today. The Miskito place window openings, typically accompanied by wooden shutters, on all sides (Conzemius 1932; Helms 1971).

External kitchens exhibit much variation in form and materials and may be attached as an additional room or located in a separate building.

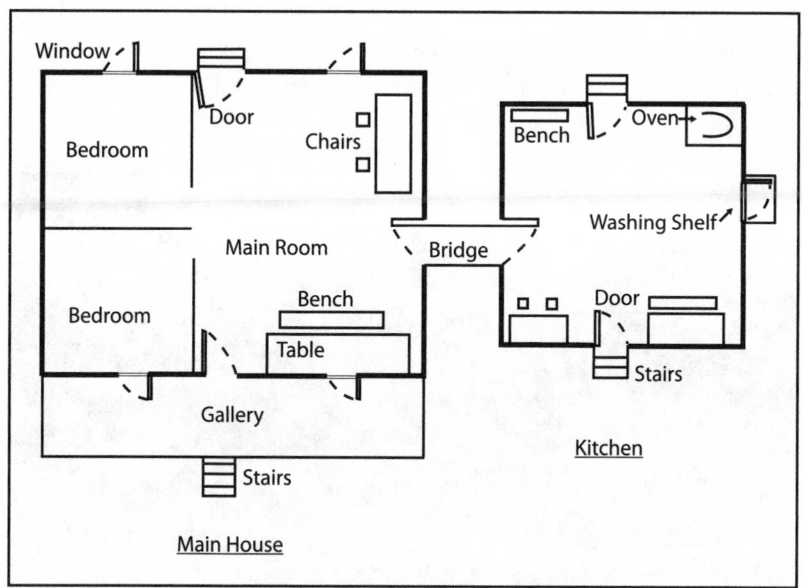

5.4 Sketch of a typical floor plan for a house and external kitchen (based on Salinas 1991).

They range from small, saw cabbage palm lean-tos to larger structures raised on posts with board floors, walls, and zinc roofs. Separate kitchens are smaller, typically fourteen by nineteen feet, than the main structure but follow the same manner of construction. Like dwellings, kitchens rest three feet above the ground on posts, and a bridge of wooden boards connects them to the main structure. Kitchens also contain one or more windows, and, typically, under one of these openings a wooden shelf used for washing dishes is attached to the outside of the building. The Miskito also use kitchens as a storage space for baskets and fishing nets, machetes, knives, and large cooking utensils. Like dwellings, separate kitchens often have full-length galleries along the front (Helms 1971).

Regional Variations in Roof and Wall Material

Regional variations in certain roof and wall materials exist in Mosquitia. Yagua dominated in coastal villages, but boards were the majority wall material in all other locations (figs. 5.5, 5.6). Boards were especially dominant in Puerto Lempira, Brus Lagoon, Mocorón, and Lisangnipura. While the status of Brus Lagoon and Puerto Lempira as ports and commercial centers explains the board dominance in these settlements, the board

5.5 A yagua-and-zinc home with an external board-and-bamboo kitchen situated on a beach ridge in Yahurabila, 1998.

5.6 A new board-and-zinc home on posts in Cocobila, with full-length gallery, 1998.

houses in Mocorón and Lisangnipura were built with the aid of the United Nations to house refugees and flood victims.

One can find a few homes with bamboo walls in nearly all villages, but they occur most often in settlements located along freshwater lagoons or rivers where bamboo grows, such as near Belén and Tasbaraya. Trunks of saw cabbage palm were the most common wall material used by the Miskito when the Moravians arrived in Honduras, but the Miskito now use them only for temporary dwellings, storage sheds, chicken coops, and, occasionally, kitchens.

Zinc has become a common roof material and is used on 30 to 45 percent of homes in most villages. Villages where zinc is the majority roofing material include Puerto Lempira, Brus Lagoon, Ahuas, Lisangnipura, and Mocorón (fig. 5.7). Zinc is also prevalent in Cocobila, Nueva Jerusalén, and Kaurkira. A few residents, most often in Cocobila, Belén, and Nueva Jerusalén, roof their homes with corrugated tarpaper.

The Miskito use two types of thatch as roofing. Suita, which grows in gallery forest along rivers, occurs more frequently in river settlements or

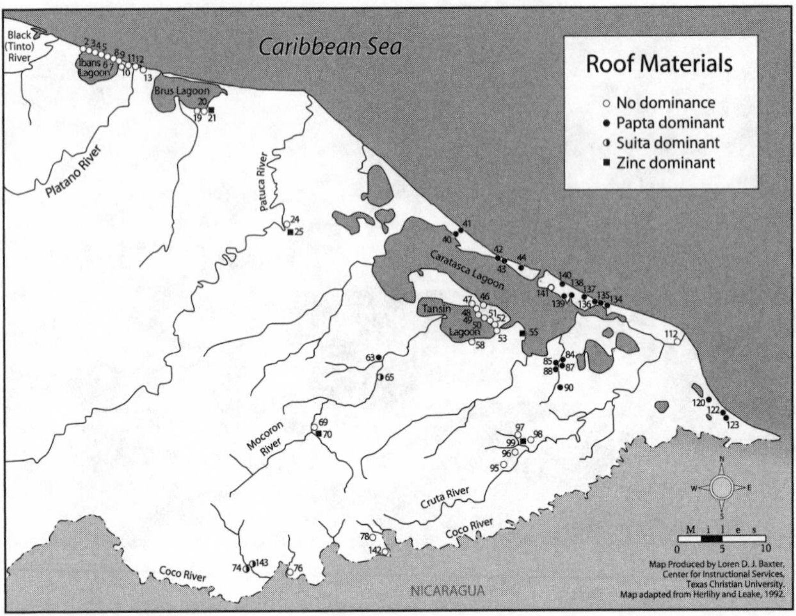

5.7 Distribution of roofing materials, 1998 (see table 1.1 for settlement names).

in settlements with agricultural plots located along portions of rivers. Fronds of saw cabbage palm dominate in villages where residents can easily obtain them from nearby savannas, or in coastal areas where the palm grows readily. Villages where saw cabbage palm thatch dominates include Katski, Prumnitara, Dapat, Kaurkira, Laka, Benk, Raya, Yahuarabila, Uhi, Pusuaia, and Krata. The main reason for this variation seemed to be availability, although sometimes suita is dominant (i.e., Mabita, Rus Rus, Ahuas, Sirsirtara), even though saw cabbage palm is available. Suita reportedly lasts only five to seven years (compared to saw cabbage palm, which lasts ten to fifteen years) but is much easier to work. Residents easily tie suita leaves side by side to long thin sticks that are then laid on top of the rafters (fig. 5.8). Saw cabbage palm fronds must be tied together in pairs with a thin vine, one on top of the other, and then each pair is tied to thin rods supported by the rafters. A roof of saw cabbage palm thatch requires more skill, dexterity, and patience, and involves additional tying. Furthermore, villagers assemble suita thatch while it is

5.8 A Miskito woman assembling suita thatch, 1998. Note the completed laths in the background.

still green, but they must let saw cabbage palm fronds dry for a period of time before thatching the roof.

The Future of Miskito Housing

The availability and use of manufactured materials in domestic architecture is an example of the Miskito's progressing incorporation into the greater Honduran economy, and their increasing interaction with economic forces originating outside the region as "global currents" reach its shores (Nietschmann 1979:1). To be sure, Miskito economic contact with the outside world, a relationship typically described as a series of boom-and-bust cycles, has been ongoing for more than three centuries (Helms 1971; Nietschmann 1973; Offen 1998). However, as indicated by changes in domestic architecture, commercial interaction increased rapidly during the past few decades. This increase is due in part to the Miskito's continuing transition from subsistence to a market economy—a change also exemplified by increasing numbers employed in wage-labor activities, such as lobster diving, and the use of cash to purchase food the Miskito formerly shared or exchanged with others (Nietschmann 1979). The coastal economy is now monetized, with many residents purchasing at least some of their food from stores. Herlihy (2006) reported that nearly a hundred small shops, most of them homes, occupied a three-mile stretch between Ibans and Barra Plátano.

The amount of variation in form and materials currently used in the construction of Miskito dwellings is the result of rapid and continual change in Miskito house types as building ideals become more westernized. Perhaps some of the increased use of manufactured construction material in Miskito housing may be a sort of modern continuation of the Miskito's historical practice of purchasing foreign manufactured products from their English trading partners (Long [1774] 1970; Roberts 1965 [1827]; Helms 1983). Helms (1971:157) believed the Miskito used manufactured items such as zinc roofs to show fellow villagers their ability to "purchase foreign goods, i.e., to consume money."

No matter the reason, my research clearly shows that the Miskito preferred manufactured materials over local, traditional materials, even though they were expensive, in addition to other negative aspects. Saw cabbage palm trunks were the least preferred wall material and are rarely used for house walls today. The Miskito consider bamboo better than saw cabbage palm trunks, but it is still not a preferred material, because it is local and traditional and therefore demonstrates the homeowner's lack of money. When I asked about the lack of bamboo-walled dwellings in Raya, a villager responded, "There is no bamboo here because the people are progressing." Similarly, yagua, while preferred over the previously mentioned materials, still ranked below boards, even though it was less expensive, resisted termites, and lasted much longer.

Among roof materials, thatch is the least desired, while zinc is the most coveted. While zinc may last longer, it is not without disadvantages. For example, many individuals complained about the heat generated by a zinc roof during the evening. A zinc roof, as one villager explained, "doesn't let you sleep at night." Accordingly, the cooler asbestos appeared to be increasing in popularity, and residents frequently used it on concrete buildings. Even though manufactured materials are more expensive and not always superior to local materials, the use of boards and zinc, along with post dwellings and external kitchens, has greatly increased since Helbig's study. Because the Miskito consider these items "a mark of modern civilized living" (Helms 1971: 51), their use will continue until replaced by newer or more modern materials. In fact, their replacement is already occurring, as concrete and asbestos are now the most modern materials available and have been used in the construction of several new homes, mainly in Puerto Lempira and Brus Lagoon, by Ladinos from the Honduran interior who moved to the Mosquitia to work in government positions or open small businesses. Most of these homes have a concrete foundation of one-foot to one-and-one-half-foot thickness, concrete walls, and a zinc or white corrugated asbestos roof (fig. 5.9).

Concrete construction has been under way for some time for churches but has only recently begun for houses. Concrete structures, including churches, schools, health centers, and houses, now exist in several villages, and I expect their numbers to increase over time. The practice of constructing concrete housing is reinforced by Hondurans who have moved into the Mosquitia from the interior and by the increased mobility of the Miskito to interior cities, which has exposed them to new architectural values and ideas. Though expensive, concrete structures are also seen by those who can afford them as better long-term investments, because of their ability to withstand hurricanes and termites. Traditional

5.9 A large modern home in Cocobila consisting of a concrete foundation and walls on the first floor, board walls on the second floor, and a corrugated white asbestos roof. Galleries are present on both levels, 1998.

houses would be less expensive to rebuild after a hurricane, but the same winds that destroy houses would also damage the natural vegetation used for thatch.

It is no coincidence that changes in Miskito domestic architecture have essentially mirrored the three stages of Moravian church construction outlined in chapter 4. The Miskito preferred missionary homes, which they considered to be "modern" and "civilized" (Helms 1971:51). Some longtime residents of Kaurkira, Brus Lagoon, and Cocobila told me how they, along with fellow villagers, admired missionary homes and desired that style of dwelling for themselves. An elderly Cocobila resident's explanation—"The house [Heath] made [in Cocobila] was like an example to the people, and it made an impression on the people, and they wanted to have one like it"—is just one example of many similar statements people made to me. Therefore, Miskito housing repeated the stages created by the missionaries when they first built churches with local materials and then replaced them with structures made of manufactured materials.

It is not unprecedented that a relatively small number of missionaries could have such a major impact on folk housing. In his study of the Texas–Mexico border area, Jordan (1988:4) found that a single person, a "Breton priest-architect," significantly altered the region's folk housing when he introduced the parapet gable from western France. Moravian missionaries were similar to the circuit priest whom Jordan described as "highly revered by the local people, . . . [he] had the expertise, background, and mobility to achieve a substantial implantation" (1988:5). The fact that Moravians often located their compounds in larger villages, where they could have an influence on the greatest number of people, also aided their ability to modify Miskito house types.

When comparing contemporary Miskito homes to past dwellings described by buccaneers, Moravians, and the Miskito themselves, one can only conclude that Miskito domestic architecture literally changed from top to bottom. The future will continue to see more homes constructed of manufactured materials, because of the increasing Hispanicization of the region and because of the area's continued transition from subsistence to a market economy.

CHAPTER 6

Missionaries for Christ, or Early Prophets of Sustainability?

Moravian Influence on Miskito Agriculture

MORAVIAN MISSIONARIES SIGNIFICANTLY INFLUENCED Miskito food production by introducing or otherwise promoting agricultural techniques and varieties of crops that they believed suitable for the Mosquito Coast environment. They also persuaded the Miskito to produce more food by encouraging them to increase the size of their dooryard gardens and fields, and by instructing them to plant more fruit trees. Many of the ideas employed by the Moravians to increase Miskito food production were similar to those found in modern-day sustainable agriculture.

The missionaries promoted sustainable development in that they attempted to increase the Miskito's standard of living without destroying the natural environment. As one Moravian writer explained, "The mission . . . seeks . . . a higher economic life, through the peaceful development of the rich resources of the land" (Mueller 1932:61). Writing in 1944, a missionary located in the Nicaraguan portion of the Mosquito Coast expressed his belief that "we must protect and improve natural resources, improve organized efforts, foster increased fruit production by having proper nurseries, reach out for untouched resources, develop new resources, [and] preserve existing resources" (General Mission Conference 1944:22). Because missionary influence on Miskito agriculture began over one hundred years before the advent of the current sustainable development and sustainable agriculture movements, missionaries merit the label of "early prophets of sustainability."

Moravians and Development

The Moravians' three-pronged approach (preaching, education, and medical work) to convert Mosquito Coast populations has been successful. Although not as organized as the above-described trajectories, the teaching of agriculture and trades was also part of their missionary effort on the Mosquito Coast and in other locations. A Moravian leader explained: "From an early day it has been the effort of Moravian missionaries in all parts of the world to instruct their converts how to utilize and develop the natural resources of their land, and to introduce to them trades and occupations as well as to provide a market for their products, if this is not otherwise at hand" (Hamilton 1912:160).

This emphasis was not uniform and was therefore more prominent in some missions than in others (Danker 1971). The Moravian mission in Nyasaland of German East Africa (Malawi) is an example of a mission where agriculture was very prominent. Missionaries introduced potatoes, wheat, rice, coffee, tea, cotton, and a variety of fruit trees. A Moravian historian described the effort:

> All manner of fruits foreign to Central Africa have been planted, and in some cases with most welcome results, the native population having also learned their value, and gladly accepting presents of young fruit-trees to plant them near their own homes--plums, peaches, apricots, oranges, lemons, grapes, mangoes, guavas, figs, pomegranates, sapodillas, dates, and even apples and walnuts. . . . (In addition, many varieties of useful timber have been set out, including the eucalyptus.) Experiments are also being made with quinces and chestnuts. Of small fruits the European strawberry, and the African blackberry and gooseberry flourish. (Hamilton 1912:162)

In addition, the Nyasaland missionaries established a large rubber plantation and imported donkeys (a breed resistant to the tsetse fly), sheep, and cattle. They also taught trades, including brickmaking, carpentry, tailoring, and shoemaking (Hamilton 1912).

Although the Nicaraguan mission did not focus on economic development as much as the Nyasaland mission (most likely because of a lack of funds and missionaries), it was still a significant part of the Moravian work among the Miskito, and individual missionaries were known for their emphasis on teaching agriculture and trades. One missionary who lived on the Mosquito Coast reflected: "Ever since their coming our brethren have labored to improve the conditions of life which they encountered here. Fruit trees and medicinal plants were imported from the West Indies. Farming was encouraged by word and example" (Hamilton 1939:41).

But if the Moravians' primary objective was to "win souls for the Lamb," why would they teach agriculture and trades? The first and most obvious answer to this question is that the Moravians sought to improve the general standard of living among the various peoples whom they were trying to convert and instill in them the "Protestant work ethic." A second and perhaps less obvious reason was that the missionaries were replicating an economy based on agriculture and trades that existed in Herrnhut and other early Moravian communities in Europe and North America that were economically self-sufficient. Finally, the ultimate goal was that each mission become a national church independently operated by the native population. Moravians realized that before an economically self-sufficient national church could be established, the members must also be economically self-sufficient. This last point was especially true for Honduras. In 1962 the superintendent of the Moravian mission in Honduras wrote, "The yearly discussion of our low financial output gets tiresome. One reason for our difficulties . . . is . . . we have not taught our people better methods of farming so that they would be able to have more to give. I continue to believe that until the Honduras Mission gets a dedicated agricultural missionary, there will be no self-supporting Church" (Marx 1963:13).

Early Moravian Influence on Miskito Agriculture

Unfortunately, we know little about the Miskito's agriculture before their interaction with Europeans. Early travelers identified important crops such as bananas, plantains, manioc, sweet potatoes, pineapples, maize, coconut, sugarcane, and cacao, cultivated in small fields that were often located a considerable distance inland from coastal villages (W. [1699] 1732; De Lussan 1929; Esquemelin [1684] 1951; Dampier [1697] 1970). The buccaneers, and later the Moravians, believed that Miskito fields, called plantations, were too small to provide enough food for subsistence. Although this perception may have been the result of a European lack of understanding of the Miskito slash-and-burn agricultural system, there were real food shortages on the Coast caused mainly by natural disasters such as hurricanes, floods, and storms that destroyed plantations (Kaurkira Station Report 1933; Werner Marx, pers. comm., July 9, 1998). On at least one occasion a missionary attributed a food shortage to a sukia who instructed people not to plant anything, because "the kaffir-pox epidemic [a mild form of smallpox] would kill them all" (Kaurkira Station Report 1931, 4).

Stealing food from plantations was apparently common during food shortages, as the practice was mentioned by multiple observers. Nietschmann (1973) found that the Miskito responded to a period of increased theft by planting smaller plantations in an effort to reduce the amount of food stolen. This response led to a further reduction in food supplies. As a consequence of the frequent food shortages, the missionaries constantly urged the Miskito to grow more food by planting more and varied fruit trees and crops, in larger plantations and gardens (Kaurkira Station Report 1933).

Currently, in addition to wage labor, fishing, and hunting, the Miskito practice slash-and-burn agriculture on small plots of land located along rivers. Manioc, several varieties of bananas, plantains, rice, maize, and beans are the most important crops grown, with the latter three also being used as cash crops. Other common food cultigens include sweet potatoes, sugarcane, pineapple, watermelon, pumpkin, and more than thirty fruit-bearing tree species (Helms 1971; Dodds 1994). Because of gender roles, only men, working with machete and axe, clear agricultural plots. Both men and women participate in the planting and harvesting of crops. Dodds (1998) found that the average Belén household actively cultivated 1.7 acres per year.

Two studies indicate that Miskito subsistence agriculture is declining because of an increase in wage labor. Dodds (1998) found that Belén households cut down less primary forest for agriculture as men pursued lobster-diving jobs. The men, who in 1992 earned the equivalent of $1.85 per pound of lobster, made the same amount of money in twelve days of diving as they did from an entire year of agricultural work. In a study of Patuca River settlements, Cochran (2008) found that subsistence agriculture declined because residents, especially young adults, sought employment among the growing number of salaried positions in government and nongovernmental agencies.

Fruit Trees

Fruit-bearing trees, often an imposing aspect of the settlement landscape, were grown in Miskito villages before the arrival of the Moravian Church but have increased in both number and varieties cultivated as a result of missionary influence. Nietschmann (1973:38) wrote that in addition to introducing new crops and agricultural techniques, Moravian missionaries in Nicaragua caused "many fruit trees such as breadfruit, rose apple, and star apple [to be] spread from village to village." Moravian efforts to spread fruit trees were not unique among religious groups. For example, Jews spread the citron, used in religious festivals, throughout the Mediterranean, and Catholics spread grape cultivation in Europe and the Americas to produce wine for Mass (Isaac 1959; Stanislawski 1975).

Missionaries taught fruit-tree cultivation through the example of mission stations, which always contained several varieties of fruit trees (Wullschlagel 1856; Renkewitz 1874; Romig 1891). According to Miskito villagers I spoke with, missionaries planted coconut, mango, and breadfruit trees when they established stations in Kaurkira, Brus Lagoon, and Cocobila. The missionary George R. Heath described the appearance of the Kaurkira station "attractive in its setting of coconuts, eucalyptus, and fruit-trees" (Heath 1940b:27). While all Moravian compounds in Honduras contain fruit trees, the compounds in Kaurkira and Brus Lagoon are outstanding in number and variety. Mission stations also served as a direct supplier of fruit trees to villagers because missionaries often gave seeds or seedlings to others. For example, missionaries in Nicaragua organized fruit-tree distribution by requiring all stations to set aside certain trees for seed and seedling production. Furthermore, missionaries were required to plant five additional trees a year (General Mission Conference 1944).

The Moravians also increased the number of fruit trees in Miskito settlements by abolishing a burial custom that called for the possessions of the deceased, including fruit trees, to be destroyed. Moravians sought to end this particular custom because they believed it caused increased poverty among the Miskito (Smith 1877; Ziock 1881; Werner Marx, pers. comm., July 16, 1998). A missionary explained the practice: "Often when a man died his coconut palms and other valuable fruit trees would be cut down, for he had planted them, and should others profit by his labors his spirit would return to plague the family. . . . Missionaries have fought these practices chiefly because of the heathen principles underlying them, yet nonetheless real is the material gain to the whole region in consequence" (Hamilton 1939:41).

The missionaries also actively taught the Miskito to plant more trees because they believed it would improve their diet and help individuals sustain themselves (Hamilton 1939). According to several villagers, the fruit trees the Moravians most commonly instructed the Miskito to plant included coconut palm, breadfruit, mango, orange, lemon, grapefruit, lime, cashew, and rose apple. Additional fruit trees promoted by the missionaries included peach palm, avocado, papaya, soursop, and guayaba.

Some Miskito resisted missionary requests to plant more trees, "because they may not live to eat the fruit" (Kaurkira Station Report 1933:4). Others did not plant trees for fear the fruit would be stolen (Heath 1916). According to one account, attempts by the Honduran government to help the Miskito plant more coconut trees also met with little success: "Some years ago the government distributed growing coconuts to be planted. Most of the Indians split the nuts and ate the tasty sponge that is the basis of the new plant. Then they planted what was left and showed the officials that they had obeyed orders but unfortunately the plants had dried up" (Kaurkira Station Report 1933:4).

The missionaries also used religious services as opportunities to instruct the Miskito to plant more fruit trees. Miskito villagers recalled how missionaries employed the biblical account of Adam and Eve, who had to work by the sweat of their brows, to illustrate the importance of agriculture and of growing more food. A village elder in Kruta recounted how missionaries requested that members plant a fruit tree upon the baptism of their child so that the child would be able to eat of the fruit of the tree when he or she was older.

Missionaries gave incentives to plant more fruit trees. In 1955 a Moravian missionary fenced the Kaurkira settlement and sponsored a contest whereby the individual who planted the most coconut palms would win a prize. The individual who won the prize, which consisted of a saw, a square, and other carpentry tools, planted an estimated 200–300 trees. In all, 3,500 coconut palms were planted as a result of the contest (Marx 1980). Kaurkira residents stated that similar contests continued for the next several years. To this day, the Kaurkira area is noted for its extensive coconut groves. Incentives for planting fruit trees were also used in Nicaragua. In 1943 a missionary in the Nicaraguan village of Sandy Bay encouraged the planting of breadfruit trees by inviting individuals who planted and fenced at least five breadfruit trees to be guests at his birthday party. Over twenty individuals planted the required number of trees. A similar party was held again for Christmas (Proceedings of the Society for Propagating the Gospel Among the Heathen 1943:53).

Rice

Moravian influence led to the Miskito's widespread cultivation of rice in both Nicaragua and Honduras. Although rice cultivation in both countries occurred on the Coast as early as 1780 and was subsequently reported along the Patuca River first in the early 1800s, and again in the 1920s, its widespread use by the Miskito is relatively recent (Anonymous 1885; Roberts 1965). Conzemius (1932) noted that rice was a new introduction and was rarely cultivated by the Miskito. Evidence of the Miskito's dismissal of rice in Honduras was recorded in the Kaurkira Station Diary at the time of a worsening food shortage: "Some, when they have no cassava and bananas, do not seem to appreciate rice; but rice is available" (Kaurkira Station Diary 1932:49). Rice (*rais* in Miskito) apparently did not become a significant part of the Miskito diet and economy until the 1920s, as a result of Moravian missionary influence (Helms 1971).

Missionaries in Nicaragua attempted to help the Miskito develop rice as a cash crop in 1928. Villagers were to bring their harvested rice to Pearl Lagoon, where the mission purchased and located a huller, dryer, and thresher. The project was intended to help the Miskito economically as well as to pay mission expenses and contribute to the eventual financial independence of the mission. The rice project was not successful, however, and after it sank the mission into debt, the machinery was finally sold in 1938 (Adams 1992). The failure was blamed on several factors, including inefficiency, mismanagement, lack of initiative by the villagers, and animals and floods that destroyed the crop.

Even though the project failed, individual missionaries continued to encourage their congregations to grow rice for both domestic consumption and sale on the market. One missionary wrote to another, "As much as I can do I am doing to get the people to plant . . . much more [rice]" (Haglund 1942).

In 1944, missionaries formed a rice cooperative in Kaurkira, Honduras (Kaurkira Station Diary 1944). The main objective of the cooperative was to grow large quantities of rice and ship it to La Ceiba, where it could be sold for twice as much as locally valued. The effort did not run smoothly, because of difficulties in finding transportation for the crop, and because the crop was nearly ruined by bilge oil (Marx 1980). The project was a success in Marx's opinion not only because of additional profit, but because once "people saw they could make money, they made much bigger plantations"—a constant goal of the missionaries (Werner Marx, pers. comm., July 16, 1998).

Beans

Although beans introduced by Ladinos were grown along the Coco River as early as 1905 (Helms 1971), residents in Brus Lagoon, Cocobila, and Kaurkira claimed that beans (*bins* in Miskito) were essentially unknown until missionaries brought seed to those settlements in the 1930s. When Heath arrived in Kaurkira in 1930, he promptly distributed fifty pounds of seeds for bean cultivation, and in 1941 he distributed seed for beans, corn, and rice in Cocobila (Marx 1980; Heath 1941b). Although Moravians may not have been the first to introduce beans to the Mosquito Coast, they were certainly instrumental in spreading the plant to individual villages, especially in the Honduran Mosquitia. Beans are a common part of the Miskito diet today and are also used as a cash crop.

Gardens and Fencing

Traditionally, the Miskito cultivated small dooryard gardens that included primarily a few fruit trees, chile peppers, and annatto (Conzemius 1932; Helms 1971). According to residents in Kaurkira, Cocobila, and Brus Lagoon, missionaries instructed people to cultivate a variety of plants in larger garden plots adjacent to homes and also encouraged them to raise chickens and pigs near their dwellings. Today, chickens are much more commonly seen in villages than pigs. The missionaries also imported barbed-wire fencing and encouraged the Miskito to build fences around plantations, gardens, and fruit trees to protect them from roaming livestock. The Miskito employ at least three common terms for fencing. Traditional fences made of local materials are known as either *klar* or *kral* (Marx and Heath 1992). The Miskito term for wire fencing, *pents*, is derived from English.

The reasons the Moravians instructed the Miskito to cultivate larger gardens and to raise livestock nearby are manifold. It was traditional for Moravian homes, such as those in the Moravian settlement of Salem, North Carolina (Griffen 1985), to contain backyard vegetable gardens, and therefore, the missionaries were simply propagating a common Moravian practice. The missionaries' instruction to maintain larger gardens and keep livestock nearby also was part of their overall effort to encourage the Miskito to grow more food, maintain a better diet, and become economically self-sufficient. Furthermore, in the event of bad weather or other emergency, food would be easily obtainable from the garden, and individuals would not have to travel long distances to their plantations. In addition to plants previously mentioned, current gardens typically contain manioc, banana, plantain, coconut, pineapple, papaya, guava, avocado, and a variety of citrus trees.

Modern Influence

The modern period of Moravian influence on Miskito agriculture began in 1966 with the formation of a cooperative venture between the Moravian Church, the Mennonites, and the United Church of Christ, known as Diakonia—the Greek word for "service" (Housman 1968). Under the direction of Diakonia, agricultural and other development projects were planned to raise the Miskito's standard of living. The modern period contained two principal differences from the previous period. First, during the modern period several agricultural experts were assigned to work in the Honduran Mosquitia as agricultural missionaries. Second, in addition to teaching, the agricultural missionaries were responsible for seeking funding and technical support from development agencies for various projects in the Honduran Mosquitia.

In 1977, Diakonia was replaced by MADIM (Agriculture and Development Mission of the Moravian Church), an indigenous development agency run by local members of the Moravian Church in Brus Lagoon. MADIM's objective was "to serve all communities, aiding in the promotion of the development in: agriculture, health, literacy, human improvement, community development, cooperatives, and small industries" (Molina-Cardenas 1986:94). MADIM's plan for the development of agriculture was based on the following goals: "organize the small farmers;

promote an agricultural cooperative; give technical help in modern agriculture; provide financial aid for farmers; secure better seeds and plants; locate better markets for the sale of crops; [organize] programs of community development; look for and help to provide, in whatever manner possible, ways of growth for the towns; give all economic and technical aid possible in the development process; and aid each community [to] discover and develop its own program of growth" (Molina-Cardenas 1986:96–97).

The Pelipita

Perhaps the most important Moravian contribution to Miskito agriculture in Honduras has been the introduction of a banana known locally as the pelipita. While on a 1967 fishing trip to the Caratasca Lagoon, Dr. Robert H. Stover, chief plant pathologist of the United Fruit Company, donated two hundred pelipita suckers to Howard Housman, superintendent of the Honduran mission (Housman 1968). The company developed this particular variety of banana to resist the three most prevalent banana diseases in Honduras–Moko, Sigatoka, and Panama. In a March 3, 1998, interview, Honduran bishop Stanley Goff explained how he and other Moravian leaders subsequently distributed the pelipita to their congregations and other interested residents with the understanding that the initial recipients would later share new suckers with their neighbors and friends. The plant was so successful that it quickly spread throughout the region. The pelipita is reportedly the dominant variety of banana grown in the Honduran Mosquitia today. Whereas the banana is a staple food of the Miskito, and whereas the dominant variety of banana cultivated is the pelipita, one might conclude that every person and plantation in the Honduran Mosquitia reaped the benefits of Moravian agricultural introductions.

Gardens

Missionary emphasis on dooryard gardens intensified during the 1960s and 1970s, when missionaries planted demonstration vegetable gardens to teach the cultivation of such vegetables as tomato, watermelon, pepper, lettuce, cabbage, cucumber, and eggplant (Flowe 1979). Agricultural missionaries encouraged the Miskito to plant larger garden plots, and a variety of seeds was distributed to encourage individuals to diversify crops for better nutrition (The Gospel under Palm and Pine 1977:28, 1980:18). In addition, composting and grafting were also taught (Housman 1968).

Livestock

The agricultural missionaries sought to improve cattle production by distributing worm medicine, experimenting with new grasses used for grazing, and importing Brahman bulls for breeding purposes (The Gospel under Palm and Pine 1967, 18; Housman 1968). Another project attempted to expand cattle ownership by simply giving a cow to families who did not own cattle. The families were allowed to pay for the cow by donating her first calf to MADIM. The organization continued the process by giving the calf to another family (Marx 1980). The Rhode Island Red, a breed of chicken known as a good producer of both meat and eggs, was distributed throughout Miskito villages (Housman 1968).

Additional Projects

Moravians taught alternative uses for local crops. For example, when several thousand pounds of corn were produced in Brus Lagoon as a result of a cooperative project, the missionaries showed Miskito women how to make tamales, cornbread, tortillas, and other dishes (The Gospel under Palm and Pine 1971:21). In another experiment, the missionaries attempted the processing and marketing of locally produced cashew nuts (the tree grows abundantly in many settlements) and encouraged the planting of more cashew trees (Worman 1972). Missionaries oversaw the introduction of improved varieties of rice, corn, beans, and manioc, and also distributed seeds for tomatoes, green pepper, eggplant, cucumbers, and melon (Housman 1968, 1970; Flowe 1978). Other agricultural projects included the distribution of tools, insecticides, and barbed wire, and the construction of a thirty-four-by-twenty-eight-foot, 20,000-pound-capacity granary at Brus Lagoon (Housman 1970; Molina-Cardenas 1986; Marx 1980, 1984; The Gospel under Palm and Pine 1980:18).

Additional agriculture-related projects conducted by the missionaries included the establishment of cooperatives aimed at both providing goods to villagers at cheaper prices and finding markets for their products. Another project called for the construction of a boat (named *Baltimore*) to transport people and agricultural products, and the purchase of an additional cargo boat to serve the Patuca River region (Worman 1972).

Moravian agricultural missionaries also organized the manufacture of handicrafts and artwork using *tunu* bark cloth. The coarse cloth is made from the bark of the tunu tree and was used to make pot holders, purses, bags, place mats, and other articles for sale in tourist outlets in La Ceiba, San Pedro Sula, Tegucigalpa, and the United States (Anonymous 1970). Interestingly, the Moravian Church, which now supports the manufacture of articles made of tunu bark cloth for sale in the tourist industry as a method of sustainable development, previously discouraged the Miskito's original use of the cloth as clothing during the late 1800s and early 1900s (Mueller 1932; Helms 1971).

Trades

To help the Miskito become economically self-sufficient, Moravian missionaries often taught various trades. In Nicaragua the teaching was originally conducted by individual missionaries and was not an organized effort by the entire mission. But by 1928 a more or less successful "industrial school" in Wasla prompted the mission to consider sponsoring such a school. The school was to teach trades that would produce items that had a local market and that could be made with local resources. Boys were educated in carpentry, shoemaking, and the tanning of cow hides, while girls were to be taught cooking, sewing, and how to milk cows and to make cheese and butter (Haglund 1928). Although the Miskito had cattle, they did not traditionally consume dairy products and reportedly did not like the taste of milk. Responding to missionary encouragement, the Miskito began drinking milk and making cheese (Heath 1942).

Heath wanted to start an industrial school in Honduras but did not, because of a lack of funds and because he worried succeeding missionaries might not continue the teaching of such skills (Kaurkira Station Report 1931). According to Miskito in Brus Lagoon, trades were occasionally taught in that village under the direction of the missionary Werner G. Marx during the 1940s and 1950s. The teaching of trades still continues in Brus Lagoon. During a visit in May 1996, I observed a group of young men attending carpentry school and young women in a sewing school.

Moravian contributions to Miskito agriculture in Honduras resulted in increased food production, including increased fruit tree, rice, and bean cultivation. The traditional Miskito diet was altered by the introduction of new crops—the pelipita, rice, and beans being the most important. Moravian emphasis on increased food production also made an impact on Miskito settlements in the form of larger and denser fruit tree canopies and the cultivation of larger dooryard gardens. While many agricultural alterations promoted by Moravians resembled elements of the modern sustainable-development agricultural movement (e.g., emphasis on fruit trees, and other crops and trades that were compatible with the Mosquito Coast environment), other items (e.g., use of insecticides, importation of barbed wire, and emphasis on the production of rice for markets) did not. Nevertheless, missionary attitudes concerning resources and the physical environment support the notion that, for the most part, the Moravians were early prophets of sustainability.

CHAPTER 7

Uncommon Ground

The Material Culture of Miskito Cemeteries

WHY STUDY CEMETERIES? Cemeteries are important components of the religious landscape, and scholars classify them as sacred space (Tuan 1978). According to Fred Kniffen (1967), cemeteries preserve past traditions and folkways because they are space that is set apart and used very little by the living. They reflect traditional values and religious beliefs, as well as economic and social status through the medium of material culture. The material culture of cemeteries varies geographically and by ethnicity (Jordan 1982, 1993; Jordan-Bychkov 2003). I agree with Francaviglia (1971b:509), who wrote, "Cemeteries, as the visual and spatial expression of death, may tell us a great deal about the living people who created them." In this chapter, I will discuss traditional Miskito burial customs, Moravian interventions, and locational aspects of Honduran Miskito cemeteries. I will also examine items of material culture currently present in Honduran Miskito cemeteries and, where possible, identify their historical antecedents.

Traditional Miskito Burial Customs

According to Bell ([1899] 1989) and Conzemius (1932), upon the death of an individual, women closely related to the deceased tried to injure themselves by banging their heads on posts, or they attempted suicide by hanging or drowning. Conzemius claimed that these efforts to injure themselves were not sincere, as they knew others nearby would prevent them. Bell (1862, [1899] 1989) recorded that females near the deceased also cut off their hair so that the dead individual would be the last person to have touched it. The Miskito considered the mentioning of a dead person in the presence of his or her relatives an offense. In the evening following a death, the entire village participated in a wake by butchering a cow and consuming food and alcohol. The women also took turns wailing over the body of the deceased, "crying" the history of the person and proclaiming the individual's good qualities. The Moravian missionary George Heath described a wake in Kaurkira, Honduras, as an "all-night dance before the funeral. If possible a gramophone is borrowed, and the dancing and feasting takes place in the presence of the corpse" (Kaurkira Station Report 1933:2).

In one of the earliest accounts of Miskito customs, Esquemelin ([1684] 1951) described how Miskito women exhumed the bodies of their husbands. A Miskito widow would open the grave about a year after the death of her husband, and then scrape the remaining tissue off the bones to wash and dry them in the sun. The widow would then wrap the bones in a satchel and carry them on her back during the daytime and sleep with them at night for another year. Only then was she allowed to remarry. Writing in the 1700s, Sloane (1740) and Jefferys ([1762] 1970) reported that the Miskito sewed their dead in tunu bark cloth and placed them in the grave standing up, facing east. Still others reported that the Miskito were buried in canoes that were cut in half and utilized as the top and bottom of a coffin (W. [1699] 1732; Bell ([1899] 1989; Conzemius 1932). Nineteenth-century writers described Miskito graves as having a shelter or "grave shed" under which plates of food and possessions of the deceased were placed (Ziock 1881; Bell [1899] 1989).

Formerly, surviving family members destroyed the deceased's possessions, including cattle, canoes, plantations, and fruit trees, so that the living would not use them and thus anger the spirit of the dead (W. [1699] 1732; Conzemius 1932). Moravian missionaries widely discouraged this practice, considering it an important cause of poverty, because the Miskito did not pass on property through inheritance (Smith 1877; Ziock 1881; Werner Marx, pers. comm., July 16, 1998). Later, Conzemius (1932) reported that the family kept the majority of the deceased's property, and only on occasion did they bury or leave less valuable items on top of the grave (which they broke to prevent stealing).

Following burial, sometimes as long as nine days, family asked a sukia, or Miskito shaman, to catch the *isingni*, or spirit of the departed. Moravian missionaries often found themselves in conflict with the sukias, who played the traditional shamanistic role in Miskito society. Missionaries opposed sukias because these shamans perpetuated "superstitious" and "heathen," non-Christian traditions. One such tradition was the capturing of the isingni. Miskito believed the spirit remained near the bed of the deceased individual and did mischief until carried to the burial ground. The sukia attempted to capture the isingni at night in the bedclothes of the deceased, a task that usually required more than one night, and for which the sukia received payment (Conzemius 1932; Mueller 1932; Helms 1971). The missionaries often challenged the isingni practice as well as the sukia performing it.

Kenneth G. Hamilton reported one such experience in a letter to a fellow missionary after having gone to the house of a deceased "Christian" to stop an isingni performance. Upon arrival, Hamilton found that the "bed was adorned by the bedding clothes, Bible, hymn books, pipe, plates, cups, etc., of the departed. Food and drink were also spread for him on the bed." Hamilton wrote that he took those items with him and told those present that if they continued with the ceremony, he would call the "civil authorities to have them punished." The next day there were two rumors in the village. The first claimed that the sukia went ahead and made connection with the spirit after the missionary left, and the spirit told the sukia that "he was a Christian and was not to be bothered by heathen rites, that his soul was in heaven etc." The other rumor claimed that when Hamilton rolled up the bedding, "the spirit fell out and landed behind the door, the sukia catching him there, the spirit later informed the sukia that if he had had a machete he would have killed me [Hamilton] for my interference. I . . . got a letter to the local police agent telling him to arrest sukias in the future if they carry on such superstitious practices, and bring the family implicated to justice too" (Hamilton 1926b).

In Kaurkira, George R. Heath emphasized that isingni ceremonies should not follow Christian funerals. He also warned his congregation that he would take part in a funeral only if it were "Christian" and if they promised there would be no isingni ceremony (Kaurkira Station Diary 1932). By June 1936, the mission had already created its own cemetery near the church in Kaurkira. Moravians did not allow non-Christians to use the mission cemetery. Non-Christian Miskito buried their dead in a nearby cemetery at Dapat. According to villagers I spoke with, Kaurkira's cemetery is no longer used exclusively by the Moravians but is now available to the entire community. Moravian influence has led to the decline of the isingni ceremony. The missionaries so widely opposed both the isingni practice and the sukias in general that even though several Miskito stated that a few sukias still practice secretly, neither exists openly today (Helms 1971).

Easter Dawn Service

The institution of the Easter dawn service is another practice related to cemeteries where the Moravians have exerted considerable influence. The first Easter dawn service took place in Herrnhut, in 1732, when a group of young men decided to express their faith in Christ's resurrection by singing hymns in the cemetery. A sunrise service consisting of hymns, scriptures, and prayers became a popular practice during the following years, and, in 1754, Count Zinzendorf included the service in the liturgy book. The church held its first Easter dawn service in North America at Bethlehem, Pennsylvania, in 1744, and in the church's Southern Province at Bethabara (North Carolina), in 1758. Eventually, several Protestant denominations adopted the practice (Atcheson 1953; Dreydoppel 1955).

The service itself, entitled "Service for Easter Morning" in the Moravian liturgy book, consists of prepared text, scriptures, and hymns, and is carried out in two parts, the first in the church, and the second in the cemetery, which Moravians refer to as "God's Acre" (Dreydoppel 1955). Variations exist but generally the congregation meets in the church at four in the morning to hold the first part of the service, and then the congregation walks to the cemetery, where the second part of the service takes place as the sun rises. A brass band accompanies the congregation. The symbolism of the Easter dawn service includes the reenactment of the disciples' finding of the empty tomb (Atcheson 1953), and the transition from dark to light during the service illustrates the "transfer from the darkness of sin and death to the glories of the kingdom through the death and resurrection of Jesus Christ" (Dreydoppel 1955:35).

Because the Miskito believed in evil spirits, and because Moravians hold the Easter dawn service in the cemetery, which the Miskito considered a place of many spirits, it took some time before missionaries in Nicaragua were able to institute the service on the Coast. Moravians first held the Easter dawn service at Bluefields in 1859, and then in the island community of Rama in 1861 (Grunewald 1859; Moravian Church 1849–89, 24:357). Missionaries later instituted Easter dawn services at Wounta

Haulover in 1863, Tasbapauni in 1865, and Sandy Bay in 1897 (Moravian Church 1849–1889, 24:656; Moravian Church 1849–1889, 25:393; Moravian Church 1890–1956, 3:322).

The missionaries in Honduras also had to wait a number of years before they could hold an Easter dawn service. On Easter Sunday 1936, the Reverend George R. Heath recorded: "We have not been able, for obvious practical reasons, to have an early service; and not even this year have we thought it wise to go to the burial ground, although we now have one" (Kaurkira Station Diary 1936:113). The first statement is a reference to tardiness—something Heath repeatedly complained about in the diary—and the second refers to the Miskito belief that many spirits reside in cemeteries.

The first Easter dawn service Heath recorded in the Kaurkira Station Diary occurred on May 9, 1944. Scholars do not know when the Moravians held their first service in other locations in the Honduran Mosquitia, except for Cocobila, where an elderly woman remembered Heath conducting a sunrise service. Although she could not remember the year, Heath lived in Cocobila from 1938 to 1945, indicating an approximate date for the event.

Currently, the Miskito hold Easter dawn services at all locations in Honduras where there is a Moravian pastor. The following is a description of the April 12, 1998, service in Puerto Lempira, abstracted from field notes:

> About twenty to twenty-five people attended the 4:30 a.m. meeting at the church. The reverend spoke, hymns were sung, and then the congregation knelt down at their pews and offered their own individual prayers out loud. The prayers lasted several minutes until the reverend stood up, indicating an end to the first part of the meeting. The group then made the fifteen-minute walk to the cemetery, where a few other members were already waiting. The congregation found an open area in the cemetery and stood facing east in the form of a cross. Everyone was then given a small white flower to hold. The reverend stood facing the listeners with his back to the east and read a sermon entitled "The Passion of Christ" from a small book. The text was based on the Bible and talked about the resurrection. Several hymns were also sung during the service. When the reverend finished reading the prepared text, he stated, "We are here in the cemetery not to remember the dead, but because we have a

hope that Christ was resurrected and we too will be resurrected." Then a final prayer was offered. The members of the congregation placed the white flowers they were previously holding on the grass at their feet, the flowers then also forming a cross. About half of the congregation went home, but the other half remained at the cemetery, visiting the graves of loved ones, and talking with friends and family. A range of emotions was present. Some were grief-stricken and tearful, while others were smiling and engaged in cheerful conversation. The timing of the service was such that by the time the congregation left the church, it had begun to get light outside, but the sun was not actually visible until during the service in the cemetery.

Cemetery Location and Orientation

Miskito burial sites are located within settlements, adjacent to settlements, and in some cases several hundred yards from settlements. Those sites located away from settlements ranged from as little as one hundred yards, as in the cemeteries of Tasbaraya and Puerto Lempira, to as much as over twenty miles, as is the case for some of the Kruta River villages. They bury their dead in Daiwras located near the Caratasca Lagoon. The Laka area villages also use Daiwras as a burial ground. The majority of burial grounds located away from settlements, however, are not more than a mile distant. Of the thirty burial sites surveyed, twenty-four are located in or adjacent to a settlement, while six are located outside a settlement.

Among the burial grounds found within villages, the sites at Brus Lagoon, Sirsirtara, Suhi, Mabita, and Tikiuraya are located near or adjacent to the center of the settlement. Cemeteries in these villages (except for Mabita, which has no church) and Kaurkira, are located near or adjacent to church property. In other cases, cemeteries are located along main roads and paths within villages. Such cases included the five sites mentioned above, plus Paptalaya, Dapat, Cayo Sirpe, Auka, Yahurabila, Prumnitara, Raya, and Kaurkira. In the case of Yahurabila, the cemetery is actually bisected by the main road that connects Yahurabila with the nearby villages of Pusuaia and Krata. Still other burial sites, including those in Uhi, Wauplaya, Belén, and Kruta, are located at or very near the edge of a village. On occasion, because settlements enlarge, burial sites can change from being located adjacent to a settlement to being located well within. For example, Puerto Lempira, Tasbaraya, and Belén will soon incorporate cemeteries into their built-up areas. Cardinal directions do not seem to be an important factor in determining burial ground locations and orientations, as they are located on all sides—north, south, east, and west—of settlements. The one apparent factor in determining the location of Miskito burial grounds is topography.

The most important rule governing Miskito cemeteries, as is the case with settlements, is to locate them on relatively high ground. Because much of the Mosquitia is low-lying, only eight cemeteries (those at Suhi, Prumnitara, Cayo Sirpi, Auka, Tipi, Tasbaraya, Kokota, Mocorón-refugee, and Daiwras) stand on hills with more than five to ten feet of local relief. The highest grounds in coastal areas are the beach ridges. Not surprisingly, like the houses in such settlements, the cemeteries are also located atop the ridges. The sites in Nueva Jerusalén, Uhi, Yahurabila, Dapat, Kaurkira, Benk, and Raya are such examples.

The cemetery next to the Moravian complex in Kaurkira provides an excellent example of a beach-ridge cemetery and confirms the importance of relatively high ground for the location of Miskito burial grounds. The cemetery stretches across two parallel ridges, with each ridge having only about two feet of relative relief from the corresponding parallel swales on each side. Of the 234 graves present in the Kaurkira cemetery, only one is located in the shallow linear depression between ridges, while the rest are located along the tops of the ridges.

As in former times, cemeteries are sometimes located a short distance from settlements on the low, rounded hills out in the savanna (Bell 1989 [1899]; Ziock 1881). All three cemeteries on the island of Tansin (Palkaka, Tasbaraya, and Kokota) are located on the savanna, as are those at Puerto Lempira, Tipi, and Daiwras.

Topography also affects the shape of burial sites. For example, cemeteries located on beach ridges tend to be narrow and elongated, while those on the savanna are compact. When space is sufficient, cemeteries are more likely to be spread out with no particular shape or boundary. Because Miskito cemeteries are on high ground, many of them possess a visual quality with vistas of open savanna or a body of water (table 7.1). Those at Daiwras, Palkaka, Tipi, Kokota, and Puerto Lempira are the most impressive.

Of the thirty burial sites studied, the Kruta cemetery has the lowest elevation. The entire settlement is barely above the riverbank, so during

TABLE 7.1. Cemeteries with open views

Cemetery*	Savanna	Lagoon	River
Ahuas (25)	✓		
Auka (95)	✓		
Cayo Sirpi (96)	✓		
Daiwras (145)	✓	✓	
Kokota (52)	✓	✓	
Mocorón-refugee (144)	✓		
Palkaka (46)	✓		
Prumnitara (139)		✓	
Puerto Lempira (55)	✓	✓	
Suhi (76)			✓
Tasbaraya (116)	✓		
Tikiuraya (104)			✓
Tipimunatara (97)	✓		
Wauplaya (63)	✓		

Source: Field notes
* Parenthetical numbers are to be used in conjunction with the designations in fig. 1.2.

the rainy season the rising Kruta River floods most of the area. According to the local Moravian pastor, the Kruta cemetery is located on the highest ground available and is the only place in the area that does not flood during the rainy season. Because the water table is just below ground, during the burial someone must hold down coffins in the rising water while others pile dirt on top.

Material Culture of Miskito Cemeteries

A casual observer of a Miskito cemetery would likely notice several items, including fencing around individual graves, wooden crosses, dirt mounds, and a few sheltered graves. Upon further inspection, however, one would realize that several additional items of material culture are common to most sites.

Crosses

Crosses are the most common material culture items in Miskito cemeteries. Wooden crosses are ubiquitous, existing in all thirty cemeteries studied. The following description of a Miskito cemetery near Cape Gracias a Dios in Nicaragua, suggests that the Miskito use of the cross is due in part to Moravian missionary influence. Reichel (1908:45) observes:

> I was very much struck by a visit to the cemetery. There are a good many graves there with little huts erected over them, underneath which are old rags, plates with food on them, and various household utensils; and alongside of these, plain graves with a simple cross; then more heathen graves, and again a grave with a cross. What a great deal it means, and how grand a testimony it is, when an Indian who until a few years ago was sunk in heathenish ways, and to whom more especially death with all its terrors was a fearful riddle, now has relinquished his superstitions, and therefore also all fear and hope, since he has found salvation at the Cross of Christ!

Several different styles of crosses are present. Most possess simple rectangular shapes, while others are pointed or rounded on the ends. The majority of wooden crosses contain no inscriptions. Those crosses that do contain inscriptions consist of the name and dates of birth and death of the deceased. Engravers make most lettering with either a pen or paint, or with a series of indentations in the wood made by nail and hammer. Concrete crosses are less common than wooden crosses, occurring in thirteen out of thirty cemeteries studied. They usually occur in graves with aboveground cement tombs and slabs. Concrete crosses are both painted and unpainted, and many lack lettering (fig. 7.1).

Metallic nameplates and crosses are present in a few cemeteries and typically occur in conjunction with aboveground cement tombs. Like aboveground cement tombs and concrete crosses, metallic nameplates and crosses are traditions that Ladinos brought to Mosquitia. Therefore, it is not surprising that these items are concentrated in the cemeteries at Brus Lagoon and Puerto Lempira, the primary population nodes in Mosquitia, where many Ladinos reside, and where most contacts between the Mosquitia and the rest of Honduras occur.

An intriguing aspect of the cross in Miskito cemeteries is its location. The Miskito bury their dead oriented toward the east. Some Miskito I spoke with explained this eastern orientation as a response to Christ's second coming from the east, while others said they face the rising sun. Still others said that when someone is laid to rest, his or her head should point to the setting sun (also resulting in an east–west orientation). However, Miskito place the cross either at the head (giving the grave an apparent

7.1 Selected cross styles in Honduran Miskito cemeteries, 1998.

eastward orientation) or at the feet (giving the grave an apparent westward orientation). A Moravian missionary noticed this westward orientation in a Nicaraguan cemetery over one hundred years ago. He wrote, "Contrary to the custom of most nations, these huts [grave sheds] were all open to the west, and well closed to the east" (Ziock 1881:511). Interestingly, spatial variation exists between cemeteries with apparent eastward and westward orientations, a variation at least partially influenced by the Moravian Church (fig. 7.2). Locations where the majority of graves have an apparent orientation toward the west include Cayo Sirpe, Daiwras, Kokota, Mabita, Mocorón, Mocorón-refugee, Sirsirtara, Suhi, Tipi, and Wauplaya. Meanwhile, the cemeteries at the strongest Moravian centers, including Ahuas, Brus Lagoon, Kaurkira, and Paptalaya, do not contain a single apparent west-oriented grave. Other cemeteries such as those at Auka, Puerto Lempira, Palkaka, Raya, Uhi, Prumnitara, and Dapat, contain mainly east-oriented graves, with only a few crosses positioned at the feet. Still others, such as those at Nueva Jerusalén and

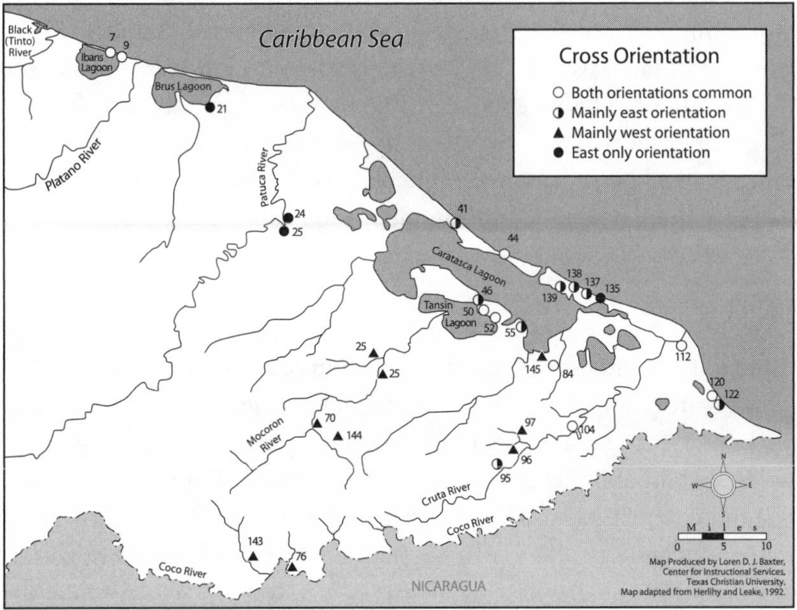

7.2 Cross orientation in Miskito cemeteries, 1998 (see table 1.1 for settlement names).

Belén, although in fairly strong Moravian areas, contain a mixture of apparently east- and west-facing graves. For example, the cemetery at Belén contains a total of ninety-eight graves, of which fifty-one apparently face east and forty-seven west.

The Prevalence of White

White is an important color in Miskito burial grounds. In addition to such built items as white picket fences, crosses, and tombs, the Miskito use white sand, pebbles, and sheets to adorn graves. The deceased's family brings white sand and pebbles, the most common of the above-mentioned white coverings, from the beach or from creek beds, and sprinkles them on the grave. Burial grounds where this practice is prominent include Palkaka, Tasbaraya, Tipi, Wauplaya, Ahuas, and Sirsirtara. The practice also occurs to a lesser extent in Brus Lagoon, Puerto Lempira, Laka Tabila, Kokota, and Paptalaya. A few people used white shells as decorations in Kaurkira and Prumnitara, where they pressed the shells into slabs before the concrete cured. White flowers and white wreaths are also common decorations in several Miskito cemeteries. Another type of white adornment used by the Miskito is a bedsheet or blanket laid over the dirt mound. This practice is most common in Raya, where white bedsheets or blankets cover twenty of approximately eighty graves. Other cemeteries where at least one white blanket or bedsheet is used to cover graves include Belén, Raya, Prumnitara, and Palkaka.

Fencing

Although Miskito do not demarcate the outside boundaries of cemeteries, they frequently fence in individual graves and family plots.[1] Barbed wire is the most common material used for fencing, but wooden sticks or poles, boards, and picket fencing are also popular. On a few occasions chain-link fencing is used, and a fence of PVC pipe surrounds a grave in the Mocorón cemetery. Wooden sticks, boards, and picket fences usually demarcate single graves, whereas wire is more practical to use for larger family plots of several graves. Wire fencing is also used for individual graves. Because of the humid, tropical climate, and roaming cattle, fencing can fall into a state of disrepair rapidly.

Personal Possessions

Early writers consistently described the Miskito tradition of placing the deceased's possessions both atop and in the grave (Bell [1899] 1989; Conzemius 1932). A Moravian missionary also described the tradition: "I remember going up on the hill to the old Indian burial ground. We saw there such things as old iron pots, calabashes, and pieces of clothing" (Anonymous n.d.). Another missionary's description indicates that the Moravians discouraged the practice. He wrote, "The little mounds are covered by small huts containing all the property of the deceased, which has not been destroyed, such articles as clothes, bottles, &c. Weapons are laid with the corpse in the grave. . . . Our Christians bury their dead as we do, and do not destroy the property of the deceased" (Ziock 1881:511). Although the Moravian Church may have discouraged these practices, they still exist today on a limited scale, with only useless or less valuable property being left at the grave site. The Palkaka cemetery was the most unusual in terms of personal effects, which included a stereo "boom box," an umbrella, a baseball cap, pots, pans, cups, and shoes. Items placed on the graves of young children included a portable crib, shoes, bedding, nursing bottles, and various plastic and glass medicine bottles for ailments such as intestinal parasites (fig. 7.3). In another example, a pit saw, broken in two pieces so that it would be useless and therefore not stolen, and a sewing machine were placed on a grave in Sirsirtara.

Grave Food

Historically, the Miskito placed food on the grave to nourish the deceased's spirit (Bell [1899] 1989; Conzemius 1932). The buccaneer Esquemelin ([1684] 1951:254) related his own experience as follows: "I have oftentimes with my own hands taken away these offerings, and eaten them instead of other victuals. To this I was moved, because I knew that the fruits used on these occasions were the choicest and ripest of all others, as also the liquors of the best sort they made use of for their greatest regale and pleasure."

The Moravians probably discouraged the Miskito from placing food on graves, because they believed the practice was evidence of "heathen superstitions" (Reichel 1908:45). The tradition continues today, however,

7.3 A child's grave in the Palkaka cemetery, containing a coconut, a toy, a portable crib and bedding, nursing bottles, and medicine for intestinal parasites and other ailments, 1998.

albeit more sparingly. Food items left on the graves in the cemeteries studied include coconuts and mangos. Opened coconuts are commonly found lying on or around Miskito graves. Some Miskito expressed a belief that "the spirit of the deceased might be thirsty and want something to drink." In some instances, people replaced coconut water with modern beverages. For example, relatives placed an empty orange juice container and a full bottle of cola on a raised concrete tomb in the Palkaka cemetery. Family members also placed empty soda cans on graves in Kokota and Puerto Lempira. Miskito residents explained that these beverages were the deceased's favorite drinks during life and that family members placed those specific drinks on the grave to refresh the deceased's spirit.

Wreaths and Flowers

Wreaths decorate sixteen out of thirty cemeteries studied. The wreaths consist of wire wrapped in thin papier mâché. The vast majority of wreaths are white, but a few in the Brus Lagoon cemetery were red and yellow. Relatives typically hang wreaths on crosses or fences, or place them directly on top of concrete tombs.

Flowering plants are common, being present in twenty of the burial sites where I collected data. Most of the plants produce white and red flowers. While people use most plants solely for decorative purposes, at times they are used as actual grave markers. Mourners also place plants in milk-can planters on top of concrete tombs. The use of wreaths and flowers appears to be relatively new and was probably encouraged by the Christian denominations present in the region.

Trees

Although trees serve as grave markers in sixteen out of the thirty cemeteries studied, the total number of graves marked by trees is not large, because a tree usually marks only a few graves in each of the sixteen cemeteries. Typical tree species used as grave markers in Miskito burial grounds include pine, cashew, mango, and coconut palm. Mourners usually plant trees atop the grave's west end.

Herbal Medicine Bottles

Protecting the grave with medicinal herbs is a Miskito tradition. The Miskito believe that by placing medicinal plants around the grave, they can protect the corpse and prevent alligators or other wild animals from digging it up. The deceased's family members place some herbs at the bottom of the grave before interment, and after the burial they mix additional herbs with water in quart-sized glass bottles and place them around the grave, typically at each corner and at the base of the cross. The water in the bottles is dark red, green, or clear. Glass bottles on graves are becoming relics of the past, as traditional beliefs slowly fade or merge with the teaching of Christian denominations now found in the Honduran Mosquitia. In the Tasbaraya cemetery, for example, family members permanently fixed empty glass bottles in the recent concrete tomb of a reportedly devout Moravian. This incident suggests that the Miskito tradition of placing glass bottles at grave corners is strong enough to continue, even though for some inhabitants, change in religious beliefs may have rendered the bottles' traditional purpose meaningless.

Dirt Mounds and Bare Earth

Burial mounds, the excess dirt remaining atop a coffin, are the most numerous features present in Miskito cemeteries. Many mounds are unmarked, having no cross, but nearly all have had grass removed from around them so that they are surrounded by a large area of bare earth. Residents maintain the bare ground adjacent to the grave by removing the vegetation once a year during Semana Santa (Holy Week). Villagers also clear grass from the area adjacent to aboveground cement tombs and concrete slabs. In the case of a fenced grave, residents scrape the entire area inside the fence clean.

"Scraping" may have multiple origins and purposes. In his study of cemeteries in the Upland South, Jordan-Bychkov (2003:76) suggested that "'scraping' to produce bare-earth expanses . . . may well be an 'Africanism.'" An entry in the Kaurkira Station Diary (1944) suggests that missionaries encouraged this practice of removing all vegetation from around the graves, perhaps in preparation for Holy Week. The Miskito probably practiced scraping as a response to frequent savanna fires. Bell

([1899] 1989: 89), who also described Miskito graves as "clean and neat," wrote, "Often in the savannas the graves get burnt by grass fires, in which case the relatives diligently seek out the originator of the fire, and make him pay the cost of a new hut." Bare earth still serves as a fire break today. At the time data were collected for this study, recent grass fires had burned right up to the bare earth surrounding graves in the Palkaka and Tipimuna cemeteries.

Concrete Slabs

I observed concrete slabs in eighteen of the thirty cemeteries studied. Most are in Kaurkira (17), Brus Lagoon (15), Puerto Lempira (11), Mocorón (10), and Raya (8). Typically, they are slabs about two feet, by five feet, by three inches, sometimes accompanied by a concrete cross or nameplate. Some slabs contain neither, and surviving family members wrote the name and dates of birth and death on the top of the slab before the concrete hardened.

The high number of slabs in Mocorón is probably related to the village's ease of contact with Puerto Lempira, and its recent history as a refugee camp. Mocorón served as a large camp run by the United Nations during the Contra war. The U.N. and other agencies regularly brought food and supplies by truck from Puerto Lempira. The Mocorón cemetery began to fill with the refugee dead, and residents created a new cemetery for refugees a few miles outside of town along the main road. It too contains several concrete slabs. I was unable to determine whether the Nicaraguan refugees preferred concrete slabs, or if the U.N. somehow encouraged their use. It is clear that the overland road between Puerto Lempira and Mocorón allowed for easier access to cement.

Concrete Tombs

I observed aboveground concrete tombs in fourteen of the thirty sites studied (table 7.2). Cement tombs occurred most frequently in the cemeteries of Brus Lagoon (174), Puerto Lempira (64), Belén (25), Ahuas (19), and Kaurkira (15). Two factors explain the large number of concrete tombs in Brus Lagoon and Puerto Lempira. Both locations have a relatively large number of Ladino residents (who are responsible for introducing the

TABLE 7.2. Selected material culture traits in Miskito cemeteries

Cemetery*	Canoes	Concrete Tombs	Grave Sheds	Grave Houses
Ahuas (25)		✓	✓	✓
Auka (95)		✓	✓	
Belén (7)		✓	✓	
Benk (120)		✓	✓	
Brus Lagoon (21)		✓	✓	
Daiwras (145)	✓		✓	✓
Dapat (137)		✓	✓	
Kaurkira (135)		✓	✓	
Kokota (52)		✓	✓	✓
Laka Tabila (84)		✓		
Mocorón (70)		✓	✓	
Nueva Jerusalén (9)		✓	✓	✓
Palkaka (46)		✓	✓	✓
Paptalaya (24)		✓	✓	
Prumnitara (139)		✓	✓	
Puerto Lempira (55)		✓	✓	✓
Raya (32)		✓		
Sirsirtara (65)	✓			
Suhi (76)		✓		
Tasbaraya (50)	✓	✓	✓	✓
Tipimunatara (97)			✓	✓
Uhi (41)		✓	✓	
Wauplaya (63)	✓		✓	
Yahurabila (44)	✓	✓	✓	

Source: Field notes. I did not include the Cayo Sirpi, Cocal, Kruta, Mabita, Mocorón-refugee, and Tikiuraya cemeteries in the table because they did not contain any of the above traits.

* Parenthetical numbers are to be used in conjunction with the designations in fig. 1.2.

custom to the Mosquitia); and they are the two main commercial centers in the Mosquitia. There, cement (a heavy bulk item) is most easily received by cargo boat from La Ceiba and other ports. The combination of a relatively large Ladino population and a greater availability of money and cement have resulted in a high number of concrete tombs in Brus Lagoon and Puerto Lempira. To a lesser extent, Kaurkira, Belén, and Ahuas also possess the above factors and therefore have higher numbers of concrete tombs than most Miskito cemeteries.

Distance and connectivity also play an important role in such matters. Even if people in isolated villages wanted to construct a concrete tomb, the cost of materials and transportation would be prohibitive in many cases. For example, it would be extremely difficult for someone to construct a concrete tomb in the Tikiuraya cemetery, because there is no overland transportation and no regular transportation by river to Puerto Lempira or any other economic center in the Mosquitia where cement is available. In light of the above discussion, one realizes it is no coincidence that Brus Lagoon, Kaurkira, and Puerto Lempira also have the highest numbers of concrete slabs, along with Mocorón. Residents' increased use of concrete tombs corresponds with the rise in concrete construction in several Miskito villages, and one should consider it part of the overall Hispanicization of the Honduran Mosquitia.

Variety is the norm in the identification or marking of tombs. Families did not always paint concrete tombs, but for those that did, popular colors were white, blue, green, and yellow. In a few cases, residents decorated concrete tombs with cement tiles. Tombs commonly contained epitaphs, but residents left several tombs unmarked. Concrete tombs usually contained concrete crosses, but on occasion residents marked concrete tombs with wooden crosses.

The Miskito sometimes construct tombs a considerable amount of time after interring a person. Concrete tombs are sometimes constructed to replace dirt mounds during Holy Week months or years after the death of an individual. Observations made at the Brus Lagoon cemetery in May 1996, and then nearly two years later, in April 1998, revealed that several dirt mounds had become concrete tombs.

The first concrete tomb constructed at Brus Lagoon, and believed to be over fifty years old, encloses the grave of a Ladino woman.[2] Brus Lagoon residents widely adopted the practice, such that Brus Lagoon's cemetery is the only Miskito cemetery where concrete tombs outnumber dirt mounds. Out of a total of 329 graves, 174 are concrete tombs, 140 are dirt mounds, and the remaining 15 are concrete slabs.

Canoe Burials

Miskito use of a dugout canoe as a coffin is a traditional method of burial that buccaneers noted as early as 1699 (W. [1699] 1732). Bell ([1899] 1989) described canoe burials in the 1850s, and Moravian missionaries and academics detailed the practice in the early to mid-1900s (Conzemius 1932; Mueller 1932; Helbig 1965). Typically, the canoe was cut in half, with the pieces forming the top and bottom of a coffin. Often, however, the Miskito cut the canoe into three pieces, using the ends as a coffin and the middle to cover the grave. A Moravian missionary described for what purpose a portion of the canoe was placed on the grave, writing, "We saw there . . . either a small dugout flat boat pitpan—or the end of one long enough to cover the top of the grave. Sometimes the graves were pretty shallow. Then the dogs, pigs, or other wild creatures would come and dig down to the bodies buried there. The dory [dugout canoe] would be some protection from that sort of thing and keep the spirits from taking away the body. Also if it was needed for crossing the lagoon to the tmisri Yapti country there would be a dory available" (Anonymous n.d.). "Tmisri Yapti" is a reference to a Miskito "hereafter" that is reached by crossing a body of water in a canoe (Conzemius 1932; Heath 1950).

Today, coffins have largely replaced canoes, but villagers in Sirsirtara, Wauplaya, and Laka (Daiwras cemetery) still practice canoe burials (fig. 7.4). Weathered remnants of canoes also cover graves in Tasbaraya and Yahurabila. Villagers in Sirsirtara, where the largest number of canoe burials are found, cut the canoe into three pieces, tying the ends together to use as a coffin and the middle to cover the grave. In one particular grave in the Daiwras cemetery, villagers buried the body in the middle section of the canoe and covered the grave with the two ends.

The Miskito tradition of sheltering, or covering their graves by constructing a shed, dates back at least 150 years and probably originated in pre-Christian times. Grave sheds were described by Conzemius (1932), Moravian missionaries (Reichel 1908; Ziock 1881), and Bell ([1899] 1989). Bell's description of a Miskito grave is as follows: "A small shed is built over the grave, in which are placed a bottle of water, a calabash, his bows, lances, and harpoons. For some time the grave is kept clean and neat, and the women now and then make offerings to the dead of a bottle of rum, a bunch of plantains, small pieces of new prints, and a few beads" (1989:89).

Interestingly, Jordan-Bychkov (2003:78) found that grave sheds were "common among the surviving remnants of southeastern Indian tribes" in the United States, and that their purpose was to "comfort the spirit

7.4 Canoe burials in Sirsirtara, 1998. The ends of these canoes are used as coffins, and the middle sections are used as grave coverings.

of the deceased." The sheds and accompanying palisades protected the decomposing corpse from animals until a shaman removed and cleaned the bones. Missionaries required southeastern tribes, upon conversion to Christianity, to practice inground burials, but grave sheds persisted as a shelter.

Grave sheds occupy twenty of the thirty cemeteries studied. The Kaurkira cemetery contains the most grave sheds (23), while Belén has eleven, Daiwras, Palkaka, and Puerto Lempira seven each, Brus Lagoon six (fig. 7.5), and Tipimuna five. Several other cemeteries contain fewer than five. Virtually all sheds are made of zinc roofing material, but a few consist of thick, black, corrugated tarpaper also used as roofing for dwellings. Although the majority of sheds are double-sided, a few single sheds are present, most notably in Palkaka, where three single sheds are found. Grave sheds may be large enough for two graves and shelter concrete tombs and slabs and dirt mounds. Ridgepoles of the sheds are usually parallel with the ridgepoles of the nearby houses.

7.5 Grave sheds sheltering concrete tombs in the Brus Lagoon cemetery, 1996.

Although written accounts prove grave sheds have been in use for at least 150 years, some Miskito believe that their use is a relatively recent practice that has developed within the past 30 years. They also believe that grave sheds reflect family wealth. When asked about the lack of grave sheds in their particular cemetery, villagers responded with the following comments: “We are too poor here for that”; “I wanted to build a shed when my daughter died but I didn’t have enough money”; and “We don’t have money.” Therefore, some Miskito believe what is actually a long-standing tradition to be a recent and increasingly popular trend practiced by individuals with disposable income. Correspondingly, Miskito construct grave sheds with modern manufactured materials only.

Grave Houses

Grave sheds, partially enclosed, which look like little houses, have existed for more than a century. In 1881, the Moravian missionary Ziock (1881:511) described “huts” in a savanna cemetery near Layasiksa, Nicaragua, as being “open to the west, and well closed to the east,” indicating that at least the eastern portion of the grave shed had been walled off. Current grave houses in the Honduran Mosquitia range from essentially grave sheds with walls to more elaborate structures with cement foundations, board walls, and doors secured with locks (fig. 7.6). Houses are present in eight of the thirty cemeteries studied and are most common on Tansin Island, where three can be seen in Palkaka, three in Tasbaraya, and two in Kokota. Also, Daiwras has two houses.

Sheltering Qualities

Whether by canoe, grave shed, house, or scrap boards, the Miskito clearly desire to protect their graves. It may be that canoes, grave sheds, and

7.6 A grave house in Palkaka with concrete block foundation, yellow board walls, red zinc roof, window, and padlocked door, 1998. Note cleared area and white sand around grave.

houses represent three concurrent phases in the evolution of Miskito grave coverings. While canoes lie directly on top of the grave, sheds provide elevated forms of shelter. Houses are a more elaborate form of enclosed grave shed. The occurrence of grave sheds (shelters without walls) and houses (shelters with walls) mirrors the change in Miskito dwellings, in that Miskito dwellings previously had no walls but have now evolved to include them.

The use of concrete tombs and slabs suggests an acceptance by the Miskito of a Ladino custom. This acceptance is enabled by the apparent sheltering or covering quality of concrete tombs and slabs. That is to say, one can also interpret the Miskito use of concrete tombs and slabs as a way of sheltering the grave site. This possibility is difficult to confirm by the current research, and in fact grave sheds sometimes sheltered concrete tombs, indicating that the concrete tomb itself was not sufficient shelter. On the other hand, the Miskito may shelter concrete tombs with grave sheds for other reasons. For example, a painted or tiled cement tomb sheltered by a grave shed and decorated with wreaths and flowers represents the largest and most expensive monument to the deceased currently found in the Honduran Mosquitia.

More Traditional versus Less Traditional

By categorizing the above traits as either "traditional" (non-European or non-Moravian in origin) or "nontraditional" (European and/or Moravian-influenced), a rough generalization is possible about the overall character of each cemetery. Items classified as traditional include: possessions of the deceased, food, bottles of herbal medicine, dirt mounds, bare earth, trees used as grave markers, cross placement at the feet, canoes, grave houses, and grave sheds. Grave sheds are problematic, because the Miskito perceive them as a new trend, but they are nevertheless a traditional item and must be classified as such. Nontraditional items include crosses, fencing, flowers, wreaths, white blankets, white sand and pebbles, and anything of concrete construction, such as tombs, slabs, and crosses.

While all cemeteries surveyed contain traditional and nontraditional traits, many cemeteries are dominated by one or the other and can therefore be characterized accordingly. "More traditional" cemeteries include:

Sirsirtara, Wauplaya, Daiwras, Tipi, Cayo Sirpe, Tasbaraya, Kokota, Palkaka, Yahurabila, Suhi, and Uhi. Cemeteries classified as "less traditional" include Brus Lagoon, Puerto Lempira, Ahuas, Kaurkira, and Dapat. The remaining cemeteries contain large numbers of both traditional and nontraditional traits and therefore fall somewhere in the middle. As one might expect, fewer traditional cemeteries are located in the larger Moravian and economic centers, which have more interaction with the Ladinos of the Honduran interior (fig. 7.7).

Additional Geographic Factors

The prominent cultural geographer Wilber Zelinsky (1994) suggested that a number of geographic factors, such as internal organization, demarcation, size, shape, ethnicity, and religious affiliation, should be examined in cemetery studies.

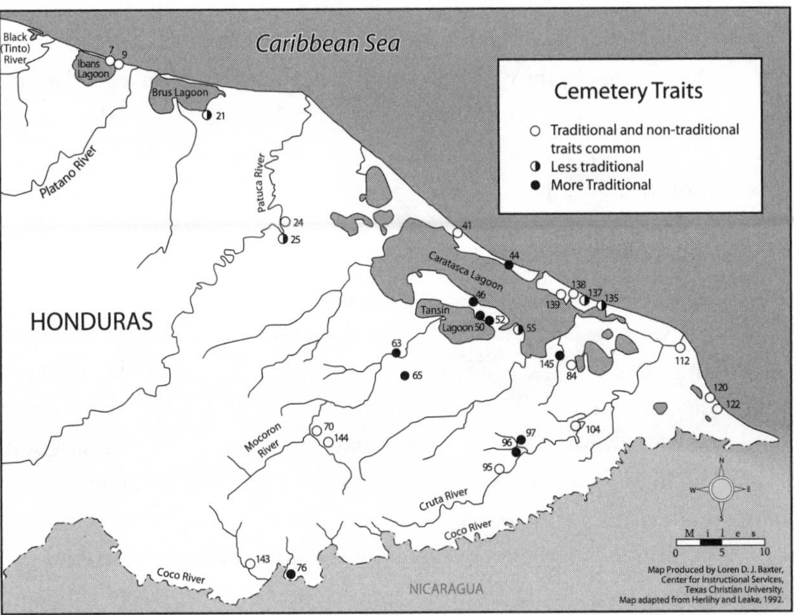

7.7 "Less traditional" and "more traditional" cemeteries, 1998 (see table 1.1 for settlement names).

Internal Organization

Aside from fenced individual and family plots,[3] much about Miskito cemeteries is random. At times individual graves are placed into "loose" rows, with the straightest rows occurring within family plots. For the most part, however, graves are situated next to each other on a more or less east–west axis as space allows.

Demarcation

In general, Miskito cemeteries are not demarcated. In only three instances are cemeteries visibly bounded. In the first case, in Palkaka, a fence consisting of one strand of barbed wire encloses half of the cemetery. In the second case, part of the refugee cemetery at Mocorón is marked by a small ditch located at the base of a hill. In Brus Lagoon, burials are fenced off from main roads with barbed wire.

Size and Shape

Miskito cemeteries do not have a standard size or shape. Size and shape are related to topography. For example, the cemeteries of Palkaka and Tipi are located on hilltops in the savanna, rounded and divided, while cemeteries on the coast are elongated and rectangular, because of their location on beach ridges.

Ethnicity

It is not always possible to determine the ethnicity of the deceased by examining the grave site. Graves with dirt mounds, crosses placed at the feet, sheds, or houses will virtually always belong to Miskito, but concrete tombs do not always represent Ladino graves (especially in Brus Lagoon, where the majority of graves were cement tombs), because some Miskito have adopted this practice.

As mentioned earlier, concrete tombs and the newer practice of metallic crosses and plates that contain epitaphs and quote scripture originate from the interior and in most cases represent Ladino Catholics. But some Miskito have already adapted these practices, as is the case of the tomb of the first Miskito-Moravian bishop.

Religious Affiliation

Likewise, religious affiliation is not perceptible in Miskito cemeteries. Aside from the cross, which is a symbol of Christianity, no items signal whether the deceased person was Catholic, Moravian, Church of God, Baptist, or of some other faith. While cemeteries in the Moravian centers of Kaurkira, Ahuas, Paptalaya, and Brus Lagoon are the only cemeteries with consistently east-facing crosses, the grave of the first Miskito Moravian bishop, located in Belén, contains a west-oriented cross (cross located at the feet). His brother claimed the family placed the cross at the feet because there was no room at the head. However, observations of the grave reveal that there is enough room to place a cross at the head instead of the feet. Whatever the reason for cross placement, this event suggests that the use of an east-facing cross is not an absolute rule among Moravians. Except for a uniquely shaped cross, the Moravian leader's tomb was similar to other graves in the Mosquitia. Likewise, the Baptist preacher's grave in Kokota, a grave house containing some of the preacher's possessions, including religious books, was similar to other Miskito grave houses and did not have any distinguishing Baptist features.

Constant Change

It is important to emphasize that Miskito cemeteries are constantly changing, due to the heat and humidity of the tropical climate, roaming cattle, and the cleaning, redecorating, and repairs that take place during Holy Week. The elements may eventually destroy grave sheds and grave houses. Cattle also wander through the cemeteries and knock down weakened fences and shelters. Hence, cemeteries commonly have a cluttered appearance, with crosses lying on the ground, fallen fences, and broken grave sheds.

Holy Week is the time family members visit cemeteries to clean and repair broken items, and to remove grass and weeds to create a "bare earth" look (Hamilton 1939). After chopping, cutting, pruning, and raking all unwanted vegetation into a pile, the family members burn it. Additionally, families repair fences, grave sheds, and grave houses; paint concrete tombs; and make dirt mounds larger. On occasion, a grave's appearance may change completely. For example, what was once a dirt mound may be replaced by a concrete slab or tomb (as in a case in Brus Lagoon discussed above). Families may construct sheds over graves where none previously existed, extensively remodel concrete tombs, and add crosses, wreaths, and flowers to grave sites.

A Distinct Region

Finally, it is important to mention two items common in Ladino cemeteries but rarely present in Miskito cemeteries—tombstones and statues or images of the Virgin Mary and Catholic saints. There were only two headstones present in the thirty cemeteries studied. One is the headstone of a North American buried in Puerto Lempira, and the other is located in Ahuas. Void of any letters or numbers, the Ahuas headstone contains the image of an opossumlike animal. Only one of the thirty cemeteries contained the image of the Virgin Mary, and that was on the tombstone of the North American. The lack of Catholic artifacts seems somewhat surprising, because according to the estimate given by the Catholic priest in Puerto Lempira, 40 percent of Mosquitia's inhabitants are now Catholic. The material culture of Mosquitia's cemeteries simultaneously displays both the persistence of, and modifications to, Miskito culture, and the distinctiveness of this Protestant region from Catholic Honduras.

Conclusion

THE FIRST MORAVIANS TO ARRIVE on the Mosquito Coast could not have envisioned the profound changes that they and subsequent missionaries would have on the region. Moravians did much more than change Miskito religious beliefs. This book demonstrates that Moravians made significant alterations to the Miskito settlement landscape in eastern Honduras—especially in settlement form, churches, housing, agriculture, and cemeteries. Missionaries altered settlement form by constructing airstrips, streets, churches, and compounds—some of which were patterned after Moravian settlements in Europe and North America. Moravian modifications to Miskito dwellings included changes to house form and construction materials. As part of the process of effecting these adaptations, the missionaries taught Miskito men carpentry and a technique for sawing lumber. Missionaries introduced new crops and livestock, such as the pelipita banana and the Rhode Island Red chicken. Moravian contributions to Miskito agriculture transformed the Miskito diet and resulted in increased fruit tree, rice, and bean cultivation. Their emphasis on increased food production impacted settlements by creating larger and denser fruit tree canopies and larger dooryard gardens. The missionaries modified Miskito burial practices by discouraging the isingni ceremony and property destruction, by propagating the use of the cross as a grave marker, and by instituting their Easter dawn service.

Today, many aspects of the Miskito-Moravian cultural landscape are more Moravian than Miskito. Missionary adaptations to Miskito society, particularly regarding housing, agriculture, and diet, were so pervasive that they even affected non-Moravian Miskito. Moravian influence resulted in a Protestant cultural region and landscape that is strikingly different from the Catholic landscapes found in the rest of the country and even those found throughout Central America.

The Moravian church compound in Honduras shows similarities but also exhibits important differences when compared with the Roman Catholic Church and colonial Spanish town planning implemented in the New World during the conquest. The typical colonial Spanish town contained a gridiron of north–south-, east–west-running streets that were centered on a plaza. The church was often located on the east side of the plaza, while the city hall, businesses, and residences were located along the remaining sides (Stanislawski 1947). Moravian town planning and Spanish colonial town planning are similar in that they are typified by a central square and a visually dominant church centrally located within the settlement. They have several important differences, however, because in the fully developed Moravian plan the principal settlement road bisects the central square, and the church is usually located within the square adjacent to the main road. Moreover, the Moravian compound contained only buildings that were used for church-related purposes, instead of privately owned stores or government offices. Furthermore, although Moravian missionaries in Honduras frequently constructed compounds, and occasionally constructed streets and landing strips, they did not implement a grid pattern. Finally, Catholic churches in Honduras are almost always oriented east–west and located on the east side of the plaza, but Moravian churches are not oriented to specific compass headings or cardinal directions. Instead, Moravian churches are commonly oriented to natural or manmade features such as rivers, lagoons, plazas, and roads (Tillman 2005, 2008).

Protestantism in Latin American countries such as Chile and those in Central America has grown to the extent that now there may be more Protestant chapels than Catholic churches, more Protestant pastors than Catholic priests, and more practicing Protestants than practicing Catholics (Clawson 2006). Future studies of this Latin American Protestant reformation should examine changes in the cultural landscape, both urban and rural, produced by Protestant growth in these areas. Scholars could use the findings in this study as a starting point to examine and compare changes in settlement landscapes of other indigenous groups in Central America where Protestant missionaries worked.

This research examined material culture change over time through the prism of landscape. The methods used in this study, namely, the documentation of the cultural landscape through extensive fieldwork, interviews with Miskito villagers, and archival research, are especially effective when there is little historical record available. Because of the Mosquitia's isolation (even the Honduran government did not have a strong presence in the region until relatively recently), there is little historical documentation of any kind. Many of the scant records that do exist originate from non-Miskito and other sources foreign to Honduras, such as archived British government reports, buccaneer and traveler accounts, and the writings of early Moravian missionaries. Geographers also employ cultural landscape study to establish the existence of, and differentiate between, cultural or ethnic regions—also known as homelands (Nostrand and Estaville 2001). This study of the Miskito settlement landscape, including settlement forms, house types, place names, material culture in cemeteries, church compounds, and church orientation, is evidence that the Mosquitia is a distinctive cultural region within Honduras (Tillman 2005, 2008).

The Miskito settlement landscape and distinct culture region documented in this study supports the efforts of land-use maps, such as the one created by Herlihy and Leake (1992) to delineate Miskito settlements and subsistence areas, and solidifies Miskito territorial claims. To document their claims to ancestral lands, the Miskito used participatory research techniques to map settlements and adjacent lands used for agriculture, hunting, pasture, and agro-forestry (Cochran 2005). These land-use maps are important because, among other things, they show the extent of territory the Miskito utilize for subsistence. Though progress toward land rights has been made in recent years, particularly in the Río Plátano Biosphere Reserve, the Honduran Miskito still do not hold individual land titles (Cochran 2008). Meanwhile, an agricultural frontier marches from west to east as Ladino colonists from the Honduran interior encroach on Miskito and Tawahka lands.

I propose that an additional method the Miskito and other indigenous peoples can employ to document their claim to land and prove their distinctiveness is to identify their ethnic landscape. While land-use maps show the "breadth" of Miskito subsistence lands, this study's identification of their ethnic landscape reveals the "depth" of shared ethnic identity, thereby demonstrating the existence of a Miskito ethnic homeland and strengthening their ancestral land claims. Future scholars and other interested parties may benefit from this study's identification and mapping of material culture elements as a methodology to help the Miskito and other groups document and strengthen their territorial claims.

Colonial practices and their associated missionary efforts impact native lands around the world in different ways. Still, this book can inform similar studies by comparison. For example, even though German colonization of the Mosquito Coast failed, the missionaries thrived, creating a new Miskito-Moravian ethnic landscape and culture region—perhaps the largest contiguous Protestant culture region in all of Spanish America. Some aspects of the Miskito settlement landscape that outside observers consider "traditional" or pre–European contact are not. The degree of Moravian influence on the settlement landscape varied geographically, because some Miskito rejected Moravian teachings, and because some villages were located far from Moravian centers. Settlements that the Moravians influenced the most exhibited a German settlement type patterned after Herrnhut and other planned Moravian communities in Europe and North America. These settlements (Brus Lagoon, Cocobila, and Kaurkira) were at the top of the hierarchy of Moravian centers and served as mission headquarters, and foreign Moravian missionaries founded and lived in their compounds.

The Moravian Church's influence on the Miskito settlement landscape has been so pervasive that a substantial period of time will pass before its contributions are eclipsed by other cultural forces. The church's influence may eventually decline, however, because of the increased presence of other religious denominations and the absence of permanently stationed foreign missionaries beginning in the late 1970s, when Honduras became an independent province of the Moravian Church. Therefore, the landscapes initiated by earlier missionaries of English and North American provenience will not be reinforced by additional foreign missionaries. Furthermore, it is too early to know what ramifications the Moravian Church's split into two factions may have on the settlement landscape.

Although the above factors are important, the current Hispanicization of the Honduran Mosquitia is the most significant factor leading to an eventual decline in Moravian influence. Puerto Lempira, the Mosquitia's center of government and main transportation hub, is the region's hearth of Hispanicization and exhibits many Ladino landscapes, including a grid pattern, plaza, and soccer field. Puerto Lempira is also the Catholic Church's main center in the region. As the capital of the Department of Gracias a Dios, Puerto Lempira has a high Ladino population and relatively strong ties to the national society. Hispanicization in Puerto Lempira, Brus Lagoon, and other Miskito settlements will grow as the region continues to be integrated into the global and national economies, attracting more Ladinos to the region. According to the 2001 census, the percentage of Ladinos residing in Gracias a Dios is increasing, corresponding with the greater government presence in the region. As the Honduran government expands, professional jobs are increasingly important in the local economy and serve to strengthen the region's links to the national economy (Tillman 2005; Cochran 2008).

Miskito is still the Coast's dominant language, but Spanish is now widely spoken. Taught in schools, Spanish is perhaps the most powerful agent of Hispanicization and is the lingua franca between indigenous groups, Ladinos, and foreigners.

Ladino influence on the Miskito settlement landscape has already manifested itself in several villages and is seen in cemeteries, in the form of large concrete tombs; in dwellings, with the growth of concrete housing (especially in Puerto Lempira); and in government health centers and public schools—both commonly constructed of concrete. The future will eventually see some Moravian contributions to the Miskito settlement landscape superseded by Ladino influences as the Mosquitia becomes increasingly assimilated into mainstream Honduras.

Appendix A

2001 Census Population of Selected Settlements in the Department of Gracias a Dios, Honduras

Settlement*	Population	Settlement	Population
Ahuas (25)	1330	Katski Almuk (140)	85
Ahuas Luhpia (89)	87	Kaurkira (135)	337**
Ahuaspahni (57)	92	Kiaskira (141)	8
Ahuastingni (91)	29**	Kinankan (134)	136
Arenas blancas (35)	24	Klauhban (18)	30**
Aurata (59)	309	Klubki (126)	431
Awasbila (73)	367	Klubkimuna (127)	252
Baikan (101)	27	Kohunta (92)	12
Barra Patuka (22)	2437	Kokota (52)	412
Belén (7)	328	Kokotingni (113)	194
Benk (120)	683	Krata (42)	432
Betania (3)	363	Kropunta (23)	453
Bilalmuk (30)	165	Kruta (112)	708
Brus Lagoon (21)	3593	Kurhpa (33)	381
Cayo Sirpi (96)	157	Kuri (Kruta River) (105)	300
Cocal (138)	63	Kuri (10)	157
Coco (61)	62	Kwihira (28)	176
Cocobila (5)	784	Laka Tabila (84)	411
Corinto (80)	34	Lakatara (88)	131
Dakratara (87)	228	Lakunka (100)	184
Dapat (137)	473	Las Marías Vieja (16)	62
El Limonal (17)	257	Leimus (142)	57
Halavar (136)	713	Limitara (72)	19
Ibans (4)	904	Lisangnipura (99)	300
Irlaya (129)	1343	Liwa (106)	136
Kalpu (111)	193	Lur (86)	50
Kanko (130)	395	Mabita (143)	30
Karaswatla (119)	145**	Mangotara (124)	586
Kasautara (128)	184	Mistruk (58)	253

Settlement*	Population	Settlement	Population
Mocorón (70)	795	Tasbaraya (Tansin) (50)	260
Nueva Guinea (114)	37	Tasbaraya (116)	184
Nueva Jerusalén (9)	584	Tawanta (47)	4
Pakwi (117)	757	Tikiuraya (104)	817
Palkaka (46)	803	Tipi Lalma (98)	329
Paptalya (24)	1084	Tipimuna (97)	369
Parada (54)	30	Titi (121)	162
Pimienta (36)	290	Tuburus (107)	277
Piñales (2)	140	Tukrun (34)	397
Plaplaya (1)	467	Tumtumtara (90)	327
Pranza (77)	246	Tusidaksa (118)	196
Priaka (56)	98	Twimawala (132)	71
Prumnitara (139)	256	Twitanta (19)	400**
Puerto Lempira (55)	3955	Uhi (41)	582
Puswaia (43)	195	Uhnuya (82)	47**
Raista (6)	110	Uhsan (110)	101
Rancho Escondido (81)	72	Uhsibila (115)	137
Ratlaya (39)	162	Uhumbila (37)	182
Raya (122)	778	Uhunuya (49)	67
Rayamuna (123)	461	Umro (102)	84**
Río Plátano (13)	460	Usupun Pura (27)	181
Rumdin (66)	117	Utla Almuk (11)	259
Rupalia (48)	41	Waha Bisban (71)	34
Rus Rus (74)	136	Waksma (26)	856
Saubila (108)	72	Walpata (53)	231
Saulala (78)	14	Wampusirpi (31)	1292
Saupani (75)	23	Wangkiawala (125)	302
Siakwalaya (103)	317	Warbantara (94)	5
Sikia Ahuia (67)	45	Warunta (60)	391
Sirsirtara (65)	374	Wauplaya (63)	129
Srumlaya (93)	116	Wawina (29)	1308
Sudin (64)	48**	Wis Wis (79)	49
Suhi (76)	509	Wisplini (62)	77
Tailibila (133)	219	Yahurabila (44)	662
Tailiyari (85)	114	Yamanta (131)	262
Tasbapauni (12)	147		

Source: 2001 census, Instituto Nacional de Estadistica, Honduras
* Parenthetical numbers are to be used in conjunction with the designations in fig. 1.2.
** 1988 census population

Appendix B

Scientific Names of Selected Vegetation

Common name	Scientific Name	Common Name	Scientific Name
Avocado	*Persea nubigera*	Pineapple	Ananas comosus
		Pumpkin	*Curcubita pepo*
Bananas	*Musa* sp.	Rice	*Oryza sativa*
Beans	*Phaseolus valgaris*	Rose apple	*Eugenia jambos*
Breadfruit	*Artocarpus altilis*	Sapodilla	*Sapota zapotilla*
Caña danta	Geonoma sp.	Saw cabbage	*Acoelorrhaphe wrightii*
Cashew	*Anacardium occidentale*	Soursop	*Annona americana*
Cedro macho	*Carapa guianensis*	Sugarcane	*Saccarum officinarum*
Coconut	*Cocos nucifera*		
Cohune	*Attalea cohune*	Suita	*Calyptrogyne sarapiquensis*
Corn	*Zea mays*		
Cortes	*Tecoma chrysantha*	Sweet potato	*Ipomoea batatas*
Grapefruit	*Citrus paradisi*	Tunu tree	*Poulsenia armata*
Guayaba	*Pisidium guajava*	Watermelon	*Citrullus lanatus*
Ironwood	*Dialium*		
Lemon	*Citrus limon*		
Lime	*Citrus aurantifolin*		
Mango	*Mangifera indica*		
Manioc	*Manihot esculenta*		
Nance	*Byrsonima crassifolia*		
Orange	*Citrus sinensis*		
Papaya	*Carica papaya*		
Pejibaye	*Guilielma gasipaes*		
Pelipita	*Musa sp.*		
Pine	*Pinus caribaea*		

Source: (Helms 1976; Dodds 1994)

Appendix C

Settlements with Catholic, Baptist, and Church of God Congregations

Settlement*	Baptist Church	Catholic Church	Church of God
Ahuas (25)	✓	✓	✓
Auka (95)	✓	✓	✓
Aurata (59)	✓	✓	
Awasbila (73)		✓	✓
Barra Patuka (22)		✓	
Benk (120)	✓	✓	✓
Brus Lagoon (21)	✓	✓	✓
Cayo Sirpi (96)		✓	
Coco (61)	✓		
Kocotingni (113)		✓	
Dakratara (87)		✓	
Dapat (137)		✓	✓
Irlaya (129)		✓	
Kalpu (111)		✓	
Kanko (130)		✓	
Karaswatla (119)		✓	
Katski (45)		✓	
Kaurkira (135)	✓	✓	✓
Klubki (126)	✓	✓	
Kokota (52)	✓		
Krata (42)		✓	
Kropunta (23)	✓		
Kruta (112)		✓	✓
Kuri (Kruta River) (10)	✓		✓
Laka Tabila (84)		✓	
Lakunka (100)		✓	
Leimus (142)		✓	
Lisangnipura (99)	✓	✓	
Liwa (106)		✓	
Lur (86)		✓	
Mangotara (124)		✓	✓

Settlement*	Baptist Church	Catholic Church	Church of God
Mistruk (58)		✓	
Mocorón (70)	✓	✓	✓
Nueva Jerusalén (9)		✓	
Pakwi (117)	✓	✓	
Palkaka (46)	✓	✓	✓
Pranza (77)		✓	
Puerto Lempira (55)	✓	✓	✓
Puswaia (43)	✓	✓	
Rancho Escondido (81)		✓	
Ratlaya (39)	✓	✓	
Raya (32)			✓
Rayamuna (123)	✓	✓	
Río Plátano (13)		✓	
Rumdin (66)		✓	
Rus Rus (74)		✓	✓
Saulala (78)		✓	
Siakwalaya (103)		✓	
Sirsirtara (65)	✓	✓	
Srumlaya (93)	✓		
Suhi (76)	✓	✓	✓
Tasbaraya (116)		✓	
Tikiuraya (104)		✓	✓
Tipi Lalma (98)		✓	
Titi (121)		✓	
Tuburus (107)		✓	
Tumtumtara (90)	✓		
Turhalaya (109)		✓	
Tusidaksa (118)		✓	
Twimawala (132)	✓		
Uhi (41)		✓	
Uhsan (110)		✓	
Uhumbila (37)		✓	
Uhunuya (49)	✓		
Uhsibila (115)	✓	✓	
Waksma (26)	✓		
Walpa Kiakira (68)		✓	
Walpata (53)	✓		
Wampusirpi (31)		✓	✓
Wangkiawala (125)		✓	

Settlement*	Baptist Church	Catholic Church	Church of God
Warunta (60)	✓	✓	
Wauplaya (63)	✓		
Waha Bisban (71)		✓	
Yamanta (131)	✓	✓	
Yahurabila (44)		✓	

Sources: Data on the location of congregations were obtained from church leaders of each denomination and field notes. Complete data for Catholic churches along and north of the Patuca River are lacking, because the region belonged to another parish, and the priest was unavailable for contact.

* Parenthetical numbers are to be used in conjunction with the designations in fig. 1.2.

Appendix D

Settlement Names

Settlement Name	Meaning, Translation
Ahuas	pine tree
Ahuas Luhpia	small pine tree
Ahuaspahni	pine tree that belongs to someone who passed away
Ahuastingni	pine tree creek
Alexandra or Cocal	personal name or coconut grove
Arenas Blancas	white sand
Auka	cortez tree
Aurata	point on the shore to where debris in the water float
Awasbila	place of many pine trees
Baikan	broken
Banaka	a tree; also, a town on Guanaja Island of the Bay Islands
Barra Patuca	bar of the Patuka (Butuk) River; Butuk was believed to be a Paya leader
Belén	Bethlehem
Benk	a temporary shelter on a riverbank; derived from English "bank"—a mahogany logger's camp on a riverbank
Betania	Bethany
Bilalmuk	old bell
Brus Lagoon	Bloody Brewer's Lagoon (Helbig 1965)
Cayo Sirpi	small sugarcane, or little island
Chiquerito	very small
Coco	coconut
Cocobila	place of many coconut trees
Corinto	Corinth

Settlement Name	Meaning, Translation
Dakratara	large round hill
Dapat	—
Dump	the stub that remains after a finger is cut off; also, possibly the place where the garbage from a nearby refugee camp was burned
El Limonal	the lemon grove
Halaver	narrow portion of land where canoes are "hauled over" from one body of water to another
Ibans	sapodilla tree
Ibatiwan	where Eve got lost
Irlaya	water where a type of small fish lives
Kalpu	—
Kanko	trunk of the saw cabbage palm
Karaswatla	lizard house
Kasautara	large cashew tree
Katski	—
Katski Almuk	old Katski
Kaurkira	place possessing bamboo
Kiaskira	—
Kinankan	"name of a Kaurikira hamlet which was burned . . . by the king to punish the insubordination of its chief man" (Heath 1947, 135)
Klauhban	part of the lagoon's shore that is now open
Klubki	—
Klubkimuna	Klubki inland
Kohunta	type of plant
Kokota	coconut tree point
Kokota Almuk	old coconut tree point
Kokotingni	coconut tree creek
Krata	—
Kropunta	crayfish point
Kruta	palm fruit point
Kurhpa	type of palm
Kuri	sapote, mamey
Kwihra	pregnant
Laka Tabila	guapinol tree point

Settlement Name	Meaning, Translation
Lakunka	lagoon of . . . (name does not specify of what or whom)
Landín	boat landing
Las Marias Vieja	the old Marias (the Marys)
Leimus	lemon
Limitara	large tiger
Liwa	spirits of the water
Lur	fishing lure?
Mabita	personal name
Mangotara	large mango tree
Mistruk	"Species of tree bearing white fragrant flowers. Its gum is very Poisonous" (Heath 1947, 244)
Mocorón	name of a river
Nueva Guinea	New Guinea
Nueva Jerusalén	New Jerusalem
Pakwi	—
Palkaka	—
Paptalaya	saw cabbage palm creek
Parada	stopping place
Payabila	place where the Paya live
Pimienta	pepper
Piñales	pineapple plantations
Pranza	—
Priaka	widow or widower
Prumnitara	big hill
Puerto Lempira	Port of Lempira—named after a sixteenth-century Lenca cacique who resisted Spanish conquistadors and is now a national hero
Pusuaia	species of mosquito
Raista	rice point—place where rice is planted
Rancho Escondido	hidden ranch
Ratlaya	rotten or putrid water
Raya	new, or curve in a river
Rayamuna	Raya inland

Settlement Name	Meaning, Translation
Río Plátano	plantain river
Rumdin	drunk rum
Rupalia	personal name
Rus Rus	name of adjacent river
Saubila	possessing cedar trees
Saulala	—
Saupauni	red cedar
Siakwalaya	small freshwater turtle
Sikia Ahuia	avocado beach
Sirsirtara	large carbon tree used for firewood
Sisinaylanhkan	place where the spirit of the ceiba (silk cotton) tree strangled itself
Srumlaya	water possessing the srum tree
Sudin	—
Suhi	flat sharpening stone
Tailibila	place possessing taili trees
Tailiyari	long taili tree
Tapamlaya	water possessing tarpon
Tasbapauni	red earth
Tasbaraya	new land
Tawanta	point of town
Tikiuraya	bend in the river where the tikiu tree grows
Tipi Lalma	east Tipi
Tipimunatara	large west Tipi
Titi	—
Tuburus	ear tree (*guanacaste*)
Tukrung	gualiqueme tree (*Inga* sp.)
Tumtumtara	large water lily
Turhalaya	water full of crocodiles
Tusidaksa	—
Twimawala	on the other side of the weeds
Twitanta	flat savanna
Uhi	type of tree

Settlement Name	Meaning, Translation
Uhnuya	—
Uhsan	type of fish
Uhsibila	place where the uhsi plant grows
Uhumbila	place where the oil palm grows
Uhunuya	—
Umro	type of tree
Usupun Pura	oak hill
Utla Almuk	old house
Waha Bisban	shredded leaf
Waksma	type of bird
Walpa Kiakira	spiny or thorny rock
Walpata	pebble beach point
Wampusirpi	little Wampu (the river upstream)
Wangkiawala	our river; also, Coco River Miskito are known as "Wangkis"
Wapniyari	along straight stretch in a river
Warbantara	large whirlpool
Warunta	White-collared peccary mountains
Wauplaya	where the trunk of the yagua palm meets the ground
Wawina	someone who calls
Wisplini	animal
Wiswis	type of bird
Yahurabila	place of much cassava
Yamanta	savanna point

Sources: The majority of Miskito settlement names were translated by Elmor Wood. Additional names were translated by Tom Keough, Carla Boscath, and various Miskito villagers. Further information was also derived from Dodds (1994) and Heath (1947). An entry with a line indicates the meaning was unknown.

Appendix E

Names of Selected Miskito House Parts and Construction Materials

English	Miskito	Spanish
asbestos	siment pankataya	asbesto
beam; rafter	bim	viga
board	tat*	tabla
cement	siment	cemento
clay stove	kubus; stov	fogón
corner post	upright	parales
corner brace	breses	pieza de refuerzo
door	dorunta	puerta
yagua palm bark	wauh	yagua
floor	plor	piso
foundation post	utla playa	poste
house	utla	casa
joist	jaist	viga; cabio
king post	utla masa	poste principal
kitchen	kitchen	cocina
nail	silak	clavo
outhouse	claset; toilet	servicios; letrina
oven	uven	horno
ridgepole	lalmukya	caballete
roof	bana	techo
room	rumbila	cuarto
saw cabbage palm thatch	papta	hojas de tique
saw cabbage palm trunk	kanku	tronco de tique
shelf for washing dishes	plet sikbaia	lavatrasto
sill	sil	solera, alféizar
split bamboo	kauhru	tarro
stairs	step	escaleras

English	Miskito	Spanish
suita thatch	ahtak	suita
truss	tauhbaya	tijera
veranda	veranda	corredor
wall	klar, kral	pared
wall plate	wal plet	viga de apoyo
window	windar	ventana
zinc roofing	pan taya*	zinc

Sources: Atto Wood, of Brus Lagoon, translated most of the words from Miskito into English and Spanish. I found additional information in Heath's (1947) unpublished "Miskito Lexicon," and Marx and Heath's (1992) Miskito dictionary. I translated the few remaining terms from Spanish to English.

*Although less obvious than several terms in this appendix, *pan taya* and *tat* are foreign-derived terms. Pan taya (*pan* means "metal pan" or "plate," and *taya* means "skin" or "feather") is the term for sheets of zinc roofing (Marx and Heath 1992). *Tat* is the term for lumber used as wall material. According to Heath (1947), *tat* and *tart* mean "board" and were derived from the English word *thwart*, which is a flat board seat (such as a rower's seat) in a small boat or canoe. *Tat* is also the Miskito word for a flat board used as a seat in a canoe (*dori tat*).

Notes

Chapter 2

1. Sources recorded the Miskito population to be approximately 1,500 in 1684 (Esquemelin [1684] 1951), 3,000 in 1711 (Peralta 1898), 7,000 by the late 1700s (White 1789), 15,000 by the 1920s (Conzemius 1932), 35,000 in 1969 (Nietschmann 1969), and 95,900 for the early 1980s (Davidson and Counce 1989: 38). Davidson and Counce estimated the Honduran Miskito population at 25,000 for the early 1980s. Although the 1988 Honduran census did not list population by ethnicity, I added the population of each Miskito village to arrive at an estimate of 31,478. The 2001 census reported 47,120 Miskito living in Gracias a Dios.

2. In 1960 the World Court ruled that the Coco River was the official boundary between Honduras and Nicaragua. This decision meant that land between the Coco and Kruta rivers became part of Honduras's national territory. This area became known by Hondurans as the zona recuperada. Moravian congregations in this area changed from being under the jurisdiction of the Nicaraguan Moravian Church to Honduran control. Some congregations in the zona recuperada, such as those in Irlaya, Benk, Kruta, Pakwi, and Raya, were established in the early 1900s.

3. The Catholic Church organized the Honduran Mosquitia into two parishes divided by a boundary that mainly followed the Warunta River, one parish headquartered in Puerto Lempira, and the other based in the village of Barra Patuka.

Chapter 3

1. Instituto Geográfico Nacional de Honduras, aerial photography, Department of Gracias a Dios series, 1:50,000 scale.

Chapter 4

1. During my 1998 fieldwork, the Moravian Church provincial headquarters in Honduras would not release data on congregation size. Membership for each zone (a zone typically includes four or five congregations) in Honduras was available for 1995 from a publication by the Moravian Church in Nicaragua entitled *Yua Banira Aisi Kaikaia Bila* (Iglesia Morava, Nicaragua, 1997). Figures for each zone consisted of: Ahuas 1,852; Auka 565; Benk 901; Brus Lagoon 1,233; Cocobila 491; Kaurkira 656; Kruta 301; La Ceiba 207;

Mocorón 324; Nueva Jerusalén 609; Puerto Lempira 587; Rio Patuka 117; San José de la Punta 168; Sico 181; Uhi 213; Wampusirpi 491 (total = 8,896). Local pastors recited congregation membership numbers from memory, but these data were not always consistent, and their accuracy was questionable.

Chapter 7

1. As is common in the Mosquitia, cattle are not fenced into a particular area for grazing but are allowed to roam and are therefore "fenced out" of areas such as private yards, plantations, church property, and individual graves.

2. I could not determine the exact date because relatives recently repaired the tomb, covering the epitaph with new concrete and a fresh coat of white paint.

3. In the past, Moravians divided their congregations into "choirs," or groups according to age, sex, and marital status. Congregations contained groups for young boys and girls, older boys and older girls, single men and single women, married individuals, and widowers and widows. Moravian missionaries did not perpetuate their tradition of burying the dead in choirs in the Honduran Mosquitia (Fries 1962). Most individuals are typically buried alongside family members.

References

Unpublished Primary Sources

Annual Report of the Province, Nicaragua. 1919. Annual Reports of the Mission 1914–1936, Moravian Church Archives, Bethlehem, PA.

Anonymous n.d. R. Bishop's Historical Notes, Rufas and Pearl Bishop's Personal Papers 1917–1956, Nicaragua Records, Moravian Church Archives, Bethlehem, PA.

Dreger, Wilford. 1978. Wilford Dreger's Field Notes. Nicaragua Records, Moravian Church Archives, Bethlehem, PA.

General Mission Conference. 1944. Mission Conference Minutes 1861–1944, Nicaragua Records, Moravian Church Archives, Bethlehem, PA.

Haglund, David. 1942. Letter to A. O. Danneberger 7 July. Haglund's Personal Letters 1942–1944, Nicaragua Personal Files, Moravian Church Archives, Bethlehem, PA.

Hamilton, Kenneth G. 1926a. Letter from Kenneth G. Hamilton to Conrad Shrimer, 8 March. K.G. Hamilton Personal Correspondence 1925–1927, Nicaragua Records, Moravian Church Archives, Bethlehem, PA.

——. 1926b. Letter from Kenneth G. Hamilton to Conrad Shrimer, 7 July. K.G. Hamilton Personal Correspondence 1925–1927, Nicaragua Records, Moravian Church Archives, Bethlehem, PA.

Heath, George Reinke. 1947. *Miskito Lexicon*. Moravian Church Archives, Bethlehem, PA.

Kaurkira Station Diary. 1930–1945. Vols. 1–3. Honduras Records, Moravian Church Archives, Bethlehem, PA.

Kaurkira Station Report. 1931. Reports of Individual Stations 1924–1937, Nicaragua Records, Moravian Church Archives, Bethlehem, PA.

——. 1933. Reports of Individual Stations 1924–1937, Nicaragua Records, Moravian Church Archives, Bethlehem, PA.

——. 1935. Reports of Individual Stations 1924–1937, Nicaragua Records, Moravian Church Archives, Bethlehem, PA.

Kruta and Raya Station Report. 1933. Reports of Individual Stations 1924–1937, Nicaragua Records, Moravian Church Archives, Bethlehem, PA.

Molina-Cardenas, Gilberto. 1986. Madim. In From Nicaragua to Honduras. Unpublished manuscript written by Warren D. Wenger, Moravian Collection, Reeves Library, Moravian College, Bethlehem, PA.

Old Cape Annual Report. 1930. Individual Station Reports 1924–1937, Nicaragua Records, Moravian Church Archives, Bethlehem, PA.

Published Primary and Secondary Sources

Adams, Anna. 1992. *Moravian Missionaries in Nicaragua: The American Years, 1917–1974*. PhD diss., Temple University. Ann Arbor: UMI.

Annis, Sheldon. 1987. *God and Production in a Guatemalan Town*. Austin: University of Texas Press.

Anonymous 1885. Report on the Mosquito Territory. In *The Kemble Papers*, vol. 2, 1780–1781. Collections of the New York Historical Society for the year 1884, 419–31. New York: The Society.

——. 1970. Tunu from Tukrun. *North American Moravian* 1 (1):17–18.

Atcheson, Donald F. 1953. Distinctive Moravian Symbols and Symbolism. Bachelor of divinity thesis, Moravian Theological Seminary, Bethlehem, PA.

Augelli, John P. 1962. The Rimland-Mainland Concept of Culture Areas in Middle America. *Annals, Association of American Geographers* 52: 119–129.

Bell, C. Napier. 1862. Remarks on the Mosquito Territory, Its Climate, People, Production, Etc. *Journal of the Royal Geographical Society* 32:242–68.

——. 1989 [1899]. *Tangweera: Life and Adventures among Gentle Savages*. Austin: University of Texas Press.

Berky, Andrew S. 1953. *The Mosquito Coast and the Story of the First Schwenkfelder Missionary Enterprise among the Indians of Honduras from 1768 to 1775*. Norristown, PA.

Bodley, John H. 1982. *Victims of Progress*. Menlo Park, CA: Benjamin/Cummings.

Breckel, Jill. 1975. *The Success of the Moravian Missions in Nicaragua and Honduras*. Bethlehem, PA: Provincial Women's Board North, Moravian Church.

Brown, Scott S. 2005. La casa de azotea en el noreste mexicano: El mestizaje del Viejo Mundo y del Nuevo Mundo en el Norte NovoHispano. In *Bridging Cultural Geographies: Europe and Latin America*, edited by Robert B. Kent, Vicent Ortells Chabrera, and Javier Soriano Martí, 81–102. Collecció América 3. Castelló de la Plana, Spain: Universitat Jaume I.

Brownlee, Fambrough. 1977. *Winston-Salem: A Pictorial History*. Norfolk, VA: Donning.

Büttner, Manfred. 1974. Religion and Geography: Impulses for a New Dialogue between *Religionswissenschaftlern* and Geography. *Numen* 21:163–96.

Butzer, Karl W., and Elisabeth K. Butzer. 2000. Domestic Architecture in Early Colonial Mexico: Material Culture as (Sub)Text. In *Cultural Encounters with the Environment: Enduring and Evolving Geographic Themes*, ed. Alexander B. Murphy and Douglas L. Johnson, 17–37. Lanham, MD: Rowman and Littlefield.

Clawson, David. 1984. Religious Allegiance and Economic Development in Rural Latin America. *Journal of Interamerican Studies and World Affairs* 26 (4):499–524.

——. 1989. Religion and Change in a Mexican Village. *Journal of Cultural Geography* 9 (2):61–76.

——. 2006. *Latin America and the Caribbean: Lands and Peoples*. New York: McGraw-Hill.

Cochran, David. 2005. The Sustainability of Shifting Cultivation in Rain Forest Conservation: Participatory Mapping the Cultural Geography of Native Peoples in the Río Plátano Biosphere Reserve. PhD diss., Department of Geography, University of Kansas.

——. 2008. Who Will Work the Land? National Integration, Cash Economies, and the Future of Shifting Cultivation in the Honduran Mosquitia. *Journal of Latin American Geography* 7 (1):57–84.

Conzemius, Eduard. 1932. *Ethnographical Survey of the Miskito and Sumu Indians of Honduras and Nicaragua*. Bureau of American Ethnology vol. 106. Washington, DC: Smithsonian Institution.

Cornebise, M. 1990. Geographical Aspects of Social and Economic Changes among the Belizean Mennonites: Twenty Years after Sawatzky. Master's thesis, Louisiana State University.

Cruz-Sandoval, Fernando L. 1984. Los indios de Honduras y la situación de sus recursos naturales. *América indígena* 44 (3):423–46.

Dampier, William. 1970 [1697]. *New Voyage Round the World*. London: Da Capo Press.

Danker, William J. 1971. *Profit for the Lord*. Grand Rapids, MI: William B. Eerdmans.

Danneberger, A. O. 1919. The Regions Beyond. *Periodical Accounts Relating to the Foreign Missions of the Church of the United Brethren, Second Century* 10 (117):297–302.

Davidson, William V. 1976. Black Carib (Garífuna) Habitats in Central America. In *Frontier Adaptations in Lower Central America*, edited by Mary Helms and Franklin O. Loveland, 85–94. Philadelphia: Institute for the Study of Human Issues.

——. 1984. Geography of Minority Populations in Central America. In *Latin America, Case Studies*, edited by Richard G. Boehm and Sent Visser, 31–37. Dubuque, IA: Kendall-Hunt.

——. 1992. Commentary: The Status of Geographical Research on the Aboriginal and Peasant Communities of Latin America. *Benchmark 1990, Conference of Latin Americanist Geographers* 17/18:189–190.

——. 1993. Territorial Changes among Indigenous Populations in Central America, 1500 to Present. Paper presented at the annual meeting of the Association of American Geographers—Southwest Division, New Orleans, LA.

——. 2002. La Costa Caribe de Honduras: Su geografía, historia y etnología. In *Colón y la Costa Caribe de Centroamérica*, edited by Jaime Incer Barquero, 61–108. Managua: Fundación Vida.

——. 2009. Reubicación de asentamientos indígenas en Centroamérica. In *Etnología y etnohistoria de Honduras: Ensayos*, edited by William V. Davidson, 293–301. Tegucigalpa: Instituto Hondureño de Antropología e Historia.

Davidson, William V., and Melanie A. Counce. 1989. Mapping the Distribution of Indians in Central America. *Cultural Survival Quarterly* 13 (3):37–40.

Dawson, Frank Griffith. 1986. Robert Kaye y el Doctor Robert Sproat: Dos Britanicos Expatriados en la Costa de los Mosquitos 1787–1800. *Yaxkin* 9 (1):43–63.

De Schweinitz, Edmund. 1901. *The History of the Church Known as the Unitas Fratrum or the Unity of the Brethren*. 2nd ed. Bethlehem, PA: Moravian Publication Concern.

Dennis, Philip A. 2004. *The Miskitu People of Awastara*. Austin: University of Texas Press.

Dennis, Philip A., and Michael D. Olien. 1984. Kingship among the Miskito. *American Ethnologist* 11 (4):718–37.

Dixon, Clifton. 1993. Costa Rica's Italian Agricultural Colony. In *Culture, Form and Place: Essays in Cultural and Historical Geography*, edited by Kent Mathewson, 287–302. Geoscience and Man vol. 32. Baton Rouge: Geoscience Publications.

Dodds, David. 1989. Miskito and Sumo Refugees: Caught in Conflict in Honduras. *Cultural Survival Quarterly* 13 (3):3–6.

——. 1994. The Ecological and Social Sustainability of Miskito Subsistence in the Rio Platano Biosphere Reserve, Honduras. PhD diss., University of California Los Angeles.

——. 1998. Lobster in the Rain Forest: The Political Ecology of Miskito Wage Labor and Agricultural Deforestation. *Journal of Political Ecology* 5:83–108.

Dozier, Craig. 1985. *Nicaragua's Miskito Shore: The Years of British and American Presence*. Birmingham: University of Alabama Press.

Dreydoppel, Otto. 1955. The Celebration of the Resurrection in the Moravian Church. Bachelor of divinity thesis, Moravian Theological Seminary, Bethlehem, PA.

Eidt, Robert C. 1968. Japanese Agricultural Colonization: A New Attempt at Land Opening in Argentina. *Economic Geography* 44 (1): 1–20.

Esquemelin, John. 1951 [1684]. *The Buccaneers of America*. London: George Allen and Unwin.

Everitt, John. 1983. Mennonites in Belize. *Journal of Cultural Geography* 3:283–93.

Fellechner, A. 1845. *Bericht über die im hochsten Auftrage Seiner koniglichen Hoheit des Prinzen Carl von Preuben und Sr. Durchlaucht des Herrn Fürsten v. Schoenburg-Waldenburg bewirkte Untersuchung einiger Theile des Mosquitolandes erstattet von der dazu ernannten Commission*. Berlin: Alexander Dunker.

Fellmann, Jerome Donald, Arthur Gettis, and Judith Gettis. 1995. *Human Geography: Landscapes of Human Activities*. 4th ed. Dubuque, IA: Wm. C. Brown.

Feurig, G. 1858. From Br. Feurig. *Periodical Accounts Relating to the Missions of the Church of the United Brethren, Established among the Heathen* 22:346–347.

Flowe, Michael G. III. 1978. Agriculture and Development Mission. *North American Moravian* 9 (5):26.

——. 1979. Community Development for Honduras. *North American Moravian* 10 (9):21.

Floyd, Troy S. 1967. *The Anglo-Spanish Struggle for Mosquitia*. Albuquerque: University of New Mexico Press.

Francaviglia, Richard V. 1971a. Mormon Central Hall Houses in the American West. *Annals of the Association of American Geographers* 61:65–71.

——. 1971b. The Cemetery as an Evolving Cultural Landscape. *Annals of the Association of American Geographers* 61:501–9.

——. 1978. *The Mormon Landscape*. New York: AMS Press.

Fries, Adelaide L. 1962. *Customs and Practices of the Moravian Church*. Rev. ed. Winston-Salem, NC: Board of Christian Education and Evangelism.

Fuson, Robert H. 1969. The Orientation of Mayan Ceremonial Centers. *Annals of the Association of American Geographers* 59:494–511.

Garrard-Burnett, Virginia. 1998. *Protestantism in Latin America: Living in the New Jerusalem*. Austin: University of Texas Press.

——. 2000. *On Earth as It Is in Heaven: Religion in Modern Latin America*. Wilmington, DE: Scholarly Resources.

Gollin, Gillian. 1967. *Moravians in Two Worlds*. New York: Columbia University Press.

Gordon, Edmund. 1998. *Disparate Diasporas: Identity and Politics in an African Nicaraguan Community*. Austin: University of Texas Press.

The Gospel under Palm and Pine: Annual Report of the Board of Foreign Missions of the Moravian Church in America, Inc. 1952–1987. Bethlehem, PA: The Board.

Griffen, Frances. 1985. *Old Salem: An Adventure in Historic Preservation*. Winston-Salem, NC: Winston Printing.

Grossman, Guido. 1988. *La Costa Atlántica de Nicaragua*. Managua: La Ocarina.

Grunewald, F. E. 1859. From Br. E. Grunewald. *Periodical Accounts Relating to the Missions of the Church of the United Brethren, Established among the Heathen* 23:10–12.

Haglund, David. 1928. How Should an Industrial School Be Kept and What Trades Should Be Taught for the Best Advantage of Our Indian Boys and Girls? *Proceedings of the Society for Propagating the Gospel among the Heathen* 103–7.

——. 1930. A Missionary Trip to Honduras. *Moravian Missions* 28 (11):88.

Hale, Charles R. 1994. *Resistance and Contradiction: Miskitu Indians and the Nicaraguan State, 1894–1987*. Stanford, CA: Stanford University Press.

Hamilton, John Taylor. 1900. *A History of the Moravian Church*. Bethlehem, PA: Times.

——. 1901. *A History of the Missions of the Moravian Church during the Eighteenth and Nineteenth Centuries*. Bethlehem, PA: Times.

——. 1912. *Twenty Years of Pioneer Missions in Nyasaland*. Bethlehem, PA: Society for Propagating the Gospel.

——. 1918. Report of the Mission for 1917. *Periodical Accounts Relating to the Foreign Missions of the Church of the United Brethren, Second Century* 10 (115):236–46.

Hamilton, John Taylor, and Kenneth G. Hamilton. 1967. *A History of the Moravian Church: The Renewed Unitas Fratrum 1722–1957*. Bethlehem, PA: Interprovincial Board of Christian Education, Moravian Church in America.

Hamilton, Kenneth G. 1939. *Meet Nicaragua*. Bethlehem, PA: Comenius Press.

Hansen, Marcus L. 1940. *The Atlantic Migration, 1607–1860*, ed. Arthur M. Schlesinger. Cambridge: Harvard University Press.

Heath, George Reinke. 1904. Indian Life in Nicaragua. *Moravian Missions* 2 (7):101.

——. 1916. By-Paths in Honduras. *Moravian Missions* 14:171–73.

——. 1931. Beginnings in Honduras. *Moravian Missions* 29(11):86–87.

——. 1939a. *Periodical Accounts Relating to the Foreign Missions of the Church of the United Brethren, Second Century*, no. 107:102–7.

——. 1939b. Report of the Honduras Mission Province for 1938. *Proceedings of the Society for Propagating the Gospel among the Heathen*, 46–58.

——. 1940a. Mission Travelogues. *Moravian Missionary* 825 (3):19–21.

——. 1940b. Mission Travelogues. *Moravian Missionary* 826 (4):27–29.

——. 1941a. Honduras: Provincial Report, 1941. *Periodical Accounts Relating to the Foreign Missions of the Church of the United Brethren, Second Century*, no. 150:62–69.

——. 1941b. Annual Report for the Year 1941. *Proceedings of the Society for Propagating the Gospel among the Heathen*, 54–62.

——. 1942. Annual Report for the Year 1942. *Proceedings of the Society for Propagating the Gospel among the Heathen*, 58–63.

——. 1949. Beginnings in Honduras. *Moravian* 94 (23):1–2.

——. 1950. Miskito Glossary, with Ethnographic Commentary. *International Journal of American Linguistics* 16:20–34.

——. 1958. Moravian Beginnings in Honduras. *Moravian* 103 (4):21.

Helbig, Karl M. 1965. *Areas y paisajes del nordeste de Honduras*. Tegucigalpa: Banco Central de Honduras.

Helms, Mary W. 1969. The Cultural Ecology of a Colonial Tribe. *Ethnology* 8 (1): 76–84.

——. 1971. *Asang: Adaptations to Cultural Contact in a Miskito Community*. Gainesville: University of Florida Press.

——. 1976. Domestic Organization in Eastern Central America: The San Blas Cuna, Miskito, and Black Carib Compared. *Western Canadian Journal of Anthropology* 6 (3):133–63.

——. 1983. Miskito Slaving and Culture Contact: Ethnicity and Opportunity in an Expanding Population. *Journal of Anthropological Research* 39 (2):179–97.

Henderson, Gavin B. 1944. German Colonial Projects on the Mosquito Coast, 1844–1848. *English Historical Review* 59:257–71.

Herlihy, Laura H. 2002. The Mermaid and the Lobster Diver: Ethnic and Gender Identities among the Río Plátano Miskito Peoples. Unpublished PhD diss., University of Kansas, Lawrence.

——. 2006. Sexual Magic and Money: Miskitu Women's Strategies in Northern Honduras. *Ethnology* 45 (2):143–59.

——. 2008. Neither Black nor Indian: The Discourse of Miskitu Racial Identity in Honduras. In *Ethno- and Historical Geographic Studies in Latin America: Essays Honoring William V. Davidson*, edited by Kent Mathewson, Peter Herlihy, and Craig Revels, 129–144. Geoscience and Man vol. 40. Baton Rouge: Geoscience Publications, Louisiana State University.

Herlihy, Peter H. 1995. La revolución silenciosa de Panamá: Las tierras de comarca y los derechos indígenas. *Mesoamerica* 16 (29):77–94.

Herlihy, Peter H., and Gregory Knapp. 2003. Maps of, by, and for the Peoples of Latin America. *Human Organization* 62 (4):303–14.

Herlihy, Peter H., and Andrew P. Leake. 1992. *Tierras indígenas de la Mosquitia Hondureña: Zonas de subsistencia*. Map produced for the Primer Congreso sobre Tierras Indígenas de La Mosquitia, Tegucigalpa, Honduras, September 1992.

——. 1997. Participatory Research Mapping of Indigenous Lands in the Honduras Mosquitia. In *Demographic diversity and Change in the Central American Isthmus*, ed. Anne R. Pebley and Luis Rosero-Bixby, 707–36. Santa Monica, CA: Rand Books.

Highfield, Arnold R. 1994. Patterns of Accommodation and Resistance: The Moravian Witness to Slavery in the Danish West Indies. *Journal of Caribbean History* 28 (2):138–64.

Holm, John A. 1978. The Creole-English of Nicaragua's Miskito Coast: Its Sociolinguistic History and a Comparative Study of Its Lexicon and Syntax. PhD diss., University of London.

Horst, Oscar. 1998. Building Blocks of a Legendary Belief: The Black Christ of Esquipulas, 1595–1995. *Pennsylvania Geographer* 36 (1):135–47.

Houseal, Brian, Craig Mcfarland, Guillermo Archibold, and Aurelio Chiari. 1985. Indigenous Cultures and Protected Areas in Central America. *Cultural Survival Quarterly* 9(1):10–20.

Housman, E. Howard. 1958. With Their Own Eyes. *Moravian* 103 (4):24–31.

——. 1968. God Help Us If We Say, God Bless You. *Moravian*. 113 (5):6–8.

——. 1970. Honduras. *Viewpoint from Distant Lands* 178:13–14.

Hutton, J. E. 1922. *A History of Moravian Missions*. London: Moravian Publication Office.

Iglesia Morava, Nicaragua. 1997. *Yua Banira Aisi Kaikaia Bila*. Puerto Cabezas: Oficina Provincial, Educación Cristiana, Estadística.

Isaac, Erich. 1959. Influence of Religion on the Spread of Citrus. *Science* 129:179–86.

Jackson, J. B. 1952. Human, All Too Human Geography. *Landscape* 2:2–7.

Jackson, Richard H., and Roger Henrie. 1983. Perception of Sacred Space. *Journal of Cultural Geography* 3:94–107.

Jackson, Richard H., and Robert L. Layton. 1976. The Mormon Village: Analysis of a Settlement Type. *Professional Geographer* 28:136–41.

Jefferys, Thomas. 1970 [1762]. *A Description of the Spanish Islands and Settlements on the Coast of the West Indies*. New York: AMS Press.

Jett, Stephen C. 1997. Place-Naming, Environment, and Perception among the Canyon de Chelly Navajo of Arizona. *Professional Geographer* 49:481–93.

Johnson, R. Burke. 1972. A New Church for Kaurkira. *North American Moravian* 3 (4):3–5.

Jones, David R. W. 1970. The Caribbean Coast of Central America: A Case of Multiple Fragmentation. *Professional Geographer* 22:260–66.

Jordan, Terry G. 1966. On the Nature of Settlement Geography. *Professional Geographer* 18:26–28.

——. 1982. *Texas Graveyards: A Cultural Legacy*. Austin: University of Texas Press.

——. 1988. A Gabled Folk House Type of the Mexico–Texas Borderland. *Yearbook, Conference of Latin Americanist Geographers* 14:2–6.

——. 1993. The Anglo-American Mestizos and Traditional Southern Regionalism. In *Culture, Form, and Place: Essays in Cultural and Historical Geography*, edited by Kent Mathewson, 175–95. Geoscience and Man vol. 32. Baton Rouge: Geoscience Publications.

Jordan, Terry G., and Matti Kaups. 1989. *The American Backwoods Frontier*. Baltimore: Johns Hopkins University Press.

Jordan-Bychkov, Terry. 2003. *The Upland South: The Making of an American Folk Region and Landscape*. Santa Fe: Center for American Places.

Kalfus, Radim. 1957. *Unitas Fratrum in Pictures 1457–1957*. Prague: Moravian Church.

Kent, Robert B., and Randall J. Neugebauer. 1990. Identification of Ethnic Settlement Regions: Amish-Mennonites in Ohio. *Rural Sociology* 55:425–41.

Kirchhoff, Paul. 1948. The Caribbean Lowland Tribes: The Mosquito, Sumo, Paya, and Jicaque. In *Handbook of South American Indians*, edited by Julian H. Steward, 4:219–229. Bureau of American Ethnology, Bulletin 143. Washington, DC: Smithsonian Institution.

Klingberg, Frank J. 1940. The Efforts of the SPG to Christianize the Mosquito Indians, 1742–1785. *Historical Magazine of the Protestant Episcopal Church* 9 (4):305–21.

Kniffen, Fred B. 1965. Folk Housing: Key to Diffusion. *Annals of the Association of American Geographers* 55:549–77.

———. 1967. Necrogeography in the United States. *Geographical Review* 57:426–27.

———. 1990. The Study of Folk Architecture: Geographical Perspectives. In *Cultural Diffusion and Landscapes, Selections by Fred B. Kniffen*, edited by H. Jesse Walker and Randall A. Detro. Geoscience and Man, vol. 27, 35–47.

Kong, Lily. 1990. Geography and Religion: Trends and Prospects. *Progress in Human Geography* 14:355–71.

Kortz, Edwin W. 1958. Honduras—from Mission Field to Associate Province. *Moravian* 103 (4):13–14.

Krüger, Bernhard. 1966. *The Pear Tree Blossoms*. Genadendal, South Africa: Genadendal Printing Works.

Lewis, Peirce. 1979. Axioms for Reading the Landscape. In *The Interpretation of Ordinary Landscapes: Geographical Essays*, edited by Donald W. Meinig, 11–32. New York: Oxford University Press.

———. 1983. Learning from Looking: Geographic and Other Writing about the American Cultural Landscape. *American Quarterly* 35:242–61.

Ligon, W. 1968. House Types of the Black Caribs and Miskito Indians of Honduras. Master's thesis, Louisiana State University.

Long, Edward. 1970 [1774]. *The History of Jamaica*. London: Frank Cass.

Lundberg, J. E. 1870. From Br. Lundberg. *Periodical Accounts Relating to the Missions of the Church of the United Brethren, Established Among the Heathen* 27:404–406.

———. 1872. From Br. Lundberg. *Periodical Accounts Relating to the Missions of the Church of the United Brethren, Established Among the Heathen* 28:196–197.

Lussan, Raveneau de. 1929. *Raveneau de Lussan, a Buccaneer of the Spanish Main and Early French Filibuster of the Pacific: A Translation into English of his Journal of a Voyage into the South Seas in 1684 and the Following Years with the Filibusters*. Translated and edited by Marguerite Eyer Wilbur. Cleveland: Arthur H. Clark.

Martin, David. 1990. *Tongues of Fire: Explosion of Protestantism in Latin America*. Cambridge: Basil Blackwell.

Marx, Elizabeth. 1937. Nicaragua. *Moravian Missions* 35 (4):29.

Marx, Samuel. 1998. Bishop Stanley Goff Dedicates New Ahuas Church and Provincial Offices. *Onward: Moravian Missions* 16 (3):1.

Marx, Werner G. 1942. North of Panama: George Reinke Heath. In *Answering Distant Calls*, edited by Mabel H. Erdman, 97–104. New York: International Committee of Young Men's Christian Associations.

———. 1963. Honduras. *Viewpoint from Distant Lands* 170:12–13.

———. 1980. *Un pueblo que canta: Historia de las Iglésias Evangélicas Moravas en la República de Honduras*. Cocobila: Iglésias Evangélicas Moravas.

———. 1984. The Moravians in Honduras. *Transactions of the Moravian Historical Society* 23 (3–4):1–15.

Marx, Werner G., and George Reinke Heath. 1992. *Diccionario Miskito–Español, Español–Miskito*. Bethlehem: Moravian Church in America.

Matson, G. Albin, and Jane Swanson. 1963. Distribution of Hereditary Blood Antigens among Indians in Middle America: IV in Honduras. *American Journal of Physical Anthropology*. 21:319–33

McSweeney, Kendra. 2004. The Dugout Canoe Trade in Central America's Mosquitia: Approaching Rural Livelihoods through Systems of Exchange. *Annals of the Association of American Geographers* 94:638–61.

Meinig, Donald W. 1965. The Mormon Culture Region: Strategies and Patterns in the Geography of the American West, 1847–1964. *Annals of the Association of American Geographers* 55:191–220.

——. 1979. *The Interpretation of Ordinary Landscapes: Geographical Essays*. Oxford: Oxford University Press.

Merian, Hans. 1975. Einfuhrung in die Baugeschichte der Evangelischen Brudergemeinen ausgehend vom Modell der Gemeine herrnhaag. In *Unitas Fratrum*, edited by Mari P. Van Buijtenen, Cornelius Dekker, and Huib Leewenberg, 465–82. Utrecht: Rijksarchief.

Minkel, Clarence. 1967. Programs of Agricultural Colonization and Settlement in Central America. *Revista Geografica* 66:19–22.

Minkel, Thomas A. 1967. Mennonite Colonization in British Honduras. *Pennsylvania Geographer* 5:1.

Moravian Church. 1849–1889. *Periodical Accounts Relating to the Missions of the Church of the United Brethren, Established among the Heathen*, vols. 19–34.

——. 1890–1956. *Periodical Accounts Relating to the Foreign Missions of the Church of the United Brethren, Second Century*, vols. 1–17.

——. 1972. *Herrnhut: Ursprung und Auftrag*. Berlin: Evangelische Verlagsanstalt.

——. 1994. *Directory*. Bethlehem, PA: Moravian Church.

Mueller, Karl A. 1932. *Among Creoles, Miskitos, and Sumos*. Bethlehem, PA: Comenius Press.

Murtagh, William J. 1967. *Moravian Architecture and Town Planning: Bethlehem, Pennsylvania, and Other Eighteenth-Century American Settlements*. Chapel Hill: University of North Carolina Press.

Naylor, Robert. 1989. *Penny Ante Imperialism: The Mosquito Shore and the Bay of Honduras, 1600–1914*. Rutherford: Fairleigh Dickinson University Press.

Newton, Arthur P. 1914. *The Colonising Activities of the English Puritans: The Last Phase of the Elizabethan Struggle*. New Haven: Yale University Press.

Nietschmann, Bernard. 1969. The distribution of Miskito, Sumu and Rama Indians, Eastern Nicaragua. *Bulletin of the International Committee on Urgent Anthropological and Ethnological Research* vol. 11, 91–102. Vienna: International Union of Anthropological and Ethnological Sciences.

——. 1973. *Between Land and Water: The Subsistence Ecology of the Miskito Indians, Eastern Nicaragua*. New York: Seminar Press.

——. 1979. Ecological Change, Inflation, and Migration in the Far Western Caribbean. *Geographical Review* 69:1–24.

——. 1987. The Third World War. *Cultural Survival Quarterly* 11 (4):1–16.

——. 1995a. Conservación, autodeterminación, y el area protegida Costa Miskita, Nicaragua. *Mesoamérica* 16 (29):1–56.

——. 1995b. Mapping the Miskito Cays with GIS. *Cultural Survival Quarterly* 18 (4): 34–37.

Noble, Allen G. 1986. Landscape of Piety/Landscape of Profit: The Amish-Mennonite and Derived Landscapes of Northeastern Ohio. *East Lakes Geographer* 21:34–48.

Nostrand, Richard, and Lawrence Estaville Jr. 2001. *Homelands: A Geography of Culture and Place across America*. Baltimore: Johns Hopkins University Press.

Offen, Karl H. 1998. An Historical Geography of Chicle and Tunu Gum Production in Northeastern Nicaragua. *Yearbook, Conference of Latin Americanist Geographers* 24:57–74.

——. 2002. The Sambo and Tawira Miskitu: The Colonial Origins and Geography of Intra-Miskitu Differentiation in Eastern Nicaragua and Honduras. *Ethnohistory* 49 (2):319–72.

——. 2003. Narrating Place and Identity, or Mapping Miskitu Land Claims in Northeastern Nicaragua. *Human Organization* 62 (4):382–92.

Olien, Michael D. 1983. The Miskito Kings and the Line of Succession. *Journal of Anthropological Research* 39 (2):198–241.

——. 1987. Micro/Macro-Level Linkages: Regional Political Structures on the Mosquito Coast. *Ethnohistory* 34 (3):256–87.

——. 1988a. After the Indian Slave Trade: Cross-Cultural Trade in the Western Caribbean Rimland, 1816–1820. *Journal of Anthropological Research* 44 (1):41–66.

——. 1988b. Imperialism, Ethnogenesis and Marginality: Ethnicity and Politics on the Mosquito Coast, 1845–1864. *Journal of Ethnic Studies* 16 (1):1–29.

Park, Chris C. 1994. *Sacred Worlds: An Introduction to Geography and Religion*. London: Routledge.

Parsons, James J. 1954. English Speaking Settlement of the Western Caribbean. *Yearbook of the Association of Pacific Coast Geographers* 16:3–16.

——. 1955. The Miskito Pine Savanna of Nicaragua and Honduras. *Annals, Association of American Geographers* 45:36–63.

Peralta, Manuel M., ed. 1898. *Costa Rica y Costa de Mosquitos*. Paris.

Pim, Bedford, and Berthold Seemann. 1869. *Dottings on the Roadside, in Panama, Nicaragua and Mosquito*. London: Chapman and Hall.

Pineda, Baron L. 2006. *Shipwrecked Identities: Navigating Race on Nicaragua's Mosquito Coast*. New Brunswick: Rutgers University Press.

Platino, Julian. 1996. Garifuna Outreach Expands. *Moravian* 27 (4):14–15.

Potthast-Jutkeit, Barbara. 1994. El impacto de la colonización alemana y de las actividades misioneros moravas en la Mosquitia, durante el siglo XIX. *Mesoamerica* 28:253–88.

Proceedings of the Society for Propagating the Gospel Among the Heathen. 1905–1947. Bethlehem, PA: The Society.

Prorok, Carolyn. 1988. Hindu Temples in Trinidad: A Cultural Geography of Religious Structures and Ethnic Identity. PhD dissertation, Louisiana State University.

——. 1991. Evolution of the Hindu Temple in Trinidad. *Caribbean Geographer* 3:73–93.

Rapoport, Amos. 1969. House Form and Culture. Englewood Cliffs, NJ: Prentice-Hall.

Reichel, L. 1908. Visitation of the Northern Stations by Rev. L. Reichel. *Periodical Accounts Relating to the Foreign Missions of the Church of the United Brethren, Second Century* 7 (73):41–55.

Reinke, Theodore A. 1913. Present Day Needs and Opportunities. *Periodical Accounts Relating to the Foreign Missions of the Church of the United Brethren, Second Century* 8 (93):460–64.

Renkewitz, F. 1874. From Br. Renkewitz. *Periodical Accounts Relating to the Missions of the Church of the United Brethren, Established among the Heathen* 29:220–24.

Revels, Craig. 2008. Banks and Booms in the Mid-day Sun: Place Names and the Honduran Mahogany Trade. In *Ethno- and Historical Geographic Studies in Latin America: Essays Honoring William V. Davidson,* edited by Kent Mathewson, Peter Herlihy, and Craig Revels, 223–35. Geoscience and Man, vol. 40. Baton Rouge: Geoscience Publications, Louisiana State University.

Richardson, Miles. 1994. Looking at a World That Speaks. In *Re-reading Cultural Geography,* ed. Kenneth Foote, Peter Hugill, Kent Mathewson, and Jonathan Smith, 156–63. Austin: University of Texas Press.

Roberts, Brian K. 1996. *Landscapes of Settlement: Prehistory to the Present.* New York: Routledge.

Roberts, Orlando W. 1965 [1827]. *Narrative of Voyages and Excursions on the East Coast and in the Interior of Central America.* Gainesville: University of Florida Press.

Romig, Br. 1891. Official Visitation by Br. Romig. *Periodical Accounts Relating to the Foreign Missions of the Church of the United Brethren, Second Century* 1:368–71, 390–409, 428–50.

Rossbach, Lioba. 1987. "Die armen wilden Indianer mit dem Evangelium bekannt machen." Herrnhuter Brüdergemeine an der Mosquito-Küste im 19. Jahrhundert. In *Mosquitia, die andere Hälfte Nicaraguas: Uber Geschichte und Gegenwart der Atlantikkuste,* edited by Klaus Meschkat et al., 65–97. Hamburg: Junius Verlag.

Rowntree, Lester B. 1996. The Cultural Landscape Concept in American Human Geography. In *Concepts of Human Geography,* edited by Carville Earle, Kent Mathewson, and Martin Kenzer, 127–59. Lanham, MD: Rowman and Littlefield.

Salinas, Iris Milady. 1991. *Arquitectura de los grupos étnicos de Honduras.* Tegucigalpa: Editorial Guaymuras.

Sauer, Carl O. 1925. The Morphology of Landscape. *University of California Publications in Geography* 2:19–54.

———. 1927. Recent Developments in Cultural Geography. In *Recent Developments in the Social Sciences,* ed. Edward C. Hayes, 154–212. Philadelphia: Lippincott.

———. 1966. On the Background of Geography in the United States. In *Heidelberger Studien zur Kulturgeographie. Festgabe zum 65. Geburstag von Gottfried Pfeifer,* edited by Hans Graul and Hermann Overbeck, 59–71. Heidelberger Geographische Arbeiten 15. Wiesbaden: F. Steiner.

Sawatzky, Harry Leonard. 1971. *They Sought a Country: The Mennonite Colonization in Mexico.* Berkeley: University of California Press.

Schattschneider, Allen W. 1956. *Through Five Hundred Years: A Popular History of the Moravian Church.* Bethlehem, PA: Comenius Press.

Shilhav, Yosseph. 1983. Principles for the Location of Synagogues. *Professional Geographer* 35:324–29.

Shortridge, James R. 1976. Patterns of Religion in the United States. *Geographical Review* 66:420–34.

Sieborger, M. 1884. From Br. M. Sieborger. *Periodical Accounts Relating to the Missions of the Church of the United Brethren, Established Among the Heathen* 33:175–76.

Sloane, Sir Hans. 1740. *A New History of Jamaica from the Earliest Accounts, to the Taking of Porto Bello by Vice-Admiral Vernon*. 2nd ed. London.

Smith, F. 1872. From Br. F. Smith. *Periodical Accounts Relating to the Missions of the Church of the United Brethren, Established Among the Heathen* 28:313–15.

———. 1877. From Br. F. Smith. *Periodical Accounts Relating to the Missions of the Church of the United Brethren, Established Among the Heathen* 30:281–84.

Smutko, Gregorio. 1996. *La presencia capuchina entre los miskitos, 1915-1995*. Catargo: Imprenta A. G. Covao.

Sopher, David E. 1967. *Geography of Religions*. New York: Prentice-Hall.

Stanislawski, Dan. 1947. Early Spanish Town Planning in the New World. *Geographical Review* 37:94–105.

———. 1975. Dionysus Westward: Early Religion and the Economic Geography of Wine. *Geographical Review* 65:427–44.

Steinberg, Michael K. 1996. Folk House–Types as Indicators of Tradition: The Case of the Mopan Maya in Southern Belize. *Yearbook, Conference of Latin Americanist Geographers* 22:87–92.

Stoll, David. 1990. *Is Latin America Turning Protestant?* Berkeley: University of California Press.

Stoll, David, and Garrard-Burnett, Virginia. 1993. *Rethinking Protestantism in Latin America*. Philadelphia: Temple University Press.

Stouse, P.A.D. Jr. 1970. Settlement Geography in Latin America. *Benchmark, Conference of Latin Americanist Geographers* 1:95–103.

Stump, Roger W. 1984. Regional Divergence in Religious Affiliation in the United States. *Sociological Analysis* 45:283–99.

Tillman, Benjamin F. 2005. The Moravian Church Compound: A German Settlement Type in the Honduran Mosquitia. In *Bridging Cultural Geographies: Europe and Latin America*, edited by Robert B. Kent, Vicent Ortells Chabrera, and Javier Soriano Martí, 103–24. Collecció América 3. Castelló de la Plana: Universitat Jaume I.

———. 2008. Not Always Oriented: Honduran Plaza–Church Locational Relations. In *Ethno- and Historical Geographic Studies in Latin America: Essays Honoring William V. Davidson*, edited by Kent Mathewson, Peter Herlihy, and Craig Revels, 177–92. Geoscience and Man, vol. 40. Baton Rouge: Geoscience Publications, Louisiana State University.

Tuan, Yi-Fu. 1978. Sacred Space: Explorations of an Idea. In *Dimensions of Human Geography: Essays on Some Familiar and Neglected Themes*, edited by K. Butzer, 84–99. Chicago: University of Chicago, Department of Geography, Research Paper No. 186.

von Oertzen, Eleonore, Lioba Rossbach, and Volker Wunderich, eds. 1990. *The Nicaraguan Mosquitia in Historical Documents, 1844–1927*. Berlin: Dietrich Reimer Verlag.

W., M. 1732 [1699]. The Mosqueto Indian and His Golden River; Being a Familiar Description of the Mosqueto Kingdom of America. In *A Collection of Voyages and Travels*, edited by Awnsham and John Churchill, 6:297–312. London.

West, Robert C. 1974. The Flat-Roofed Folk Dwelling in Rural Mexico. In *Man and Cultural Heritage*, edited by H. J. Walker and W. G. Haag. Geoscience and Man, vol. 5, 111–32. Baton Rouge: Louisiana State University.

West, Robert C., and John P. Augelli. 1989. *Middle America: Its Lands and Peoples*. Englewood Cliffs, NJ: Prentice-Hall.

White, Robert. 1789. *The Case of His Majesty's Subjects Having Property in and Lately Established upon the Mosquito Shore in America*. London: T. Cadell.

Wilson, John F. 1990. *Obra morava en Nicaragua: Trasfondo y breve historia*. Managua: Editorial Union.

Winberry, John J. 1974. The Log House in Mexico. *Annals of the Association of American Geographers* 64:54–69.

Worman, Fred. 1972. Economic Development in Department Gracias a Dios, Honduras. *North American Moravian* 3 (1):12–13.

Wullschlagel, H. R. 1856. Extract from the Report of a Visit to the Mission on the Mosquito Coast. *Periodical Accounts Relating to the Missions of the Church of the United Brethren, Established Among the Heathen* 22:33–36.

Zelinsky, Wilber. 1961. An Approach to the Religious Geography of the United States: Patterns of Church Membership in 1952. *Annals of the Association of American Geographers* 51:139–93.

——. 1994. Gathering Places for America's Dead: How Many, Where, Why? *Professional Geographer* 46:29–38.

Ziock, H. 1881. From Br. H. Ziock. *Periodical Accounts Relating to the Missions of the Church of the United Brethren, Established Among the Heathen* 31:509–12.

Zollhofer, F. 1911. My First Evangelistic Tour to Kruta. *Periodical Accounts Relating to the Foreign Missions of the Church of the United Brethren, Second Century* 8 (88):191–97.

Index

agriculture, 1, 8, 9, 21, 25, 104, 105; cooperatives, 114–15; crops, 110–11, 155(table); food shortages, 106–7; fruit tree, 107–10; gardens, 113–14; modern, 112–13; subsistence, 11–12
Agriculture and Development Mission of the Moravian Church (MADIM), 112–13
Ahuas, 37, 46, 60, 61, 169n1(ch. 4); cemetery, 127, 128, 133, 134, 141, 143, 144; church, 66, 68, 71, 72; houses, 91, 97; Moravian structures, 76, 80, 82–83
Asang, 43, 66, 68
Auka, 47, 68, 72, 91, 169n1(ch. 4); cemetery, 122, 123, 127

bananas: pelipita, 9, 113, 116, 145
Baptist Church, 35, 77, 157–59(table)
Bawihka, 12–13
beach ridges, 37, 39, 41, 51, 123, 142
beans, 111, 116, 145
Belén, 46, 47, 48, 66, 72, 93, 97; cemetery, 122–23, 128, 133, 134, 137, 143; description, 49–50
Benk, 40, 47, 66, 98, 123, 169n2(ch. 2), 169n1(ch. 4)
Bluefields, 1, 42, 74, 89, 120; mission, 24, 26–27, 34
board houses, 91, 92, 96–97
British. *See* English
Brus Lagoon, 4, 21, 43, 148, 149, 169n1 (ch. 4); cemetery, 122, 125, 127, 128, 133, 135, 137, 141, 142, 143; church, 66, 68, 69–70, 72; compounds, 76, 80, 81(fig.); fruit trees, 46, 108; houses, 91, 93, 94, 96, 97, 101, 102; structure of, 62–64; trades, 115–16
buccaneers, 12, 13–14
Bulow, Freiherr von, 24
burial customs, 108, 145, 170n3; canoes, 135–36; grave cleaning, 132–33; grave sheds, 136–38; Miskito, 9, 21, 117–20. *See also* cemeteries

canoe burials, 118, 135–36, 137(table)
Cape Gracias a Dios, 28, 34, 125
carpentry, 91, 145
Catholic Church, 1, 18, 53, 142, 144, 169n3; on Mosquito Coast, 11, 34–35, 148–49, 157–59(table); in Puerto Lempira, 60, 77
cattle production, 114, 170n1
Cayo Sirpe, 37, 122, 123, 127, 141
cemeteries, 1, 117, 140–41; canoe burials, 135–36; concrete in, 133–34; crosses, 124–28; Easter dawn service, 120–22, 145; grave houses, 138–39; grave sheds, 136–38; items left, 129, 130(fig.), 131; Miskito, 1, 9, 119; mounds in, 132–33; orientation of, 122–24, 142; seasonal changes in, 143–44
chickens, 111, 114, 145
churches, 49, 50, 53, 60, 87; architecture, 68–73; names and adornments, 83–85; orientation of, 65–68, 79–80
Church of God, 35, 77, 157–59(table)
climate, 11
Cocal, 7–8, 37, 47
Cocobila, 47, 76, 108, 121; and Belén, 49–50; church, 66, 68, 69–70, 72–73, 83,

84; description, 48–49; houses, 91, 97, 102; mission compound, 78–80; structure of, 42, 44, 148
Coco River, 28, 29, 169n2
colonization, 10; German, 23–25; missionaries, 2, 25–26
compounds: Moravian, 44, 63(fig.), 74, 76, 77–83, 103, 146
concrete, 101–2, 133–34, 138(fig.), 140, 142
cooperatives: agricultural, 110–11, 112–13, 114–15
crops, 9, 107, 110–11, 116, 145
crosses: style of, 124–28, 142, 143

Daiwras: cemetery, 122, 123, 127, 136, 137, 139, 141
Dakratara, 66, 68, 72, 91
Dapat, 37, 52, 72, 98; cemetery, 122, 123, 141; church, 66, 68
decorations: Moravian church, 83–85
Diakonia, 112

Easter dawn service, 9, 120–22, 145
encampments, 57, 58
English, 13, 14, 16, 17, 22
English language, 11
ethnicity, 142; Miskito, 147–48
ethnogenesis: Miskito, 12–15
evil spirits, 21, 120

False Cape. *See* Kruta
feasting: burial customs, 17–18
fencing, 111–12, 128, 170n1
Flores, Sico, 57
food: grave, 129, 131; shortages, 107–10
food production, 116; crops, 110–12; fruit trees, 107–10
footpaths, 46, 52; Cocobila, 48–49
fruit trees, 9, 44–46; introduced, 107–10, 145, 155(table)

Garcia, Armundo, 57
gardens, 9, 104, 107, 111–12, 113–14
Garifuna, 31–32
geography: cultural landscape, 3–4
Germans, 22; colonies, 1, 23–25, 148
Gracias a Dios, Department, of, 5(fig.), 10, 59, 151–53(table)
grave houses, 138–39
graves, 5, 142; canoe, 135–36; cleaning, 132–33; items on, 129–31; orientation, 118, 125, 127–28; protection, 139–40
grave sheds, 118, 127, 136–38
Great Britain, 17, 23. *See also* English

Heath, George R., 8–9, 22, 68, 70, 108, 111, 121; on burial customs, 118, 119; missions, 77, 78–79
Hermhut, 18–19, 43, 73, 106, 120, 148
Hispanicization, 11, 135, 148–49
Holy Week, 132–33, 143–44
hospital: in Ahuas, 60, 62, 82, 83
houses, 1, 8, 21; changes, 92–96, 100–101; concrete, 101–2; construction, 167–68(table); Moravian influences, 87–92; traditional, 86–87; village structure, 41–42
Housman, Howard, 113
hurricanes, 38, 40, 41
Hus, John, 18

Ibans, 66, 72, 83

Jeremy I, 17

Katski Almuk, 69, 70(fig.), 72
Kaurkira, 44, 52, 53(fig.), 76, 121, 148, 169n1(ch. 4); cemetery, 119, 122, 123, 127, 128, 133, 134, 135, 137, 141, 143; church, 66, 68, 69, 70, 72; fruit trees, 46, 108, 109; houses, 89, 91, 97, 98, 102; as Moravian center, 77–78; rice, 110–11
kings: Miskito, 17
kitchens: external, 89, 91–92, 95–96
Kokota, 127, 128, 131, 139, 141, 143
Konigsberg: colonists from, 23–25
Krata, 50–51, 52(fig.), 98

Kruta, 42, 47, 66, 72, 169n2, 169n1(ch. 4); cemetery, 122, 123–24; location, 38–41
Kruta River, 37, 56, 122

labor, 16; wage, 12, 107
La Ceiba, 4, 110–11, 169n1(ch. 4)
Ladinos, 101, 142, 144, 149; and concrete tombs, 133–34, 140; in Moravian Church, 32–33
lagoons: villages and, 36–37
Laka region, 37–38, 122
Laka Tabila, 46, 54–55, 56(fig.), 93, 128
landing strips, 50, 53, 63–64
land rights, 3, 23, 24, 147–48
landscape, 9; churches on, 66–68; cultural, 3–4, 65; ethnic, 147–48
Layasiksa: grave houses, 138–39
Lisangnipura, 55–57, 96, 97
livestock, 111, 112, 114

MADIM. *See* Agriculture and Development Mission of the Moravian Church
Marx, Samuel, 60, 82
Marx, Werner, 43, 91, 115
Mathilde, Princess, 27
medicine: herbal, 9, 132
Mendez, Juan, 50–51
Miskito, 3, 42, 145; agriculture, 11–12; ethnogenesis, 12–15; expansion, 15–17; land claims, 147–48; in Moravian Church, 33–34; religion, 21–22; settlement patterns, 1–2, 36–38
Miskito language, 11, 14–15, 21, 27, 149
Miskito reservation, 17
missionaries, 2, 8–9, 13, 34–35, 76, 145; dooryard gardens, 113–14; to Garifuna, 31–32; influence of, 42–43, 87–92; Moravian, 1, 19–21, 22, 24–25, 39–40, 148
missions/mission stations, 39–40, 74; churches, 66, 68; establishment, 25–34; fruit trees, 108–10; goals, 104–5; Kaurkira, 77–78
Mocorón, 48, 57–58, 169–70n1; cemetery, 123, 127, 128, 133; church, 66, 71, 72; houses, 96, 97
Moravian Church, 5, 8, 24, 60, 112, 169–70nn1, 3; architecture, 68–69; in Bluefields, 26–27; central communities, 77–83; churches, 66–73, 83–85; establishment, 18–19; houses, 87–92; independent churches, 22–23; influence, 2–3, 42, 145–46; missions, 1, 19–21, 25–34, 39–40, 104–5; planned communities, 43–44, 73–74, 146, 148; settlement hierarchy, 75–77. *See also* missions/mission stations

Nicaragua, 1, 18, 20, 22–23, 29, 32, 33, 169n2
Nueva Jerusalén, 2, 48, 66, 97; cemetery, 123, 127; church, 83, 169–70n1

Palkaka, 68, 72; cemetery, 127, 128, 129, 131, 133, 137, 139, 141, 142
palms, 86, 89, 97, 98, 100–101, 109, 131
Paptalaya, 37, 46, 72; cemetery, 122, 127, 128, 143
Patuka River, 34–35, 37
Pearl Lagoon, 110
personal possessions: burial customs, 108, 118, 129, 130(fig.)
pines, 12, 37, 60, 131
place names: settlement, 46–48, 161–65(table)
population, 169n1(ch. 2); Department of Gracias a Dios, 151–53(table)
Post, Christian Frederick, 34
post houses, 89, 92
posts: house, 86, 87, 92
potions: supernatural, 21–22
poverty: and burial customs, 118
property: personal, 108, 118
Protestantism, 1, 10, 18, 35, 145, 146, 148
Prumnitara, 37, 41, 47, 68, 72, 98; cemetery, 122, 123, 127, 128
Prussia, 23, 24–25

Puerto Lempira, 4, 21, 37, 41, 47, 72; Catholic Church, 35, 169n3; cemetery, 122–23, 125, 127, 128, 133, 135, 137, 141, 144; fruit trees, 45–46; Hispanicization, 148–49; houses, 96, 97, 101; Moravian Church, 66, 68, 77, 121–22, 169–70n1; structure of, 59–60, 61(fig.)

raiding, raids: Miskito, 16
Rama Indians, 27, 32
Raya, 40, 46, 53, 54(fig.), 66, 72, 98, 169n2; cemetery, 122, 123, 127, 128, 133
refugee camps, 58, 127, 133
refugees: Nicaraguan, 35, 58
religion, 26; cemeteries, 142, 143; geography of, 4, 65, 157–59(table); Miskito, 21–22. *See also* Moravian Church
research methods, 4–5, 7–8
resettlement/relocation, 42, 43
rice production, 110–11, 116, 145
Río Plátano, 15, 37, 41, 47
Río Plátano Biosphere Reserve, 147
roads, 46
roofs, 91, 93, 96; thatch, 90(fig.), 97–100; zinc, 89, 92, 94, 101, 137

Salem (N.C.): plan, 73–74
Sambo Miskito, 13, 15, 16, 17
Sandy Bay, 87, 109, 121
savannas: cemeteries on, 132–33; villages, 37–38, 44–45, 54–55
Schönburg-Waldenburg, Prince, 23, 24, 25
settlements. *See* villages
shamans, 9, 21, 106–7, 118–19
Sirsirtara, 47, 57; cemetery, 122, 127, 128, 129, 136, 141
Spanish language, 11, 149
Stover, Robert H., 113
Suhi, 47, 122, 123, 127, 141
suita, 90(fig.), 97, 98–100
sukia, 9, 21, 106–7, 118–19
Sumu, 12–13, 16, 28, 32, 43
symbols: Moravian Church, 83–85

Tansin Island, 123, 139
Tasbapauni, 27, 41, 46, 47, 66, 72, 121, 132; church, 83, 84–85
Tasbaraya, 71, 97; cemetery, 122–23, 128, 136, 139, 141
Tawahka, 13, 16, 32
Tawira Miskito, 13, 15, 16, 17
territory: Miskito, 15–17
thatch, 90(fig.); types of, 97–100
Tikiuraya, 37, 53, 55(fig.), 122, 135
Tipilalma, 38, 47; cemetery, 123, 127, 128, 141, 142
tombs, 133–35, 138(fig.), 140, 142
town planning, 73–74, 146, 148
trade, 14, 15, 17
trades: teaching, 105, 106, 115
transportation routes, 41, 46, 59
trees, 131. *See also* fruit trees
Twitanta, 46, 66, 71(fig.), 72

Uhi, 66, 98, 169–70n1; cemetery, 122, 123, 127, 141
United Nations, 55–56, 58, 133

vegetation canopies, 44–46
villages, 1, 9, 147; agglomerated, 41–43; churches, 65–68; and encampments, 57–58; fruit trees, 44–46; hierarchy, 75–77; location, 36–41; Miskito, 1–2, 6–7(table), 145; Moravian, 73–74, 77–83; names, 46–48, 161–65(table). *See also by name*

Walker, Patrick, 24, 25
walls: house, 88–89, 90(fig.), 93, 96–97, 100–101
Wauplaya, 38, 122, 127, 128, 136, 141
Wounta Haulover, 27, 42–43, 88, 120–21

yagua, 93, 96, 101
Yahurabila, 51, 66, 72; cemetery, 122, 123, 136, 141; houses, 91, 98
Yapti Misri, 21

zinc roofing, 89, 92, 94, 97, 100, 101, 137
Zinzendorf, Louis Von, 18–19, 120
zona recuperada, 29, 37, 41, 169n2

About the Author

Benjamin F. Tillman is an associate professor of geography at Texas Christian University, Fort Worth, Texas. He received his PhD in Geography from Louisiana State University in 1999. He is the author of *La Influencia Morava en el Paisaje de la Mosquitia Hondureña* (2004). His research interests are centered on the cultural and historical geography of Central America's eastern coast. His current research examines the spread of the breadfruit tree from the South Pacific to the Caribbean, and its use among indigenous peoples in Central America.